# AMBEDKAR
# AND
# CASTE POLITICS IN INDIA

# AMBEDKAR AND CASTE POLITICS IN INDIA

Dr. Shyam Shanker Prasad Gupta

CENTRUM PRESS
NEW DELHI-110002 (INDIA)

**CENTRUM PRESS**
**H.O.:** 4360/4, Ansari Road, Daryaganj,
New Delhi-110002 (India)
Tel: 23278000, 23261597, 23255577, 23286875
**B.O.:** No. 1015, Ist Main Road, BSK IIIrd Stage,
IIIrd Phase, IIIrd Block, Bangalore-560085 (INDIA)
Tel: 080-41723429
*Email:* centrumpress@gmail.com
*Visit us at:* www.centrumpress.com

*Ambedkar and Caste Politics in India*



First Edition, 2011
ISBN 978-93-80836-46-1

PRINTED IN INDIA

---

*Printed at* Mehra Offset Press, Delhi

# Contents

# Preface

Ambedkar fought for the rights of workers and peasants. In the late 1920s and especially in the 1930s when he had formed his Independent Labour Party, he took up the cause of tenants (from both the dalit Mahars and the caste Hindu Kunbis) in the Konkan region of Maharashtra. With the support of radicals then in the Congress Socialist Party, the Independent Labour Party organized a huge march of 20,000 peasants to Mumbai in 1938, the largest pre-independence peasant mobilization in the region. In the same year, Ambedkar joined with the Communists to organize a strike of Mumbai textile workers in protest against a bill about to be introduced by the British Government to curve labour strikes. Ambedkar took the lead in condemning the bill in the assembly and argued that the right to strike was simply another name for the right to freedom of assembly.

The demand for safeguards and protection of Scheduled Castes (earlier called Depressed Class) has a long history dating to Montague-Chelmsford Reform of 1919 during the British Raj period. Ambedkar had been closely involved in the struggle to give Scheduled Caste people solid statutory safeguard. He was a delegate at the Round Table Conference in London, where he asked for separate electorate for the Dalits. It is not a surprise that subsequently Ambedkar saw to it that the welfare of the Scheduled Caste people were guaranteed in the 1949 Constitution of India in the form of reservation in legislative, employment and educational fields.

Ambedkar was a great champion of the dalit cause because he succeeded in turning the depressed class movement into a revolutionary movement throughout India. Today India has witnessed the oppressed classes walking on the streets of cities and villages with confidence and poise, of course many despicable acts of discrimination and violence against the dalits still occur. Yet the juggernaut of equality is rolling on remorselessly and forcefully.

The book, which provides a rare opportunity to debate and discuss the contribution of Dr. Ambedkar in nation-building, will be great interest to all sections of people.

*—Dr. Shyam Shankar Prasad Gupta*

# 1

# Ambedkar Views on Roots of the Problem in Casteism

## Parallel Cases

Social inequality is not confined to Hindus only. It prevailed in other countries also and was responsible for dividing society into higher and lower, free and unfree, respectable and despised. It would be interesting to compare the condition and status of the untouchables in India with the condition and status of the unfree and the despised classes in other countries ancient and modern. For an intelligent understanding of the differences and similarities it is essential to have some idea of the history of such parallel cases before any comparison can be instituted. It is not possible to give a survey of all such classes in all parts of the world. Nor is it necessary. A few typical cases can only be taken as illustrations.

In studying the relationship between the Hindus and the Untouchables three questions at once come to one's mind. Why has untouchability not vanished? Why does the Hindu regard lawlessness against the Untouchables as legitimate and lawful? Why does the Hindu feel no qualms of conscience in his dealings with the Untouchables?

Classes, which like the Untouchables were lowly and despised have at one time existed in other societies also. For instance, they existed in once ancient Rome. The population of ancient Rome fell into five classes: (1) Patricians, (2) Plebians, (3) Clients, (4) Slaves and (5) Freemen.

The Patricians were the ruling class. They were the civics in every sense. The rest were all servile in status. The Plebs and the Clients were destroyed by war. Those of the new comers who invoked the protection of the heads of Patrician families of repute and were ready to become their vassals were known as clients. Those who were too independent to brook submission to a private patron put themselves under the direct protection of the sovereign and became royal tenants and were known as Plebians.

The Plebians had the right to hold property both movable and immovable to transfer it by quirtian modes of conveyance, and to have the protection for it of the tribunals. But the Plebian had no share in the Government of the City.

He was a half-fledged citizen—*civies sine suffragio*. The Plebs were denied any participation in the religion of the city and as men to whom the suspicion were incompetent, any intermarriage between the Patrician and the Plebian was out of question. The client had to look to his Patrician patron for support and maintenance.

The Patrician patron had to provide all that was necessary for his sustenance and that of his wife and children. This relation was a hereditary one, a client passed on from father to son. The client had not only to depend upon his Patrician patron for his maintenance but he had also to depend upon him for his legal protection. Not being a civic, a client had no right of suit and his Patrician patron had to assist his client in his redress for him for his injuries and represent him before the tribunals when he became involved in litigation.

As to the slaves there were millions of them. A single rich landholder might own hundreds and even thousands, and it was a poor man that did not have several at least. They were just things to be owned. They were not persons in the eye of the law and had therefore no rights.

They received kind treatment from a few humane masters. But generally they were treated with the greatest cruelty. "If a slave coughs or sneezes during a meal, if he lets a key fall noisy to the floor, we fall into a great rage...... Often we strike too hard and shatter a limb or break a tooth," said Senecca. One rich Roman used to punish his slaves for carelessness by casting them into a fishpond as food for lampreys. The slaves who displeased their masters were ordinarily sent to an underground prison. During the day, they had to work loaded with heavy iron chains.

Many were branded with red-hot iron. The mill where the slaves had to work is thus described by a Roman author; 'Gods! What poor shrunken up men? With white skins striped with blows of the whip..... They were only the shreds of tunis; bent forward, head shaved, the feet held in a chain, the body deformed by the heat of the fire, the eyelids eaten away by the fumes, everything covered with grain dust'.

English society also had at one time its servile classes. One has only to turn to the Domesday Book to see what the state of English Society was at the time of the Norman conquest.

The Domesday Book which is a social survey of the land in England and its various kinds of tenants made by William the Conqueror immediately after his conquest in 1086 shows the following classes in which the population was divided:

| | | | | |
|---|---|---|---|---|
| 1. Gentry & Clergy | Made up of | Tenants in Chief<br>under tenants | 1,400<br>7,900 | 9,300 |
| 2. Freeholders Yeomen | Made up of | Freemen Socmen | 12,000<br>32,000 | 44,000 |
| 3. Half-free or Unfree | Made up of | Villeins Cottars<br>and Borders | 169,000<br>90,000 | 259,000 |
| 4. Slaves | | | | 25,000 |

Out of a total of 3,37,000 souls as many as 2,84,000 were either unfree or slaves.

These are examples of servility in which race or religion played no part. But examples of servility by reason of race or religion are not wanting in history. The principal one is that of the Jews. On account of the belief that the Jews were responsible for the death of Christ, the Jews have been subjected to persecution. During the Middle ages in almost all the European towns, the Jews were compelled to reside within a restricted quarter in a separate part of the town, and this Jewish quarter came to be known as the 'Ghetto'. A Council held in Coyanza in Australia in 1050 enacted 'that no Christian shall reside in the same house with Jews, nor partake of the food; whoever transgresses this decree shall perform penances for seven days, or, refusing to do it, if a person of rank, he shall be excommunicated for a year; if of an inferior degree, he shall receive 100 lashes."

The Council of Falencia in 1388 enacted that "Christians must not dwell within the quarters assigned to the Jews and Moors, and those that resided within them were to remove therefrom within two months after the publication of this decree in the Cathedral and if they did not, were to be compelled by Ecclesiastical censure." In the Middle ages the Jews were obliged to have communal baths. No Jewish community could be destitute of such baths because the State often forbade the Jews to bathe in the rivers which the Christians used. In the fourteenth Century the Jews of Augers were readmitted to the town on several onerous conditions, one being that they would not bathe in the river Maine.

The State also levied certain taxes upon the Jews. They were of three kinds—poll taxes, and particular fines and dues for individual transactions and privileges. The age at which Jews or Jewesses became liable to the poll tax varied considerably but the age was very young, and in Spain, as in England in 1273, every Jew above the age of ten was rateable. The billeting of soldiers on Jews in times of peace was a frequent species of exaction. So many were the vexatious dues exacted from the Jews everywhere throughout the Middle ages that it would be impossible to enumerate them all. To crown all this Pope Innocent III decided in 1215 that thenceforward the Jews must be marked off from the Christians by a badge prominently fastened to their outermost garment. Clear and emphatic in its demand that the Jews must wear badges, the Laternan council nevertheless avoided details. It left the definition of the size, colour, and character of the degrading mark to the taste of local Governors and States. Each Governor and State devised a badge of its own pattern. On account of the extraordinary number of modification, size and shape the badge sometimes became obsolete and the Jews managed to evade it. As the badge was often hidden, in 1525 Pope Clement VII changed it for a yellow hat or bonnet.

A consideration of the position of the Untouchables reminds one of the positions of the Catholics in England. The Catholics were subjected to many disabilities. The catalogue of their disabilities is given below:

1. That of Catholic marriages or of marriages Catholics celebrated by Catholic priests being deemed invalid by the existing laws, so that if one of the parties quit the other *quicumque de causa* (from any reason whatsoever), the deserted party receives no relief from the parish, nor redress from the law of his or her country. The priest, also it is said, may be transported, or put in prison and condemned to transportation for having married the parties.
2. That of foundations or of moneys appropriated for the maintenance of priests, or to support the Catholic worship, being deemed by the existing laws to be appropriated to *superstitious purposes* and as such are liable to confiscation; and when alienated or seized upon by malevolent person cannot be recovered by law; Instances of such alienation and seizures might be adduced.
3. That of Catholics serving in His Majesty's Army and Navy being withheld from attending Divine Service according to the rite of their own religion on Sundays and festivals, and of their being compelled to go to Protestant Churches on those days against their will, an evil which leads brave and loyal subjects to complain and be discontented at a time when every heart and hand should be united to oppose the enemy; and the United Kingdom should be as one man.
4. By the 13th Charles II, commonly called the Corporation Act, their whole body is excluded from offices in cities and corporations.
5. By the 25th Charles II, commonly called the Test Act, their whole body is excluded from civil and military offices.
6. By the 7th and 8th William III, c. 27 Roman Catholics are liable to be prevented from voting at elections.
7. By the 30th Charles II, s. 2. c. 1, Roman Catholic peers are prevented from filling their hereditary seats in Parliament.

8. By the same statute Roman Catholics are prevented from sitting in the House of Commons.
9. By several statutes Roman Catholics are disabled from presenting to advowsons, a legal incident of property which the law allows even to the Jew.
10. Though a considerable proportion of His Majesty's fleets and armies was Catholic, not only is no provision made for their religious comforts etc., but by the articles of war they are liable to the very heaviest pains and penalties for refusing to join in those acts of conformity to the religious rites of the Established Church. By the articles of war, section I, a soldier absenting himself from Divine service and sermon is liable, for the first offence, to forfeit one Shilling, and for the second and every other offence, to forfeit one Shilling and to be put in irons. By the same articles section 2, article 5,' if he shall disobey any lawful command of his superior (and of course if he shall disobey any lawful command of his superior to attend Divine Service and Sermon) he shall suffer death or such punishment as by general court martial shall be awarded.
11. In common with the rest of his Majesty's subjects the Roman Catholics contribute to the support of the Established Religion; they have also to support their own religious functionaries; and thus have a double religious establishment to defray. Of course, however, they do not complain; but they think it a serious grievance that their own religious endowments are not legalised like those of the Protestant Dissenters.
12. In hospitals, workhouses, and other public institutions the attendance of the ministers of their own communion is sometime denied to the poor of the Roman Catholic religion, and the children of the Roman Catholic poor are sometimes forced into Protestant schools under the eyes of their parents."

Like Catholics, the Untouchables also suffer from certain disabilities.

Providence it seems has inexorably doomed the continent of Africa to be only a nursery of slaves for the free and civilised peoples of Asia and Europe. The Negro was imported as a slave by the Arabs into Asia long before he was introduced as a slave by the Europeans into America. Although this is so, Negro slavery in America and in the English Colonies has had a sorrowful history which has made people forget the importation of the Negro as a slave in Asia and quite naturally because Negro slavery in America as carried on by the Europeans was a most revolting thing. It began in the first decade of the 16th Century and lasted till the middle of the 19th Century.

In the half century after Columbus first landed in the Bahama Island in 1492, the Spaniards conquered and partly occupied a huge area stretching from Mexico through Peru to Uruguay and including all the larger west Indian Islands, while in 1531 the Portuguese began the colonisation of Brazil. At once the new comers, the Portuguese and the Spaniards, set themselves to exploit the great natural wealth of their acquisitions, to work the gold and silver mines on the main land and to lay out plantations of tobacco indigo and sugar in the rich soil of the island.

But they were soon confronted by the difficulty of procuring the requisite supply of labour. A great deal of it was needed, and the cost of white men's wages and the heat of the tropical sun made it virtually impossible for the Europeans to provide it for themselves. The only labour supply of a non-European character available on the spot consisted of the native Indians. The Portuguese and the Spaniards had massacred many Indians during the conquest. Many had fled to the mountains and forest from the scourge of the invaders. Those that were available were made slaves and made to work in the mines. Under the lash of the Portuguese and the Spaniards and the relentless labour that was exacted from them in the mines and in the fields the Indians sickened and died.

The conquistadors—as the Spanish pioneers in South America were called—under the leadership of Nicholas de Ovando who followed promptly the trail of Columbus, brought with them a young priest Batrolome' de Las Casas who was well known for his piety. Las Casas was charged by the Court of Spain to deal lovingly with the Indians in the hope of bringing them to a knowledge of the sacred Christian faith. Las Casas was the first Bishop of Mexico. In performing the duty with which he was charged Las Casas while in Haiti witnessed the cruelties that were practised by the conquistadors upon the Indians and engaged himself passionately to the end of his life in preserving the pitiable remnants of the Caribbeans as the Indians of Haiti were called, from the inevitable destruction at the hands of their masters.

The Caribbeans were a gentle, un-offending and hospitable race. They numbered no less than 1,000,000 persons when Columbus found them, formed into kingdoms and ruled peacefully by their caciques. Under the systematic cruelty of these Spanish adventurers who came after Columbus their numbers were reduced to a bare 60,000. It is recorded that entire villages committed suicide inviting others to join them as the only way of escaping this scourge and this tyranny. Las Casas was a spectator to many of these scenes of self immolations. He protested in righteous anger. But his protests went in vain and were bound to go in vain.

The clearing of the forest, the tilling of the soil and the working of the mines had to go on. Without this the kingdom given by God could not become the Paradise of man. Las Casas realised this. But he was also overwhelmed with grief at the thought of what the Indians would have to go through if this plan was to be realised. His benevolent instincts led him to petition the King of Spain to allow the free importation of Negroes. The Spanish Government in 1511 decreed that a large number of Negroes should be transported to the New World. In pursuance of this there came ships laden with African Negroes as cargo to make the New World a Paradise for man. For a few years both worked under the Conquistadors, Indians as well as Negroes.

The sturdiness of the Negroes as compared with the Indians was soon proved. One of the Conquistadors has testified that when he prepared his timbers for the four brigantines that pass through the Isthmus from the Atlantic to the waters which flowed into the Pacific, he had used several hundred Indians and thirty Negroes, and, in the execution of this task, he found that 500 Indians perished and the thirty Negroes survived. The Negroes not only survived but prospered so much that it came to be a common opinion "that unless a Negro should happen to be hanged he would never die; for as yet, none had been known to perish from infirmity". The Negro by his own conduct and character gave evidence that he was a more efficient tool than the Indian. The result was that the Indian was let go and the Negro was preferred for the labour, the former because God made him less sturdy and the latter because God made him more sturdy. The result was that the Indian escaped slavery and the Negro took over the destiny which was intended by the Conquistadors to apply to him a destiny to which he was invited by the pious and benevolent priest Las Casas and for which the Negro showed his own credentials of fitness.

Having found that "one Negro does more work than four Indians" there was opened at once a regular market for trading in Negroes. The market which was opened by the Portuguese on the West Coast of Africa began immediately to show its profits and quite naturally because the exploitation of the untold wealth of the New World was impossible without Negro labour. People became so engrossed in this new business in human beings that the search for a new route to the East, which began it all, was abandoned.

There was a keen competition between the various nations of Europe for a share in this new line in commerce. A papal Bull of demarcation had created for Spain and Portugal a monopoly on the wealth flowing in from the New World. The English and the Dutch feared there was danger to all Europe in this monopoly of American resources and were determined not to allow it.

The English took a good hand in securing this trade for the benefit of their nation. The first deal took place in 1553 when 24 Negroes were brought from the Coast of Africa and quietly sold in the English market. The most intrepid, and who later became the most heartless of man stealers known to history was John Hawkins. Under Elizabeth he sailed forth in the good ship *Jesus* to get Negroes from Africa whom he sold into the Spanish Colonies. Bent on breaking the monopoly of Spain Sir Francis Drake followed Hawkins. International disputes over the pirating of these adventures arose which culminated in the clash and destruction of the Spanish Armada. It is interesting to bear in mind that in these disputes each nation shamelessly asserted that these acts of piracy committed by their subjects in stealing Negro slaves were "no private but public actions" supported by the respective states. As though the irony involved in using the Ship *Jesus* for carrying the Negroes for enslavement was not enough there occurred another event which also was full of irony. It was the simultaneous landing of the Pilgrim Fathers on Plymouth Rock in the *Mayflower,* and the landing of twenty Negroes at Jamestown in Virginia from a barnacled and sea worn brig which sailed up the James river and brought them for the use of the gentlemen adventurers of the first successful English Colony of Virginia in America.

Thus were introduced into America the Negroes and the Pilgrim Fathers who stepped into it almost at the same time, the Pilgrim Fathers for preserving their liberty and the Negro for losing his freedom. For a long time the Negro formed a dominant element in the population of the American Colonies so far as numbers were considered. In a real sense America including its islands was settled chiefly from Africa and by Negroes. Before 1800 the number of Negroes brought in America was more than twenty times that of all Europeans combined. This was inevitable. The population of Europe was small, reduced further by its long wars and just emerging itself from a backward culture. For a long time the status of the imported Negro was undefined. The twenty Negroes brought by the Dutch and who landed in Jamestown were not immediately stamped in the Colony as slaves.

They were accepted on much the same basis as the indentured servants. It has been found that in the muster rolls of the Colony of Virginia in 1624 and 1625 there were recorded 23 Negroes all of whom were listed as 'servants' as were the whites of the same class. It is also recorded that thirty-four years after the arrival of the twenty Negroes one of them Anthony Johnson got a judgment from the Court sustaining his claim to perpetual service of John Caster, another Negro. The status of slavery was not crystallised for fifty years and steps by which it became crystallised were very gradual.

To begin with there was the law of servitude which applied to all servants whether they were Negroes or whites. In course of time a distinction came to be made in the treatment of the Negroes and white servants due to the fear of an alien and pagan people which as they became traditional and gained the sanction of custom, gradually modified the status of the African and transformed Negro servitude into Negro slavery. The slavery of the Negro in the American Colonies grew by the gradual addition of incidents modifying the law and custom of servitude. In this transition from servitude to slavery there are two principal steps.

The first step in the transition was taken when the custom of holding Negroes "servants for life" was recognised. As has been observed, the distinguishing mark of the state of slavery is not the loss of liberty, political and civil but the perpetuity and absolute character of that loss, whether voluntary or involuntary in origin. It differs then from other forms of servitude limited in place or time, such as medieval vassalage, villeinage, modern serfdom, and technical servitude, in degree rather than in kind. The efforts of the planters to lengthen the terms of the service of their servants which failed with the white servants succeeded with the black. Public opinion supported the change because the blacks were regarded as dangerous if left uncontrolled.

The second step by which Negro servitude was converted into Negro slavery was taken when the condition and status of the mother was extended to and continued in her offspring. The transmission from mother to child of the conditions of slavery for life grew naturally out of the fact that the master necessarily controlled the child, controlling the mother. It was evident that parents, under an obligation of life service, could make no valid provision for the support of their offspring and that a just title to the service of the child might rest on the master's maintenance. This change which had undoubtedly been effected in custom long before it was formally sanctioned by law was recognised by statute in the different states of America between 1662 and 1741.

This is how the Negro who was originally only a servant became a slave. It is to be noted that slavery in Africa the home of the Negro is a native institution and is very ancient. The most common ways of becoming a slave were: (1) By being born a slave, (2) by being sold into slavery for debt, (3) by becoming a slave through capture in war and (4) by kidnapping individuals and selling them into slavery due to revenge or greed and gain. The Negro was really familiar with the slave system and tasted the pleasures of a slave owner. One therefore may not feel the same sympathy with the Negro when he was made to give up the status of a master and made to occupy the position of a slave. But looked at even as a case of retribution well deserved, his condition as a slave in the New World to which he was transplanted, cannot fail to excite a righteous indignation for the miseries to which he was subjected by his new and alien masters.

How great were the miseries of the Negro in the New World when he became subject to the system of slavery, it is not possible for the inhabitants of Europe or Asia to imagine. They may be described under three heads. The miseries of his capture, the miseries of travel and the miseries of his toil. First as to the ways of capturing Negroes for enslavement. In the early days Negroes could be rounded up by sudden landings on the coast: but in time the Negroes learned to watch for the coming of the ships and take refuge in the bush; and, though adventurous traders sometimes penetrated inland themselves, their usual custom was to do business with professional native or half caste dealers who took the cheap goods they had bought from Europe cloth, beads, hardware, muskets and powder, spirit—and bartered them for slaves with chiefs upcountry. There is nothing to show that the chiefs, of the stronger tribes at any rate, resisted or wanted to resist the fascination of these wares, especially the guns and drink. Enslavement within a tribe, it was observed, became the penalty for less and less serious offences; and inter-tribal warfare with slaves for its motive as well as the kidnapping of women and children in peacetime became a more or less constant feature of African life, spreading steadily into the interior of the continent with the steady infiltration of the trade.

Secondly as to the mode of transporting the Negro to America. Having bought his slaves, the dealer marshalled them, men, women and children, in a caravan for the march, sometimes a very long march to the coast. Usually fetters were put on them to prevent escape and often they were locked in the "slave stick"—a long pole with a crutch at the end for fastening round the neck. They carried on their heads the loads of foodstuffs and other baggage required for the journey or the ivory or other native produce which the dealer might have bought. The rigours of the march were often too much for the weaker members of the party. Slaves who fell sick were killed or left to die. The more frequented slavetracks were strewn with human bones. Arrived at the coast, they were stowed on board the slave ships, which were specially fitted for their transport. The hold was divided horizontally by decks about three feet apart with a gangway down the middle. On these shelves the slaves were laid, handcuffed in pairs, men and women in separate holds. Since the bigger the cargo, the bigger the profit, they were some times packed so tightly that they could scarcely turn round.

In a ship of 150 tons as many as 600 slaves were carried. The direct voyage to Brazil was fairly short, but the so-called "Middle Passage" to the West Indies—the main centre of distribution—might be protracted for several weeks by adverse or dropping winds. If it was calm enough, the slaves were brought up on deck and urged or forced to dance for exercise. In rough weather conditions of the slaves in the hold may be imagined. Disease of course, was rife on board. Though instruments were provided for forcibly feeding those who refused to eat, it was reckoned in the latter eighteenth century that on the average at least one-sixth of a cargo died on the voyage.

As the end of the voyage approached, the slaves were examined and prepared for sale. Wounds, caused by storm or ill usage, were doctored up and as far as possible concealed. But the agents at the ports often complained that the "parcels of Negroes" landed were "bad" or "mean" or "much abused". Finally, on shipboard or in the public slave market, the slaves were put up for sale by "scramble" or auction. The price of a healthy man rose as high as £ 60 during the eighteenth century.

The sick and injured were lumped with feeble women and children and sold off cheap as "refuse". Even when at last they reached the plantations, the slaves had to face one more ideal before they settled down to endure what was left to them of life. The first months of employment were known as the period of "seasoning" and during it no less on an average of one third of the novices failed to adjust themselves in body or spirit to the new conditions of climate or food or labour and died. Taking all the deaths together in the slave-catching wars or raids, on the march to the sea, during the "Middle Passage" and in "seasoning"--it has been moderately reckoned that for every

African Negro who became "seasoned" at least one other Negro was killed.

Thirdly as to the actual conditions of life which a "seasoned" Negro slave had to undergo. The Negro slavery gave the Master two rights, which were indisputably established, the right to own and the right to punish. The right to own was given a wide meaning. By virtue of it the Master had not merely a right to the services of the Negro as a servant, but he had also the right to sell those services, to transmit by inheritance and to alienate them in any way he liked. The effect of this conception of the right was "to completely confound and identify the person of the slave with the thing owned." The conception of the slave as property made the Negro liable to be seized in payment of his master's debts. Even after such slaves had been emancipated they were still liable to seizure for the payment of debts contracted prior to their emancipation.

The conception of a slave as property rather than as person added further disability to the legal or civil status. He could neither own nor enjoy property in his own right. This was unlike the Roman Law, which did allow the slaves to own property, which was called peculiar. It was a limited right but it was still an important right because it shows that the Roman Law did recognise that a slave I though property was also a person. Not being a person a Negro as a slave could neither engage in trade nor marry. The right of the Master to punish a slave was also given a very cruel interpretation in its application to the Negro. In a case which arose in the state of North Carolina Court in 1829 the Chief Justice in acquitting the Master who was indicted for beating his slave observed:

> *"It was a mistake to say that the relations of Master and slave were like those of parent and child. The object of the parent in training his son was to render him fit to live the life of a free man, and, as a means to that end, he gave him moral and intellectual instruction. With the case of the slave it was very different. There could be no sense in addressing moral considerations to a slave. The end of slavery is the profit of the Master, his security and public safety; the subject, one doomed in his own person and his posterity to live without knowledge and without capacity to make anything his*

*own, and to toil that neither may reap the fruits. What moral consideration shall be addressed to such a being to convince him, that it is impossible, but that the most stupid must feel and know can never be true—that he is thus to labour on a principle of natural duty, or for the sake of his own personal happiness? Such services can only be expected from one who has no will of his own, who surrenders his will in implicit obedience to that of another. Such obedience is the consequence only of uncontrolled authority over the body. There is nothing else, which can operate to produce the effect. The power of the Master must be absolute to render the submission of the slave perfect."*

The result of such an interpretation of the Master's right to punish was that for a long time in the U.S.A. if a Negro slave chanced to die as a consequence of "a lawful correction" it was regarded by law as a lamentable and accidental homicide. How mercilessly this right to punish was exercised by the masters will be realized by a perusal of the extracts from letters written by a resident in Antigna in 1787. Says the writer:

*"The Negroes are turned out at sunrise, and employed in gangs from twenty to sixty or upwards, under the inspection of white overseers, generally poor scotch lads, who by their assiduity and industry frequently become masters of the plantations, to which they make out as indentured servants. Subordinate to these overseers are drivers, who are mostly black or mulatto fellows of the worst dispositions; these men are furnished with whips, while on duty, which they are obliged on pain of severe punishment to have with them, and are authorised to flog wherever they see the least relaxation from labour; nor is it a consideration with them, whether it proceeds from idleness, or inability, paying at the same time, little or no regard to age or sex. At twelve they are turned in (that is leave off work) to get what they can to refresh nature with; at half past one the bell rings, when they turn out and resume their labour until sunset......*

*"The punishments inflicted on slaves in this island, are various and tormenting..... Among which is the*

*thumbscrew, a barbarous invention to fasten the thumbs together, which appears to cause excruciating pain. The "iron necklace' "is a ring, locked and riveted about the neck; to these, collars are frequently added..... Which prevent the wearers from laying down their heads with any degree of comfort. The "boots" are strong iron rings, full four inches in circumference:. Closed just above the ankles; to these some owners prefix chain, which the miserable sufferers, if able to work, must manage as well as they can, and it is not un frequent to see in the streets of this town, at midday, Negroes chained together by these necklaces, as well as the boots.... The 'spurs' are rings of iron, similar to the boots, to which are added spikes from three to four inches long, placed horizontally. A chain fastened about the body with a padlock is another mode of tormenting this oppressed race of being."*

It would be a great mistake of judging a whole class of slave owners by the vice of individuals. Often enough, the attitude of slaves to their Masters was quite friendly and equally often the attitude of the Masters to their slaves was kindly. None the less the system was a system founded on a purely economic basis making it inevitable that human being be created as mere tools to be used without being influenced by any considerations of humanity.

It is unnecessary to adduce any more cases to illustrate the fact that the lowly, unfree and unprivileged classes have existed in the past in countries other than India. What is of importance is that these unfree, unprivileged classes have disappeared as a separate class and have become part and parcel of the great Society. The question is: Why has untouchability not disappeared?

## Hindus and Want of Public Conscience

The cases in which the Hindus have indulged in violence against the Untouchables are cases of fight for equal freedom to all. If the Untouchables want to go in procession, they have no objection to the Hindus doing the same. If the Untouchables want to wear gold and silver ornaments, they do not object to the Hindus having the same right. If the Untouchables want to send their children to schools, they are not against the children of the Hindus having full freedom for education. If the Untouchables wish to draw water from the well, they have no objection to the Hindus exercising their right to take water. One can go on *ad infinitum*. But it is unnecessary. The point is easy and simple to grasp. It is that whatever freedom the Untouchables claim is not exclusive to them and is not inconsistent with the right of the Hindus to equal freedom. Why then does the Hindus use violence to put down such innocent and perfectly lawful acts? Why does he regard his lawlessness as lawful? Who cannot see that the acts and omissions of the Hindus in his dealings with the Untouchables cannot be called by any other name except that of social wrongs. The acts and omissions are not mere inequities; they are not mere indignities. They are gross instances of man's inhumanity to man. For a doctor not to treat a patient because the patient is an Untouchable, for a body of Hindu villages to burn the houses of the Untouchables, to throw human excreta in their well if these are not acts of inhumanity, I wonder what can be? The question is why has the Hindu no conscience?

There is only one answer to these questions. The class composition in other countries were based on economic and social considerations. Slavery and serfdom had no foundation in religion. Untouchability though it can give and does economic advantages to the Hindus, is primarily based on religion. There is nothing sacrosanct in economic and social interests. They yield to time and circumstances. This is the broad explanation why slavery and serfdom have vanished and why untouchability has not. The same is the answer to the two other questions. If the Hindu observes untouchability it is because his religion enjoins him to do so. If he is ruthless and lawless in putting down the Untouchables rising against his Established Order, it is because his religion not only tells him that the Established Order is divine and therefore sacrosanct but also imposes upon him a duty to see that this Established Order is maintained by all means possible. If he does not listen to the call of humanity, it is because his religion does not enjoin him to regard the Untouchables as human beings. If he does not feel any qualms of conscience in assaulting, looting, burning and other acts of atrocities against the Untouchables, it is because his religion tells him that nothing is sin, which is done in defence of the social order. Many Hindus would regard this as a travesty of their religion.

The best way to meet the charge is to quote Chapter and verse from Manu who is the architect of Hindu Society. Let anyone, who denies what I have said, read the following Commands of Manu regarding untouchability. Untouchables and the duties of the Hindus in regard to them:

1. All those tribes in this world, which are excluded from (the community of) those born from the mouth, the arms, the thighs, and the feet (of Brahman), are called Dasyus, whether they speak the language of the Mlenchhas (barbarians) or that of the Aryans.
2. Near well known trees and burial ground, on mountains and in groves, let these (tribes) dwell, known (by certain marks), and subsisting by their peculiar occupations.
3. But the dwellings of the Chandalas and Shwapakas shall be outside the village, they must be made Apatras and their wealth (shall be) dogs and donkeys.
4. Their dress (shall be) the garments of the dead, (they shall eat) their food from broken dishes, black iron (shall be) their ornaments, they must always wander from place to place.
5. A man who fulfils a religious duty shall not seek intercourse with them; their transactions (shall be) among themselves, and their marriages with their equals.
6. Their food shall be given to them by others (than an Aryan giver) in a broken dish; at night they shall not walk about in villages and in towns.
7. By day they must go about for the purpose of their work, distinguished by marks at the king's command, and they shall carry out the corpses (of persons) who have no relatives, that is a settled rule.
8. By the king's order, they shall always execute the criminals in accordance with the law, and they shall take for themselves the clothes, the beds and the ornaments of (such) criminals.
9. He who has had connection with a woman of one of the lowest castes shall be put to death.

10. If one who (being a member of the Chandalas, or some other low caste) must not be touched, intentionally defiles by his touch one who (as a member of a twice born caste) may be touched (by the other twice born persons only) he shall be put to death." Can anybody, who reads these Commandments of Manu deny that it is Hindu religion, which is responsible for the perpetuation of untouchability and for the lawlessness and want of conscience on the part of the Hindus towards the Untouchables? Indeed, if the acts of omission and commission which have been detailed in the this books of this book were correlated to these ten Commandments, it will be found that the Hindus in committing these acts are merely following the Commandments of Manu. If the Hindu will not touch an Untouchable and regards it as an offence if an Untouchable touches him, it is because of the Commandments Nos. 5 and 10. If the Hindus insist upon the segregation of the Untouchables, it is because of Commandment No. 3. If the Hindu will not allow the Untouchable to wear clean clothes, gold ornaments, he is only following Commandment No. 8. If the Hindu will not tolerate an Untouchable acquiring property and wealth, he is only following Commandment No. 3.

It is really unnecessary to labour the matter further. It is incontrovertible that the main cause which is responsible for the fate of the Untouchables is the Hindu religion and its teachings. A comparison between Paganism and Christianity in relation to slavery and Hinduism in relation to untouchability reveals how different has been the influence of the two religions on human institutions, how elevating has been the influence of the former and how degrading that of the latter. Those who are fond of comparing slavery with Untouchability do not realize that they are facing a paradox. Legally the slave was not a freeman. Yet, socially he had all the freedom necessary for the growth of his personality. Legally the Untouchable is a freeman. Yet, socially he has no freedom for the growth of his personality.

This is indeed a very glaring paradox. What is the explanation of this paradox? There is only one explanation of this paradox. It is that while religion was on the side of the slave, religion has been against the Untouchables. The Roman law declared that the slave was not a person. But the religion of Rome refused to accept that principle, at any rate, refused to extend that principle to social field. It treated him I as a human being fit for comradeship. The Hindu Law declared that the Untouchable was not a person. Contrary to Paganism, the Hindu religion not only accepted the principle but also extended it to the social field. As the Hindu Law did not regard the Untouchable a person, Hinduism refused to regard him as a human being fit for comradeship.

That the Roman religion saved the slave from the social degradation consequent upon his legal degradation is beyond question. It saved him from such degradation in three different ways. One way by which the Roman religion saved the slave was to keep the most sacred place open for the slave to occupy. As has been observed:

> *"Roman religion was never hostile to the slave. It did not close the temple doors against him; it did not banish him from its festivals. If slaves were excluded from certain ceremonies the same may be said of freemen and women—men being excluded from the rites of Bona Dea, Vesta and Ceras, women from those of Hercules at the Ara Maxima. In the days when the old Roman divinities counted for something, the slave came to be informally included in the family, and could consider himself under the protection of the Gods of the household..... Augustus ordered that freed women should be eligible as priestesses of Vesta. The law insisted that a slave's grave should be regarded as sacred and for his soul Roman Mythology provided no special heaven and no particular hell. Even Juvenal agrees that the slave's soul and body, is made of the same stuff as his master."*

The second way in which the Roman religion helped the slave was equivalent to lodging a complaint before the City Prefect whose duty it became to hear cases of wrong done to slaves by their masters. This was a secular remedy. But the Roman religion had provided another and a better remedy. According to it, the slave was entitled to throw himself before the altar and demand that he should be sold to a kinder master. The third way in which the Roman religion saved the slave by preventing the Roman Law from destroying the sanctity of his personality as a human being. It did not make him unfit for human association and comradeship. For the Roman slave this was the greatest saving grace. Suppose Roman society had an objection to buy vegetables, milk, butter or take water or wine from the hands of the slave; suppose Roman society had an objection to allow slaves to touch them, to enter their houses, travel with them in cars, etc., would it have been possible for the master to train his slave to raise him from semi-barbarism to a cultured state? Obviously not; it is because the slave was not held to be an Untouchable that the master could train him and raise him. We again come back therefore to the same conclusion, namely, that What has saved the slave is that his personality was recognised by society and what has ruined the Untouchable is that Hindu society did not recognise his personality, treated him as one whose personality was unclean which rendered him as unfit for human association and common dealing.

There was no gulf, social or religious, which separated the slave from the rest of the society. In outward appearance he did not differ from the freeman; neither colour nor clothing revealed his condition; he witnessed the same games as the freeman; he shared in the life of the Municipal towns and got employed in the State service, engaged himself in trade and commerce as all freemen did. Often apparent equality in outward things counts far more to the individual than actual identity of rights before the law. Between the slave and the freed there seems often to have been little social barrier, Marriage between the slave and freed and even freed and slave was very common. The slave status carried no stigma on the man in the slave. He was Touchable and even respectable. All this was due to the attitude of the Roman religion towards the slave.

There is no space to describe at length the attitude of Christianity to slavery. But it was different from Paganism. It is not known to many that during the period of slavery in America, Christian priests were not prepared to convert Negro slaves to Christianity because of their view that it would degrade Christianity if the convert remained a slave. In their opinion, one Christian could not hold another Christian as a slave. He was bound to offer him fellowship.

To sum up. Law and Religion are two forces which govern the i conduct of men. At times, they act as handmaids to each other. At other times, they act as check and counter-check. Of the two forces, Law is personal while religion is impersonal. Law being personal it is Capable of being unjust and iniquitous. But religion being impersonal, it can be impartial.

If religion remains impartial, it is capable of defeating the inequity committed by law. This is exactly what happened in Rome in regard to the slave.

That is why religion is believed to ennoble man and not to degrade him. Hinduism is an exception. It has made the Untouchable sub-human. It has made the Hindu inhuman. There is no escape to either from the established order of the sub-human and the inhuman.

## Hindus and Their Want of Social Conscience

Everyone who feels moved by the deplorable condition of the Untouchables begins by saying: "We must do something for the Untouchables". One seldom hears any of the persons interested in the problem saying: "Let us do something to change the Hindu."

It is invariably assumed that the object to the reclaimed is the Untouchables as though untouchability was due to his depravity and that he alone is responsible for his condition. If there is to be a Mission, it must be to the Untouchables. Nothing requires to be done to the Hindu. He is sound in mind, manners and morals. He is whole, there is nothing wrong with him. He is not the Sinner.

What is the real state of affairs? This argument that there is nothing wrong with the Hindus and that the Untouchable is responsible for whatever wrong he suffers is very much the argument that is used by the Christians for defending themselves against the inhuman treatment accorded by them to the Jews. A very crushing reply has been given by Mr. Louis Goulding to the Christians on behalf of the suffering Jews. In discussing the source of the Jewish Problem Mr. Louis Goulding says:

"I beg leave to give a very homely instance of the sense in which I consider the Jewish Problem in essence a Gentile

Problem. A close acquaintance of mine is a certain Irish Terrier of mixed pedigree, the dog Paddy, who is to my friend John Smith as the apple of both his eyes. Paddy dislikes Scotch terriers; it is enough for one to pass within twenty yards of Paddy to deafen the neighbourhood with challenges and insults. It is a practice which John Smith deplores, which, therefore, he does his best to check—all the more as the object of Paddy's detestation are often inoffensive creatures, who seldom speak first.

Despite all his affection for Paddy, he considers, as I do, that Paddy's unmannerly behaviour is due to some measure of original sin in Paddy. It has not yet been suggested to us that what is here involved is a Scotch Terrier Problem and that when Paddy attacks a neighbour who is peacefully engaged in inspecting the evening smells it is the neighbour who should be arraigned for inciting to attack by the fact of his existence."

If we equate Paddy to the Hindu and Scotch Terrior to the Untouchable the argument of Goulding will apply to the Hindus no less than it does to the Christians. If for the reasons given by Mr. Goulding the Jewish Problem is in reality a Christian Problem then the Problem of the Untouchables is primarily a Hindu Problem.

Are the Hindus conscious, do they recognise that the Untouchables are a problem to them? Are they worried about it? Is it weighing on their minds? Certain obvious tests may be applied in order to ascertain the truth. One test is the volume of literature on the subject.

One can take the volume of literature issued on the Negroes of America as a standard measure. One is amazed at the huge amount of printed material that exists in the United States on the subject of the Negroes. It is said that a really complete bibliography on the Negro Problem would run up to several hundred thousand titles. The literature is really immeasurable. This proves as nothing else can, how much it is a problem to the Whites. It has disturbed through several generations all classes of people in America, the religious moralists, the political philosophers, the Statesmen, the philanthropists, the social scientists, the politicians, the businessmen and the plain ordinary citizen as well.

What is the amount of literature on the Untouchables that exists in India? Not more than half a dozen pamphlets! Another test would be the test of social behaviour. I give below two cases reported in the papers. One is from the '*Pratap*' of 5th March 1926. It gives the following news:

> *"On the 23rd of February at about 11 O'clock in the day, a group of about 12 or 13 were digging earth in Begumganj, Lucknow when the quarry collapsed and they were all buried under heaps of earth. One boy and six women were rescued after the earth had been removed out of whom only one woman turned out to be alive, who belonged to Mirpur. She had received grievous injuries and her condition was very critical. The Hindu inhabitants of Begumganj however refused to give a bed to lay that woman on. At last a Muslim offered a bed; now there was no Hindu prepared to help to carry the poor woman as far as her house. At last, a sweeper was called and he undertook to carry the woman to her home as she lay on the bed."*

The best illustration of the absence of conscience in the Hindu towards the Untouchables is to be found in the following incident which is reported by the Correspondent of the '*Sangram*' and published in its issue of 10th July 1946. The correspondent says:

> *"A woman died on the 8th of July 1946 in the Anath Ashram (Beggars Home) called Azil situated in a village called Mhapse (in Goa) and maintained by Christians. The woman was believed to be a Hindu. She was alone and had no relations. Seeing that there was no one to dispose of the dead body and to perform funeral rites, the Hindus of the village came together and raised a subscription for the purpose. They brought the dead body out of the Beggars' Home. Just about that time some Untouchables, who knew the woman came there and recognized the dead body. The moment the Hindus came to know that the woman belonged to the Untouchables the Hindus who had gathered there deserted the dead body and started walking away. The Untouchables who had come requested the Hindus to give them the amount they had collected for buying the*

*coffin and the shroud. The Hindus refused to part with the money saying that the money was collected from the subscribers on the representation that the deceased woman was a Hindu woman. As she is not a Hindu but an Untouchable, they can't spend the money on her funeral. The Untouchables had to do their best to dispose of their dead body. The Untouchables had good evidence of the love and affection the Hindus bear towards them.*

The following is from the '*Milap*' of 2nd October 1925. Its correspondent reports:

*"News has been received from Ruddurprayag that one evening in the first week of September a Harijan came to the Dharmashala (or monastery) of Ruddurprayag. When he learnt that a tiger came there every night, he requested the pastor of the Dharmashala to let him lie hidden in some corner of the Dharmashala for the night, so that he may remain safe from the tiger. The callous pastor, however, paid no heed to the request and closed the gates of the Dharmashala. The ill-starred Harijan laid himself down outside in one corner, full of apprehensions of the tiger. Towards the end of the night the tiger came and attacked the Harijan. As the man was quite strong and healthy and despair made him fearless, he caught hold of the tiger's neck and shouted 'I have grabbed the tiger. Come and kill him'. But the high caste pastor did not open the door, nor did he offer any sort of help, so that very soon the grip of the Harijan loosened and the tiger also ran away. At present the man is lying wounded in Shrinagar (Garhwal) where he is getting himself treated. His condition is said to be critical."*

The heartlessness disclosed by these instances shows that the Hindu does not bother about what he does to the Untouchables or about what happens to the Untouchables.

A third test would be the test of service and sacrifice for the uplift of the Untouchables.

Here again, one may adopt the service and sacrifice of the Americans for raising the Negroes as our standard measure. Here are some figures.

Consider the requests made by the Whites for the benefit of the Negro education.

| Testator | Amount (in Dollars) | Testator | Amount (in Dollars) |
|---|---|---|---|
| Kane | 50.000 | Mason | 1.00.000 |
| Harton | 5.000 | Naunbert | 40.000 |
| Troughton | 1.60.600 | Harrison | 2.30.000 |
| Ottinger | 500 | Munger | 75.000 |
| Gambrille | 35.000 | Corliss | 45.000 |
| Jarepki | 1.000 | Rosenbanin | 1.000 |
| Strock | 500 | Burton | 1.000 |
| Kidder | 5.000 | Conroy | 1.00.000 |
| Clodin | 10.000 | Kent | 10.000 |
| Wood | 500 | Duke | 1.40.000 |
| Harkness | 12.50.000 | Marciliat | 5.000 |
| Beatie | 2.90,000 | Masey | 25.000 |
| Marquant | 5.000 | Nicholas | 20.000 |
| Newton | 5.000 | Garretson | 15.00.000 |
| Hummington | 25,000 | Hatcher | 20.000 |
| Phelps-Stokes | 2.80.000 | Wright | 10.000 |
| Butler | 30.000 | | |

These figures relate to the period before 1930. They do not take account of residuary bequests.

Compare the Educational funds that exist for the advancement of education among the Negroes. They are:

(i) The Avery Fund.

(ii) The Vilas Bequest.

(iii) The African Fund.

(iv) The Buckingham Fund.

(v) The George Washington Educational Fund.

(vi) The Miner Fund.

(vii) The Steward Missionary Foundation.

(viii) The Daniel Hand Fund.

(ix) The John Slater Fund.

(x) The Phelps-Stokes Fund.

In addition to this, there are general Funds such as the

Carnegie Corporation Julius Rosenwald Fund and the Rockfeller Foundation which also help the Negroes. The amounts distributed by these funds is not known. But they must be amounting to millions.

Compare the amount spent by Religious organizations on the education of the Negroes. Here are some interesting figures.

| | **Annual Expenditure (In Dollars)** | **Permanent fund for Negro Education (In Dollars)** | **Value of school plants, etc. (In Dollars)** |
|---|---|---|---|
| American Baptist Home Mission Board | 116,247 | 1.597,700 | 3.594,251 |
| American Church Institute for Negroes (Episcopal) | 185.100 | 450,000 | 3,000,000 |
| American Missionary Association | 368.057 | 3.228.421 | 3.200.000 |
| Church of Christ (Disciples) United Christian Missionary Society | 91,072 | | 500,000 |
| Lutheran Evangelical Synodical Conference of North America Board Colored Mission | 74,900 | | 175,000 |
| Methodist Episcopal Church Board of Education. Institutions for Negroes | 259.264 | 1,962.729 | 5,000.000 |
| Methodist Episcopal Church Woman's | 104,975 | | 360,000 |
| Home Missionary Society of Presbyterian Church in the U.S.A. Division of Missions for Colored People | 405,327 | 1,994.032 | 3.560.000 |
| United Presbyterian Church Board of Mission for Freemen | 98,000 | 645,000 | 1.000.000 |

It is estimated that the total amount spent for the religious and philanthropic organizations between 1865 and 1930 comes to 135,000,000 dollars on the advancement of the Negroes. Of this amount, 85,000,000 dollars have been contributed by the Whites.

What is the measure of service and sacrifice of the Hindus for the elevation of the Untouchables. The only organization the Hindus can boast of is the Harijan Sevak Sangh. Its capital fund does not probably go beyond 10 lakhs. Its annual expenditure does not go beyond a few thousand rupees on petty and insignificant and insubstantial purposes. The Fund is not a welfare fund. It is essentially a Political Fund intended to make the Untouchables vote with the Hindus.

Why is this difference? Why do the Americans exert so much in service and sacrifice for the elevation of the Negroes and why have the Hindus cared to do nothing for the elevation of the Untouchables? The answer is that the Americans have a social conscience while the Hindus have none. It is not that the Hindus have no sense of right and wrong, good and bad, moral and immoral. What is wrong with the Hindu is that his sense of moral obligation towards others is restricted to a limited class of people, namely, the members of his caste. As Mr. H. J. Paton says" Clearly a man may be a good member of a limited society without being a morally good man.

There seem indeed to be already shadows or anticipations of moral excellence even in the man who carries out coherently an individual policy of life; and we begin to find something which we may almost mistake for virtue itself, when we consider the man who is a loyal member of any society, even of a gang of thieves. Yet although there must be honour among thieves, a thief is not therefore an honourable man. The morally good man seems to be the man who is good as a member not of a limited society but of an unlimited society—of a society of societies whose purpose includes all purposes, and beyond which there is no other society to be a source of conflicting claims of duties." The Untouchable does not belong to the society of the Hindus and the Hindu does not feel that he and the Untouchables belong to one society. This is the reason why the conduct of the Hindu is marked by a moralistic unconcernedness.

Not having conscience, the Hindu has no such thing in him as righteous indignation against the inequities and injustices from which the Untouchable has been suffering. He sees no wrong in these inequities and injustices and refuses to budge. By his absence of conscience the Hindu is a great obstacle in the path of the removal of untouchability.

## The Hindu and his Belief in Caste

Among the Hindu social reformers there is a moderate section. This section holds that untouchability is separate from the caste system. Following this ideology they hold that it is possible to remove untouchability without attacking the caste system. The religious minded Hindu is as opposed to the removal of untouchability as he is to the removal of the caste system. He is as opposed to dealing with social reform in two stages as he is in dealing with it in one stage. But the politically minded Hindu is tremendously fond of the idea. That is obviously for two reasons. In the first place, it gives the Hindu the chance of showing himself in international world as a better specimen of democracy than he really is. Secondly, by leaving caste alone there is no risk of the caste Hindus forsaking the Congress.

Those who propose to deal with untouchability without damaging the caste system, rest their case on verse 4 of Chapter X of the Manusmriti. In the verse, Manu says that there are only four varnas and that there is no fifth varna. This verse is interpreted to mean that the untouchables are included in the fourth varna, that they are part of the Sudras and as there is no objection to touching the Sudras there could be no objection to touching the Untouchables. However pleasing this construction may be to the politically minded Hindu, it does accord with the intention of what Manu wanted to convey. The verse is open to another construction. It may mean that Manu was not prepared to enlarge the Chaturvarnya and make it a Panchavarnya by recognising these communities which were outside the four varnas as constituting the fifth varna.

In saying that there is no fifth varna what he means to suggest is that he did not want to incorporate those outside the four varnas into the Hindu society by making the Hindu society consist of five varnas instead of four. That he wanted to convey the latter intention is abundantly clear by speaking of a category of people as Bahyas or Varna Bahyas which means those outside the varna system. If Manu wanted to include all persons within the four varnas there was no reason for speaking of some people as varna Bahyas. Indeed, he recognises two sub-divisions within the class of Varna Bahyas. He calls them Hinas and Antayevasins . Given these facts, it is obvious that the construction sought to be placed in the verse in the Manusmriti will not deceive the orthodox Hindu into accepting that the maintenance of untouchability is contrary to the Manusmriti and that its abolition is not therefore contrary to the tenets of the Hindu religion.

The argument based on the interpretation of Manu's text is too intellectual for the ordinary uneducated Hindu. He knows only two things. One thing he knows is that there are three barriers in the matter of social intercourse which he must observe. They are (1) prohibition against inter-dining,

(2) prohibition against inter-marriage, while in untouchability there is third barrier added and (3) prohibition against physically touching certain class of people. The first two barriers make up the caste. The third forms untouchability. The caste Hindu does not bother about the number of barriers. He is particular about the observance of the barrier. When he is asked not to observe, he turns round and asks why not? His argument is that, if I am free to observe the first two barriers, what is wrong if I observe the third? Psychologically, caste and untouchability are one integral system based on one and the same principle. If the caste Hindus observe untouchability it is because they believe in caste.

Looked at from this point of view, the idea of hoping to remove untouchability without destroying the caste system is an utter futility. The underlying idea that caste and untouchability are two different things is founded on a fallacy. The two are one and are inseparable. Untouchability is only an extension of the caste system. There can be no severance between the two. The two stand together and will fall together.

There is another reason why untouchability cannot disappear by a stratagem, legal or rational. As has already been pointed out, the Hindu social order is based on the principle of graded inequality. It may not bean exaggeration to say that not many people understand the significance of this principle. The social system based on inequality stands on a different footing from a social system based on graded, inequality. The former is a weak system which is not capable of self-I preservation. The latter on the other hand, is capable of self-preservation. In a social system based on inequality, the low orders can combine to overthrow the system. None of them have any interest to preserve it. In a social system based on graded inequality the possibility of a general common attack by the aggrieved parties is nonexistent. In a system of graded inequality, the aggrieved parties are not on a common level.

This can happen only when they are only high and low. In the system of graded inequality there are the highest (the Brahmins). Below the highest are the higher (the Kshatriyas). Below the higher are those who are high (Vaishya). Below the high are the low (Sudra) and below the low are those who are lower (the Untouchables). All have a grievance against the highest and would like to bring about their down fall. But they will not combine. The higher is anxious to get rid of the highest but does not wish to combine with the high, the low and the lower lest they should reach his level and be his equal. The high wants to overthrow the higher who is above him but does not want to join hands with the low and the lower, lest they should rise to his status and become equal to him in rank.

The low is anxious to pull down the highest, the higher and the high but he would not make a common cause with the lower for fear of the lower gaining a higher status and becoming his equal in the system of graded inequality there is no such class as completely unprivileged class except the one which is at the base of the social pyramid. The privileges of the rest are graded. Even the low is a privileged class as compared with the lower. Each class being privileged, every class is interested in maintaining the social system.

Untouchability may be a misfortune to the Untouchables. But there is no doubt that it is a good fortune to the Hindus. It gives them a class which they can look down upon. The Hindus do not want a system in which nobody will be anybody. They also do not want a system in which everybody may be somebody. They want a system in which they will be some bodies and others will be nobodies. The Untouchables are nobodies. This makes the Hindus some bodies. The system of untouchability sustains the natural pride of the Hindus and make them feel as well as look big. This is an additional reason why the Hindus are not likely to give up untouchability particularly those large majority who are small men.

Untouchability will vanish only when the whole of the Hindu Social Order, particularly the caste system will be dissolved. Is this possible? Every institution is sustained by some sort of a sanction. There are three kinds of sanction, which supply life force to an institution. They are legal, social and religious. The vitality of the institution depends upon the nature of the sanction. What is the nature of the sanction behind the caste system? Unfortunately, the sanction behind the caste system is the religious sanction, for, the caste as a new form of the Varna system derives its sanction from the Vedas which form the sacred book of the Hindu religion and which are infallible. I say unfortunately because anything which has a religious sanction becomes by virtue of it sacred and eternal. To the Hindu, caste is sacred and caste is eternal. If caste cannot vanish what hope is there for untouchability to disappear?

## What the Untouchables have to Face?

***Antagonism of the Administration:*** Section 2 of the Indian Penal Code reads as follows: "Every person shall be liable to punishment under this Code and not otherwise for every act or omission contrary to the provisions thereof, of which he shall be guilty within British India." The Law Commissioners who prepared the draft Penal Code in their address to the Secretary of State thought it necessary to draw pointed attention to the words 'Every Person'. In the course of their observation, they said:

"Your Lordship in Council will see that we have not proposed to except from the operation of this Code any of the ancient sovereign houses of India residing within the Company's territories. Whether any such exception ought to be made is a question which, without a more accurate knowledge that we possess of existing treaties, of the sense in which those treaties have been understood, of the history of negotiations, of the temper and of the power of particular families, and of the feeling of the body of the people towards those families, we could not venture to decide. We will only beg permission most respectfully to observe that every such exception is an evil; that is an evil that any man should be above the law; that it is still greater evil that the public should be taught to regard as a high and enviable distinction the privilege of being above the law; that the longer such privileges are suffered to last, the more difficult it is to take them away; that there can scarcely even be a fairer opportunity for taking them away than at the time when the Government promulgates a new Code binding alike on persons of different races and religions; and that we greatly doubt whether any consideration, except that of public faith solemnly pledged, deserves to be weighed against the advantages of equal justice."

It might have been thought that this principle of equal justice would strike a death blow to the Established Order. As a matter of fact, far from suffering any damage the Established

Order has continued to operate in spite of it. It might be asked why the principle of equal justice has failed to have its effect. The answer to this is simple. To enunciate the principle of justice is one thing. To make it effective is another thing. Whether the principle of equal justice is effective or not must necessarily depend upon the nature and character of the civil services who must be left to administer the principle. If the civil service is by reason of its class bias the friend of the Established Order and the enemy of the new Order, the new Order can never come into being.

That a civil service in tune with the new order was essential for the success of the new order was recognised by Karl Marx in 1871 in the formation of the Paris Commune and adopted by Lenin in the constitution of Soviet Communism. Unfortunately, the British Government never cared about the personnel of the Civil Service. Indeed it opened the gates of the administration to those classes who believed in the old Established Order of the Hindus in which the principle of equality had no place. As a result of this fact, India has been ruled by the British but administered by the Hindus. A few statistics of the composition of the Civil Service will fully demonstrate this fact.

From the capital of India down to the village the whole administration is rigged by the Hindus. The Hindus are like the omnipotent almighty pervading all over the administration in all its branches having its authority in all its nooks and corners. There is no loophole for anyone opposed to the old order to escape. No matter what the Department, whether it is Revenue, Police or Justice it is manned by the Hindu. If the Established Order has continued to exist, it is because of the unfailing support it received from the Hindu officials of the State.

The Hindu officials are not merely administering the affairs on their merit. They are administering them with an eye to the parties. Their principle is not equal justice to all. Their motto is justice consistent with the Established Order. This is inevitable. For they carry over into administration the attitude towards different classes in society under the Established Order. This is well illustrated by the attitude of the State officials towards the Untouchables in the field of administration.

As every Untouchable will be able to testify, if an Untouchable goes to a police officer with a complaint against the caste Hindu, instead of receiving any protection he will receive plenty of abuses. Either he will be driven away without his complaint being recorded or if it is recorded, it would be recorded quite falsely to provide a way of escape to the Touchable aggressors. If he prosecutes his offenders before a Magistrate the fate of his proceedings could be foretold. The Untouchables will never be able to get Hindus as witnesses because of the conspiracy of the villagers not to support the case of the Untouchables, however just it may be. If he brings witnesses from the Untouchables, the Magistrate will not accept their testimony because he can easily say that they are interested and not independent witnesses or, if they are independent witnesses the Magistrate has an easy way of acquitting the accused by simply saying that the Untouchables compliment did not strike him as a truthful witness. He can do this fearlessly knowing full well that the higher tribunal will not reverse his finding because of the well-established rule which says that an appellate court should not disturb the finding of the trial Magistrate based upon the testimony of witness whose demeanour he had no opportunity to observe:

That such a discrimination is practised has now been admitted even by Congressmen. The annual Report of the Tamil Nadu Harijan Sevak Sangh for the year ending September 30, 1937 says:

*"The political consciousness of the Harijans having been roused by the rights in the remotest villages where it is only the policeman that reign, it is not always possible for the Harijan to do this, for the assertion of his rights means a clash between him and the castemen, in which it is always the latter that have the upper hand. The natural consequences of this scuffle is a complaint either to the police or the Magistrate. The latter course is beyond the means of a Harijan while the former resort is worse than useless. The complaints are in many cases not inquired into at all, while in others a verdict favourable to the castemen is entered. Our complaints to the Police also meet with similar fate. The trouble seems to us to be that there is no change in the mentality*

*of the lower policeman. Either he is unaware of the rights of the Harijans of which he is supposed to be the guardian or he is influenced by caste men. Or, it may also be that he is absolutely indifferent. In other cases, corruption is responsible for his taking the side of the richer caste men."*

This shows how the Hindu official is anti-Untouchable and pro-Hindu. Whenever he has any authority or discretion, it is always exercised to the prejudice of the Untouchables. The police and the Magistrate are sometimes corrupt. If they were only corrupt, things would not perhaps be so bad because an officer who is corrupt is open to purchase by either party. But the misfortune is that the Police and Magistrates are often more partial than corrupt. It is this partiality to the Hindus and his antipathy to the Untouchables which results in the denial of protection and justice to the Untouchables. There is no cure for this partiality to the one and antipathy to the other, because it is founded in the social and religious repugnance, which is inborn in every Hindu. The Police and the Magistrates by reason of their motives, interest and their breeding, do not sympathise with the living force operating among the Untouchables. They are not charged with the wants, the pains, the carvings and the desires, which actuate the Untouchables. Consequently, they are openly hostile and inimical to their aspirations, do not help them to advance, disfavour their cause and snap at everything that smacks of pride and self-respect. On the other hand, they share the feelings of the Hindus, sympathise with them in the attempt to maintain their power, authority, prestige and their dignity over the Untouchables. In any conflict between the two, they act as the agents of the Hindus in suppressing this revolt of the Untouchables and participate quite openly and shamefacedly in the nefarious attempt of all Hindus to do every thing possible by all means, fair or foul, to teach the Untouchables a lesson and hold them down in their own places.

The worst of it is that all this injustice and persecution can be perpetrated within the limits of the law. A Hindu may well say that he will not employ an Untouchable, that he will not sell him anything, that he will evict him from his land, that he will not allow him to take his cattle across his field without offending the law in the slightest degree. In doing so, he is only expressing his right. The law does not care with what motive he does it. The law does not see what injury it causes to the Untouchable. The police may misuse his power and his authority. He may deliberately falsify the record by taking down something, which has not been stated or by taking down some thing which is quite different from what has been stated. He may disclose evidence to the side in which he is interested. He may refuse to arrest. He may do a hundred and one things to spoil the case. All this he can do without the slightest fear of being caught. The loopholes of law are many, and he knows them well. The Magistrate has vested in him an enormous amount of discretion. He is free to use it. The decision of a case depends upon the witnesses who can give evidence. But the decision of the case depends upon whether the witnesses are reliable or not. It is open to the Magistrate to believe one side and disbelieve the other side. He may be quite arbitrary in believing one side, but it is his discretion, and no one can interfere with it. There are innumerable cases in which this discretion has been exercised by the Magistrates to the prejudice of the Untouchables. However truthful the witnesses of the Untouchables the Magistrates take a common line by saying I disbelieve the witnesses', and nobody has questioned that discretion. What sentence to inflict is also a matter of discretion with the Magistrate. There are sentences, which are non appealable. An appeal is a way of getting redress. But this way may be blocked by a Magistrate by refusing to give an appealable sentence.

If the Hindu society plays its part in maintaining the Established Order, so does the Hindu officials of the State. The two have made the Established Order impregnable.

## Problem of Discrimination

To the Untouchables the problem of discrimination in order of seriousness is only next to the problem of recovering their manhood. The discrimination against the Untouchables is practised by the Hindus on a scale, the extent of which it is impossible for an outsider to imagine There is no field of life in which the Untouchables and the Hindus come into competition and in which the former is not subjected to discrimination. It is also of the most virulent type. In the matter of social relationship, it takes the form of barriers against dancing, bathing, eating, drinking, wrestling, worshipping. It puts a ban on all common cycles of participation.

In the use of public facilities, the spirit of discrimination manifests itself in the exclusion of Untouchables from schools, wells, temples and means of conveyance. Public administration is most deeply drenched by the spirit of discrimination against the Untouchables. It has affected Law Courts, Government Departments, Cooperative Banks, and particularly the Police. Discrimination against Untouchables in the matter of securing land, credit, jobs exist in the most rampant form. It is in service that discrimination shows itself most strongly. Though there are no regulations, there are well-recognised rules, which govern the entry and promotion of the Untouchables in the matter of service. Most often an Untouchable will not get an entry. Whole departments are closed to them. The weaving side of the Textile Mills the whole of Army is closed to the Untouchables If did, there is a well-set limit beyond which the Untouchable may not rise, no matter what his efficiency or length of service. The principle in general is maintained that the Untouchables shall not be placed in administrative authority over the Hindus. The consequence is that unless some entire branch of service is turned over the Untouchables, there are very few posts of consequence, which the Untouchables are allowed to fill. To put it concretely, the only field of service in which there is no discrimination against the Untouchables is scavenging. There is no need for discrimination in this field because the whole of it is made over to the Untouchables and there is no competition from the Hindus. Even here discrimination steps in the matter of higher posts. All unclean work is done by the Untouchables. But all supervisory posts which carry higher salary and which do not involve contact with filth are all filled by Hindus.

In this situation rights of citizenship cannot mean the rights of the Untouchables. Government of the people and for the people cannot mean Government for the Untouchables; equal opportunity for all cannot mean equal opportunity for the Untouchables; equal rights for all cannot mean equal rights for the Untouchables. All over the country in every nook and corner the Untouchable faces handicaps, suffers discriminations, is meted injustices to the Untouchables, the most unprivileged people in India. The extent to which this is true is known only to the Untouchables who labour under the disadvantages. This discrimination is the strongest barrier against the Untouchables. It prevents them from rising out of it. It has made the life of the Untouchables one of the constant fears of one thing or another, of unemployment, assault, persecution, etc. It is a life of insecurity.

There is another form of discrimination, which though subtle is nonetheless real. Under it a systematic attempt will be made to lower the dignity and status of a meritorious Untouchable. A Hindu leader would be described merely as a great Indian leader. No one would describe him as the leader of Kashmiri Brahmin even though he be one.

If a leader who happens to be an Untouchable is to be referred to he will be described as so and so, the leader of the Untouchables. A Hindu doctor would be described as a great Indian doctor. No one would describe him as a Iyengar even though he be one.

If a doctor happens to be an Untouchable doctor, he would be referred to as so and so, the Untouchable doctor. A Hindu singer would be described as a great Indian singer. If the same person happens to be an Untouchable he would be described as an Untouchable singer. A Hindu wrestler would be described as a great Indian Gymnast. If he happens to be an Untouchable he would be described as an Untouchable gymnast.

This type of discrimination has its origin in the Hindu view that the Untouchables are an inferior people and however qualified, their great men are only great among the Untouchables. They can never be greater nor even equal to the great men among the Hindus. This type of discrimination, though social in character, is no less galling than economic discrimination.

Discrimination is merely another name for absence of freedom. For as Mr. Tawney says : "There is no such thing as freedom in the market, divorced from the realities of a specific time and place. Whatever else it may or may not imply, it involves the power of choice between alternatives a choice which is real, not merely nominal, between alternatives which exist in fact, not only on paper. It means, in short, the ability to do or refrain from doing definite things, at a definite moment, in definite circumstances, or it means nothing at all. Because a man is most a man when he thinks, wills and acts, freedom deserves the outline things, which poets have said about it; but, as a part of the prose of every day life, it is quite practical and realistic.

Every individual possesses certain requirements ranging from the material necessities of existence to the need to express himself in speech and writing, to share in the conduct of affairs of common interests, and to worship God in his own way or to refrain from worshipping him the satisfaction of which it is necessary to his welfare. Reduced to its barest essential, his freedom consists in the opportunity secured by him, within the limits set by nature and the enjoyment of similar opportunities by his fellows, to take the action needed to order to ensure that these requirements are satisfied."

It is not my intention to add yet another catalogue of essential rights to the liberties of such lists, which already exist; but these are two observations, which apply to all of them. In the first place, if the rights are to be an effective guarantee of freedom, they must not be merely formed, like the right of all who can afford it to dine at the Ritz. They must be such that, whenever the occasion arises to exercise them, they can in fact be exercised.

The rights to vote and to combine, if not wholly valueless, are obviously attenuated, when the use of the former I means eviction and of the latter the sack; the right to the free choice of an occupation, if the expenses of entering a profession are prohibitive; the right to justice, if no poor man can pay for it; the right to life, liberty, and the pursuit of happiness, if the environment is such as to ensure that a considerable proportion of those born will die within twelve months, and that the happiness investments of the remainder are a gambling stock.

In the second place, the rights which are essential to freedom must be such as to secure the liberties of all, not merely of a minority. Some sage has remarked that marriage would not be regarded as a national institution if, while 5 per cent of the population were polygamous, the majority passed their lives unsolved and unencumbered by husbands or wives. The same is true of freedom. Society in which some groups can do much what they please, while others can do little of what they ought, may have virtues of its own; but freedom is not one of them. It is free in so far, and only in so far, as all the elements composing it are able in fact, and not merely in theory, to make the most of their powers, to grow to their full stature, I to do what they conceive to be their duty, and since liberty should not be too austere to have their fling when they feel like it. In so far as the opportunity to lead a life worthy of human beings is restricted to a minority, what is commonly described, as freedom would more properly be called privilege.

The discriminations against the Untouchables are merely the reflections of that deep and strong Hindu sentiment which is carried over in law and administration which justifies the making of distinctions between Hindus and Untouchables to the disadvantage of the Untouchables. Those discriminations have their roots in fear of the Hindus that in a free field, the Untouchables may rise above the prescribed station in life and become a menace to the Hindu Social Order the cardinal principle of which is the maintenance of Hindu superiority and Hindu domination over the Untouchables. So long as the Hindu Social Order lasts, discriminations against the Untouchables continue to exist.

## Problem of Isolation

Why has the movement of the Untouchables not succeeded? Have they no allies? If there are allies why do they not help and cooperate with the Untouchables? This is a very pertinent question and it is necessary that it should be properly understood. For answering this question, it is essential to have a very clear idea of the Hindu social organisation and the classes of which it is composed.

The structure of Hindu society is a very complicated one and it would be difficult for one, whose life has not been woven into it, to know the pattern. Perhaps, a diagrammatic presentation may be helpful. I give below one which, in my judgement, facilitate the understanding of the social structure of the Hindus:

**Hindus**

| Caste Hindus<br>(Savarna Hindus)<br>(Avarna Hindus) | | Non-Caste Hindus | |
|---|---|---|---|
| Class I | Class II | Class III | Class IV |
| | | 1. Primitive Tribes<br>2 Criminal Tribes. | |
| | | | Untouchables |
| High Caste—Dvijas<br>Traivarnikas— | | Castes evolved out of the Sudra or fourth varna | Low Castes— |
| Castes evolved out of the three varnas: Brahmins, Kshatriyas and Vaishyas. | | | |

The diagram shows that although there are innumerable castes among the Hindus, they can all be grouped under four classes. Of these four, Class I forms the *Herenfolk* or the Ruling Class, Classes III and IV form the subject people.

Let us now consider which of these classes can be the natural ally of the Untouchables.

Those in Class I form the privileged classes of the Hindu society. The Hindu social order was created by them. They alone benefit by it while the aim of these in Class I is to save it. Neither by community of interest nor by reason of ideological affinity can the two friends and allies disagree.

What about the Criminal and Primitive Tribes? They have the strongest ground for overthrowing the Hindu Social Order. What about the Sudras?

The laws of the Hindu Social Order are as repulsive to Class II, the Sudras as they are to Class IV, the Untouchables. It is interesting to know the status of the Sudras in the Hindu society as prescribed by Manu the Lawgiver and the Architect of Hindu society. For an easy understanding of the subject, the rules regarding the status of the Sudras are set out below under separate heads: Manu asks the householders of the Brahmans, Kshatriyas and Vaishyas:

IV. 61 "Let him not dwell in a country where the rulers are Sudras."

A Sudra is not to be deemed to be a respectable person. For Manu enacts that:

XI. 24. "A Brahmin shall never beg from a Sudra, property for (performing) a sacrifice *i.e.*, for religious purposes." All marriages with the Sudra were proscribed. Marriage with a woman belonging to any of three other classes was forbidden. A Sudra was not to have a connection with a woman of the higher classes and an act of adultery committed by a Sudra with her was considered by Manu to be an offence involving capital punishment.

VIII. 374. "A Sudra who has an intercourse with a woman of the higher caste guarded or unguarded shall be punished in the following manner; if she was unguarded, he loses the offending part; if she was guarded then he should be put to death and his property confiscated."

VIII. 20. A Brahmana who is only a Brahman by decent *i.e.*, one who has neither studied nor performed any other act required by the Vedas may, at the king's pleasure, interpret the law to him *i.e.*, act as the judge, but never a Sudra (however learned he may be). VIII. 21. The Kingdom of that monarch, who looks on while a Sudra settles the law, will sink low like a cow in the morass. VIII. 272. If a Sudra arrogantly presumes to preach religion to Brahmins, the king shall have poured burning oil in his mouth and ears.

In the matter of acquiring learning and knowledge Manu ordains as follows:

III. 156. He who instructs Sudra pupils and he whose teacher is a Sudra shall become disqualified for being invited to a Shradha.

IV. 99. He must never read the Vedas in the presence of the Sudras.

Manu's successors went much beyond him in the cruelty of their punishment of the Sudra for studying the Veda. For instance, Katyayana lays down that if a Sudra overheard the Veda or ventured to utter a word of the Veda, the King shall cut his tongue in twain and pour hot molten lead in his ears. As to property by the Sudra, Manu enjoins as follows:

X. 129. No superfluous collection of wealth must be made by a Sudra, even though he has power to make it, since a servile man, who has amassed riches, becomes proud, and, by his insolence or neglect, gives pain to Brahmins.

VIII. 417. A Brahman may seize without hesitation, if he be in distress for his subsistence, the goods of his Sudra. The Sudra can have only one occupation. This is one of the inexorable laws of Manu. Says Manu:

1. 91. One occupation only, the Lord prescribed to the Sudra, to serve meekly these other three castes (namely Brahmin, Kshatriya and Vaishya).

X. 121. If a Sudra, (unable to subsist by serving Brahmana), seeks a livelihood, he may also seek to maintain himself by attending on a wealthy Vaishya.

X. 122. But let a (Sudra) serve Brahmans, either for the sake of heaven, or with a view to both (this life and the next) for he who is called the servant of a Brahman thereby gains all his ends.

X. 123. The service of Brahmans alone is declared (to be) an excellent occupation for a Sudra for whatever else besides this he may perform will bear him no fruit.

Service by Sudra is not left by Manu to be regulated as a free contract. If the Sudra refused to serve, there is a provision for conscription which runs as follows:

VIII. 413. A Brahmana may compel a Sudra, whether bought or unbought, to do servile work for he is created by the creator to be the slave of a Brahmana.

X. 124. They must allot to him out of their own family (property) a suitable maintenance, after considering his ability, his industry, and the number of those whom he is bound to support.

X. 125. The remnants of their food must be given to him as well as their old household furniture.

A Sudra is required by Manu to be servile in his speech and manner towards the other classes.

VIII. 270. A Sudra who insults a twice born man with gross invectives shall have his tongue cut out; for he is of low origin.

VIII. 271. If he mentions the names and castes of the (twice born) with contumely, an iron nail, ten fingers long, shall be thrust red hot into his mouth.

Manu is not satisfied with this. He wants this servile status of the Sudra to be expressed in the names and surnames of persons belonging to that community. Manu says:

II. 31. Let the first part of a Brahman's name denote something auspicious, a Kshatriya's be connected with power, and a Vaishya's with wealth but a Sudra's express something contemptible.

II. 32. The second part of a Brahmin's name shall be a word implying happiness, of a Kshatriya's (a word) implying protection, of a Vaishya's a term expressive of thriving and of a Sudra's an expression denoting service."

It is obvious that these three classes are naturally allies. There is every ground for them to combine for the destruction of the Hindu Social Order. But they have not. It is not that no attempt has been made to unite them. The non-Brahmin Party which held the field between 1919-1935 was an attempt to unite them into one political organisation to destroy the dominance of the Brahmins who are the architects of the Hindu Social Order and being the chief beneficiaries of it are its strongest supporters.

This was not the only attempt to bring about solidarity among the three classes. Another attempt is being made by the labour leaders particularly the Communists. They preached that there is an identity of interest of the working class, no matter to what community they belong. There must be developed in them class consciousness and class unity. Once united they could employ the terrifying power of their numbers to break down the economic order and once the economic order falls to the ground the social order of the Hindus is bound to go to pieces. What has been the result? The result is that the solidarity has failed to come. The Sudras and the Criminal and Primitive Tribes are more hostile to the Untouchables than they are to the Brahmins. Indeed it is the Sudras who act as the police force of the Brahmins for repelling the attack of the Untouchables on the Hindu social order. This is a strange phenomenon. But it is a fact. The atrocities that are committed upon the Untouchables, if they commit any breach of the rules and regulations of the established order and of which description has been given in this books are all the doings of the Sudras.

The reasons for this want of solidarity is not far to seek. It is to be found in the system of graded inequality whereby the Brahmin is above everybody, the Sudra is below the Brahmin and above the Untouchable. If the Hindu social order was based on inequality, it would have been overthrown long ago. But it is based on graded inequality so that the Sudra while he is anxious to pull down the Brahmin, he is not prepared to see the Untouchable raised to his level. He prefers to suffer the indignities heaped upon him by the Brahmins to join the Untouchables for a general levelling down of the social order. The result is that, there is nobody to join the Untouchable in his struggle. He is completely isolated. Not only is he isolated he is opposed by the very classes who ought to be his natural allies. This isolation is one more obstacle in the removal of untouchability.

## Matters Made Worse by Untouchability

A correspondent from Jaipur reports the following incident which occurred in June 1953: "Jaipur, June 25: The guinea worm, called *nahru* or *bala* by people here, is a disease prevalent in the State which keeps the patient suffering for months, sometimes for a year or two. Many lose the use of a limb as a result of this disease. The disease spreads through the medium of drinking water. The only preventive steps doctors advice is that water should be drunk after boiling and filtering.

The disease frequently occurs as the rains set in, which is also the time for sowing with the result that at a time when he should be preparing to earn his living a villager is confined to bed.

On investigation in the village of Kopra near Banswara it was found that in 57 families there were 125 sufferers from guinea worm. There were six members in a Harijan family, five of whom had guinea worm. They had only a few bits of dry meat to eat. Often the trouble is thrust on these people by society. A pond from which Harijans drink water was so dirty that it must have been a nursery for the guinea worm. When showed to the Collector of Banswara he was shocked and ordered the pond closed immediately. Nearby, was a pucca well from which water could be taken by entering into it. Hindu were entreated to permit Harijans, to take water from this well but they would not agree. The Collector asked them if they would drink the water from the pond, if told to. They admitted that the water was unfit for human use, yet they would not allow Harijans use of the pucca well.

Conditions are bad and Harijans are the worst sufferers. The law has made untouchability a crime. The Harijan Sevak Sangh has long been working for its oblation, but it cannot be said that the hearts and minds of caste Hindus in the countryside have undergone a change. The State Governments have not been able to do much in this connection.

It is sad to notice that the various civil disabilities of Harijans still continue to exist in our villages in spite of the Civil Disabilities Removal Act which came into force about five years ago. It is now 9 months since the All India Harijan Sevak Sangh started its intensive work for the removal of social disabilities of Harijans in Melur Taluk in Mathurai district. Several disabilities of Harijans regarding tea shops, barber saloons, wells, tanks, chavadies, etc., have been brought to light during this period. In some places it is the Village Munsifs who were expected to give wide publicity to the Act and enforce it, that are very reactionary forces standing in the way of the poor Harijans exercising their elementary rights. A few instances are cited below to show how deep-rooted is the prejudice against the Harijans in our society.

In Parli near Natham, a Harijan youth who refused to take tea in a cocoanut shell and desired to be served in the glass tumbler was kicked and shoed on the head by a caste Hindu who was subsequently convicted and fined only Rs. 10 by the Sub-Magistrate, Melur.

At Melavalvoo, when I went to a tea shop with two Harijan boys, a group of people threatened to assault me and drove away the boys. A glass tumbler was wantonly broken by the tea shopkeeper and they all demanded that I must pay for it on penalty of being thrashed. I, however, took shelter in an Elementary School nearby and the crowd disappeared only on the intervention of the President of the Panchayat Board.

At Kelavalvoo, the Harijans take water from a dirty pond in which men bathe and cattle are washed. The Harijans were encouraged to go to the public Oorani (protected water tank), but they were abused and threatened by the caste Hindus so that they dare not take water from the Oorani. There is a Police Station at Kelavalvoo, but the police here are indifferent towards the disabilities of the Harijans. In Attukulam the caste Hindus put night-soil in the public well because they could not physically obstruct the Harijans who took water from it under our directions. In Ettimangalam, the caste Hindus destroyed the paddy seedlings raised by some Harijans in Government poromboke and because the Harijans had got into the chavadi during a public meeting held in the village. No action was taken by the police on the complaint given by the poor Harijans.

In Tiruvadur when we directed Harijans to take water from the Oorani, a caste Hindu youth assaulted a pregnant Harijan woman and broke her pot as well. The caste Hindu was charged by the police and convicted by the Sub-Magistrate to pay a fine of only Rs. 15 and thereafter the Harijans are freely taking water from this Oorani. In Kottagudi, a village barber, who refused haircut to a Harijan boy was charged by the police and convicted by the Sub-Magistrate. But thereafter, the Harijans were summoned by the caste Hindus to the chavadi and warned that in case they sought the service of this barber, a collective fine would be imposed on them.

In Kidaripatti, the Harijans are not allowed to take the corpse through the public foot path and they are also not permitted to ride on cycle through the village streets. A case regarding the alleged obstruction of a Harijan from riding on cycle is pending trial in the Sub-Magistrate's Court, Melur. In Nundikovilpatti, only three furlongs from the Taluk Office, Melur, the Harijans were taking drinking water from a dirty channel because they had no access to the Oorani. Two complaints were given to the police regarding this and now the caste Hindus dare not obstruct the Harijans. In Thekkitheru, when the Harijans sat on the Manthai chavadi during a public meeting held at the chavadi, pebbles were thrown at them till they quitted the place out of fear. In Navinipatti about two miles from Melur, the village Munsif himself is alleged to have taken objection to the Harijans wearing decent dress on Pongal festival day and made two Harijan youths to remove their shirts and upper cloth. The youths were made to do Kumbidal (full prostration on the ground) and go away in loincloth only.

The most painful oppression has been in Mankulam, about ten miles from Mathurai city, where the village Munsif took a hostile attitude. Two Harijan youths went to tea shop and as they were denied admission, they complained to the police. For this, one of them was tied to a pillar and mercilessly beaten by a caste Hindu boy under instructions from the elders. Another Harijan was assaulted with a knife by a servant of the village Munsif. The Harijans were socially boycotted and denied labour because they took water from the public Oorani. The shopkeepers refused to sell provisions to them and they were put to starvation for two days.

The situation improved only after the intervention of the Revenue Divisional Officer. Recently, two Harijans and myself were brutally attacked by a band of caste Hindus and beaten with firewood cudgels for having bathed in the tank and gone into a coffee club in front of the chavadi. We were admitted and treated in the Government Hospital in Mathurai, I sustained a fracture in the right foot due to which I cannot use the right leg and walk. Sixteen persons including the village Munsif have been charged by the police for rioting. Some Congressmen are, however, trying for a compromise because some of their relations are involved in this. These friends are also known to have approached the authorities in this connection. Mahatmaji had desired us to consider the Harijans as blood brothers, but alas! blood is thicker than water.

One feels so dejected and disheartened at the attitude of the caste Hindus towards the Harijans in spite of the great sacrifices of Mahatmaji, who won Swaraj for us and desired us to concede freedom to these downtrodden people as well. The Revenue and police authorities can do a lot to remove the disabilities of the Harijans. Mahatmaji's son Manilal is offering satyagraha in South Africa for the civil disabilities of Indians. But we are denying similar liberties to the Harijans whom Mahatmaji owned as his kith and kin. Let the caste Hindus and Congressmen who adore Mahatmaji remember that his spirit will not rest in peace till the curse of untouchability is wiped out, root and branch, from the nook and corner of our land. The Government must realise the deed for greater efforts to remove this bane from our society.

## Lynch Law against Harijans

***The Chavadi Courts:*** It is a well known fact that though the Harijans are denied entry in the public chavadies in the villages in Tamilnad, they are tried by the caste Hindus at these chavadies and victimised to such an extent that they always live in fear of the caste Hindus. One of the reasons why the Harijans in the villages do not respond to our movement of the removal of their civil disabilities is their constant fear of this victimisation by the caste Hindus under the leadership of the village Periambalagar, the chief of the caste Hindus. In several places, the villagers run these chavadi courts under the colour of holding Panchayats.

The poor Harijans are summoned to the chavadi and tried like slaves. If any of them go against the order of the Periambalagar then the Lynch Law is put into operations and they are subjected to merciless beating and torture with a view to strike terror in them and to demonstrate the absolute power of the Periambalagar. The victimisation of the Harijans at the chavadi takes place in various forms according to the circumstances and the whims of the Periambalagar and his council—public whipping, imposition of heavy fines and confiscation of their properties on failure to pay the same, foisting of false cases, economic boycott by denying labour and with holding wages, social ostracism by prohibiting their taking part in social functions and religious ceremonies, denial of water by preventing access to tanks and wells, denial of foodstuffs by banning sale of articles to them in the village-shops etc. The liberation of the Harijans is possible only if the Government takes strong measure against the villagers for holding these illegal and unlawful courts in the name of the village Panchayat. No civilised Government can tolerate the persecution of a backward and minority community by the villages in the various manners mentioned above.

***Atrocities in Thumbapatti:*** The following account of the trial of Harijans at Thumbapatti on 1st August 1953 would make any heart bleed. This village is 22 miles from Madurai and it is the native place of Shri P. Kakkan, M.P., one of the prominent Harijan Leaders of Tamilnad. It is learnt that all the adults in the Harijan cherri were summoned to the mandai (common place) in front of the chavadi. The caste Hindus did obeisance to the Periambalagar and his council, in the usual manner, by doing full prostration, their belly touching the ground to pick up the dust. About a dozen Harijan youths were then picked out for trial on the charge they were suspected of the various petty thefts occurring in the village.

It is however learnt that youths who were a bit assertive and not usually submissive to the caste Hindus had been singled out for punishment. They were given blows with sticks and were asked to admit having committed the thefts. The other Harijans were questioned and under fear of victimisation they are said to have thrown all the thefts on the accused. Judgement was passed that the youths were guilty and some of them were handcuffed for being duly punished. It is learnt that one of them however remonstrated and tried to escape on some plea. This disrespect to the chavadi court was immediately resented by the villagers and it is learnt that the Periambalagar promulgated the chavadi ordinance that the Harijan youths be severely dealt with.

The Lynch law was put into operation and a most merciless attack was made on the Harijan youths. All those who had some grudge or prejudice against the Harijans got the opportunity to wreak vengeance on them with impunity. The Harijan youth who had tried to escape was dragged by his legs over the rough and stony ground. The others were beaten with sticks and tied to the trees and again beaten so mercilessly till their bones were almost broken. There they were made to stand, tied to the trees for about eight hours, as the pitable objects of public scorn. The Harijans in general appear to have been warned that they should not cooperate with the Harijan workers.

***False Case Foisted:*** What the villagers did thereafter is still more shameful. It is the usual practice to foist cases on the Harijans and to get the police to take immediate action. When it was discovered that the Harijans had sustained serious injuries, the villagers realised that they would get into trouble. It is learnt that Shri Poosari Kakkan, the Eighty-years old father of Shri P. Kakkan, M.P., who is working as the village

Thotti, was therefore asked to give a false complaint that some articles in the Harijan temple were found missing since the previous evening and a report was sent to the Police by the village Munsif, that these articles were recovered from the Harijan youths. Shri Poosari Kakkan, and his relation, another village Thotti named Etti Kakkan, are said to have brought these articles and given to the village Munsif. Immediately on receipt of the report the Police came, arrested the Harijan youths on a charge of theft and sent them to the Hospital as they were found wounded. We do not propose to publicly criticise the action of the Police. Enough to say, the atrocities on the Harijans by the villagers, did not catch the official eye of the Police!

***The Truth Known:*** The villagers were good enough to send a mass petition supporting their action to Shri A. Vaidyanatha lyer. President, Tamilnad Harijan Sevak Sangh. It was forwarded to me for enquiry and report. A small committee consisting of the President of Melur Taluk Congress Committee, the Secretary of Melur Taluk Harijan Sevak Sangh, the Secretary of the Seva Samaj, Melur and myself accordingly enquired into the matter and found that the villagers had made a merciless attack on the Harijan youths and kept them tied to the trees for about eight hours till the arrival of the Police.

The complaint given by Shri Poosari Kakkan and the Periambalagar were examined by Shri Vaidyanath lyer and they admitted to him that the complaint given to the Police was a false and concocted one.

The Periambalagar also expressed regret for the wrongs done to the Harijans. Meanwhile the police also investigated into the complaint given by Shri Poosari Kakkan and referred the case as 'undetectable'. No case was however taken against the villagers. It appears the bones of the Harijans youths had not actually broken. The marks of beatings with sticks and of the rope-tie were visible on their bodies for several days. Two of them were kept at the hospital for two days and their legs were X-rayed to make sure if their bones were broken. They were sent out with plaster bandages on their legs. They were not able to walk properly for a fortnight.

***Two Enquiries Conducted:*** An enquiry was conducted by the Dy. Welfare Officer, Madurai under orders from the Dy.

Collector and another enquiry was recently conducted by the Revenue Divisional Officer, Madurai under orders from the Government. The result is yet to be known.

***Civil Disabilities in Thumbapatti:*** There was terrible opposition from the villagers of Thumbapatti when the Harijans took water from the public Oorani in 1948. Till then the Harijans were taking water from a dirty pond where cattle are washed and men bathe. Some Harijan youths were severely beaten and an attempt was made to set fire to Harijan houses. The village Munsif and others are said to have been warned by the authorities in this connection. One case, where a Harijan was denied coffee in the glass tumbler in a teashop in Thumbapatti, was reported to the Police on 19th August 1953 and the tea shopkeeper was convicted and sentenced to pay a fine of Rs. 10 by the Sub-Magistrate.

The village barber declares that he is willing to serve Harijans. Yet the Harijans do not go to him probably because of the secret warning given to them by the caste Hindus. Some Harijans had gone to the barber on 1st July 1953 and there is reason to believe that the trial of the Harijan youths on 1st August 1953 was an arrangement made to strike terror in the Harijans.

***Our General Experience:*** It is our general experience that when the Harijans make bold to asset their elementary rights, the villagers summon them to the chavadi and persecute them in one form or other. Such happenings took place in Mangulam. Kuruvankulam, Adanoor, Pathiettamgudi and Karugakottai. The higher officials of the Police were good enough to visit these places. In some places, the Harijans were summoned to the chavadi and warned as at Kottagudi, Kidaripatti and Pullipatti. The subordinate Police officials usually support the caste Hindus and thus the latter get the freedom to apply their Lynch law and bring the Harijans to a sense of their social servility.

***Can we Tolerate This:*** The question before us is whether we can tolerate this kind of public lynching and humilitation of the Harijans in these days when we had revolted against the atrocities of the Dyers at Jallianwalla bagh. In Jallianwala, the atrocities were committed by foreign bureaucrats on men and women who had assembled in a gathering. Here similar atrocities were committed by our villagers on a few Harijan youths who were tried at the chavadi with a view to strike terror in the Harijans in general.

***What the Government must Do:*** Village Panchayats consisting of elected members including Harijans, have been formed by the Government in the villages. One wonders why the caste Hindus should be allowed to run their chavadi courts in parallel to these Government recognised Panchayats. These chavadi courts are a menace to the social, economic and political progress of the poor backward class communities in the villages. There can be no salvation or freedom to the Harijans in the villages unless these chavadi courts are banned by the Government.

All our efforts for the removal of the civil disabilities of Harijans will go in vain till the chavadi courts are prohibited from dealing with the Harijans. Before spending 3 lakhs of rupees for the eradication of untouchability, the Government must take necessary measures to stop the victimisation of the Harijans at the chavadi and enable them to raise their heads as human beings. Untouchability in public places has become a thing of the past in Kerala because of the non-existence of these chavadi courts in that part of the country.

***An Appeal:*** It was Mahatma Gandhi who made us realise the great injustice we do to poor Harijans in the villages by treating them as low castes and slaves. But for him the Harijans in the various parts of the country would have gone out of the Hindu fold because of the unbearable sufferings under the caste Hindus. It is now 21 years since Mahatma Gandhi observed the Epic Fast at Poona to create public opinion in favour of the Harijans. No doubt there has been a great awakening during the last decades and there is now general sympathy towards the Harijan movement.

The Government is pledged to the removal of all the social and civil disabilities of Harijans and it is giving full cooperation to all peaceful and legitimate efforts to improve the status of the Harijans. But we have to admit that there is still, lot of prejudice towards the Harijans in the villages. We appeal to all public workers to bring about a change of heart of the caste Hindus in the villages so that the Harijans are no longer treated as a separate Untouchable class. We appeal to all leaders to work for the eradication of untouchability and to see that the Harijans are treated as part and parcel of the Hindu society.

## Civilization or Felony

The population of India is generally classified on a linguistic or on religious basis. These are the only two ways of classifying the people of India, which have been persistently in vogue for a long time. The effect is that outsiders get the impression that, what is of interest and importance to know about the peoples of India is the religions they profess or the languages they speak. Limited by this interest, they remain content with a knowledge they get about the religions and languages that are prevalent in India. All that the outsider cares to hold in his head is that, in India there are people who are either Hindus or Mahomedans. If he is interested in religion or that there are people in India some of whom speak Marathi, some speak Gujarathi, some Bengali and some Tamil, etc.

Of the two ways of classifying people of India the religious classification is the one which is more impressive and arresting for the foreigner. He is more interested in the religions than in the languages. But even he is not aware of all the religious communities in India. He knows only of Hindus and Mahomedans. He sometimes hears of the Sikhs, very seldom of Christians although they are a growing community and never of the Buddhists who are of course nonexistent so far as India of today is concerned.

The impression of the foreigner is that there are only Hindus and Musalmans in India and that there are none others worth bothering about. That this should be his impression is quite natural. The air is filled with the din and noise of the Hindu-Moslem conflict. How gravethe conflict is, can be seen from the number of Hindu-Moslem riots that have taken place in recent years and the casualties and deaths that resulted from them.

But this struggle is a struggle for establishing an empire. There are Hindus who are agitating for establishing in India a Hindu Raj with Mahomedans as subject only. There are

Mahomedans who are dreaming of Pan Islamism and of making India a part of a Muslim Empire with a choice for the Hindus between the sword and the Koran. In between these two extremists, there are sober persons who are for a state in which both Hindus and Muslims can live as equal partners. Whether the extremists will succeed or the moderates will succeed time alone can show. In the meantime the extremes in both the camps are making headlines by their blood baths. But, be that as it may, I venture to think that there are many who will not feel much interest in this struggle between the Hindus and the Mahomedans. After all it is a struggle for mastery for dominance.

It is a struggle for liberation. It is a struggle for establishing an empire of one over the other. They will be more interested in the struggles of the down trodden, of those who are fighting to obtain the title deeds to respectable humanity. In describing the old quarrel between the Whigs and Tories in England, Francis Place in describing the political policy of the Whigs said, they were out to crush the king on the one hand and the people on the other hand and establish the aristocracy of the governing class. Those Hindus and Musalmans who are now fighting have the same policy in Indian politics. They want to establish their classes from them as the governing body. The masses whether of the Hindus or of the Musalmans are merely used for establishing the ascendency of the classes. This struggle that is going on is really a struggle of the classes. It is not a struggle of the masses.

Those who are interested in the struggle of the masses must learn to look at the population of India from another point of view. They must cease to look at it purely from the point of view of religion. They must look at the population of India from the social and economic point of view. This does not mean that one need not care to know how religion has affected the economic and social life of the people of India. Indeed no study of the Indian people, be they Hindus or Musalmans, can give an adequate picture of their life if religion is kept out of consideration. Because religion is supreme in India as was the Roman Catholic Church in the Middle Ages in Europe. Bryce has described the dominance of the Church over the lives of the people in terms that are worth recording" A life in the Church, for the Church, through the Church; a life which she blessed in mass at morning and sent to peaceful rest by the vesper hyme; a life which she supported by the constantly recurring stimulus of the sacraments, relieving it by confession, purifying it by penance, admonishing it by the presentation of visible objects for contemplation and worship, this was the life which many of the Middle Ages conceived of as the rightful life of the man; it was the actual life of many, the ideal of all"

The dominance of religion on the life of the people of India today is no whit less than the dominance of the Church over the lives of the people in the Middle Ages. It would therefore be a mistake to leave religion out of consideration. But it is equally true to say that a purely religious point of view would give only a superficial picture. What is important to know is how the masses and the classes in India live? What are the social and economic terms of their associated life? To what extent are these influenced by religion? The answer to this question is given by the condition in which we find certain classes who fall within the Hindu fold.

It is a pity that Prof. Max Muller did not visit India. On seeing the contrast between theory and practice he might have explained the contrast. For the present the contrast remains a riddle.

This is so in spite of the doctrine of Brahma, asserted by the Brahmins to be residing and pervading every human being. If there is Brahma in a Brahmin so also it is in a Primitive man, in a Criminal Tribes man and so also in an Untouchable? How are these two facts to be reconciled the theory of Brahma and as against it the existence of the Primitive Tribes, the Criminal Tribes and the Untouchables?

This sunken humanity falls into three distinct categories. One such category is comprised of people who are called Primitive Tribes. Communities listed as Criminal classes form a second and separate category and the third category is the one, which covers what are called the Untouchables.

The total population of persons who fall into these three categories is by no means small. The population of the Primitive Tribes in India according to the Census of 1931 comes in round figures to 25 millions. The total population of the Criminal classes now listed as Criminal is somewhere about 41/2 millions.

The total population of the Untouchables according to the Census of 1931 is 50 millions in India as a whole. The total of these classes comes to 791/2 millions. And the question is what is the position of these 791/2 million souls?

First as to the Primitive Tribes. In what state of civilization are they?

The name Primitive Tribes is expressive of the present state of people who are called by that name. They live in small-scattered huts in forests. They live on wild fruits, nuts and roots. Fishing and hunting are also resorted to for the purpose of securing food. Agriculture plays a very small part in their social economy. Food supplies being extremely precarious they lead a life of semi-starvation from which there is no escape. As to clothes they economise them to a vanishing point. They move almost in a state of complete nakedness. There is a tribe which is known as "Bonda Porajas" which means "naked Porajas". Of these people it is said that, the women wear a very narrow strip which serves as a petticoat almost identical with what is worn by the Momjak Nagas in Assam, the ends hardly meeting at the top on the left thigh.

These petticoats are woven at home out of the fibre of a forest tree. Girls wear a fillet of beads and of palmyra leaf and an enormous quantity of beads and neck ornaments extremely like those worn by many Komjak women. Otherwise the women wear nothing. The women shave their heads entirely..... Of the Chenchus, a tribe residing near Farhabad in the Nizam's Dominions it is said that "their houses are conical, rather slight in structure made of bamboos sloping to the central point and covered with a thinnish layer of thatch...... They have very little indeed in the way of material effects, the scanty clothes they wear, consisting of a langoti and a cloth in the case of men and a short bodice and a petticoat in the case of women, being practically all, besides a few cooking pots and a basket or two which perhaps sometimes contains grain.

They keep cattle and goats and in this particular village do a little cultivation, elsewhere subsisting on honey and forest produce which they sell". Regarding the Morias another Primitive Tribe, it is stated the men generally wear a single cloth round the waist with a flap coming down in the front. They also have a necklace of beads and when they dance, put cock's plums and peacock's feathers in their turbans. Many girls are profusely tattooed, especially on their faces, and some of them on their legs as well. The type of tattooing is said to be according to the taste of the individual and it is done with thorns and needles. In their hair, many of them stick the feathers of jungle cocks and their heads are also adorned with combs of wood and tin and brass.

These Primitive Tribes have no prohibition against eating anything, even worms and insects and in fact there is very little meat that they will not eat, whether the animal has died a natural death or has been killed four days or more before by a tiger.

The religion of these Primitive Tribes is the worship of demons of all denominations and dead ancestors of all antiquity. Witchcraft, sorcery, animal and human sacrifice make up their religion. Without education, with no idea of Science or of the knowledge of the working of nature, steeped in ignorance and superstition, these Primitive Tribes have been living on the outskirts and in close conformity with civilisation in a savage stage which has been their lot for ages. Instead of marching along, they are where they have been all along doing nothing but marking time. The Criminal Classes at one time included such well organised confederacies of Professional Criminals as the Pindharies and the Thugs.

The Pindharies were a predatory body of armed gangsters. Their organisation was an open military organisation of freebooters who could muster 20,000 fine horse and even more. They were under the command of brigand chiefs. Chitu, one of the most powerful commanders had under his single command 10,000 horse, including 5,000 good cavalry, besides infantry and guns. The Pindharies had no military projects for employing their loose hands of irregular soldiery, which developed into bodies of professional plunderers. The Pindharies aimed at no conquests. Their object was to secure booty and cash for themselves. General loot and rapine was their occupation. They recognised no rulers. They were subjects of none. They rendered loyalty to none. They respected none and plundered all high and low rich and poor without fear or compunction.

The Thugs' were a well organised body of professional assassins, who in gangs of from 10 to 200 travelled in various guises throughout India, worked themselves into the confidence of wayfarers of the wealthier class and, when a favourable opportunity occurred, strangled them by throwing a handkerchief or noose round their necks and then plundered and buried them. All this was done according to certain ancient and rigidly prescribed forms and after the performance of special religious rites, in which was the consecration of the pickaxe and the sacrifice of sugar. They were staunch worshippers of Kali, the Hindu Goddess of destruction.

Assassination for gain was with them a religious duty, and was considered a holy and honourable profession. They had in fact no idea of doing wrong, and their moral feelings did not come into play. The will of the goddess by whose command and in whose honour they followed their calling was revealed to them through a very complicated system of omens. In obedience to these, they often travelled hundreds of miles in company with, or in the wake of their 1 Encyclopaedia Britannica. 11th Ed., Vol. XXVI, p. 896. Intended victims before a safe opportunity presented itself for executing their design; and when the deed was done, rites were performed in honour of that tutelary deity and a goodly portion of the spoil was set apart for her.

The Thugs had also a jargon of their own, as well as certain signs by which its members recognised each other in the remotest part of India. Even those, who from age or infirmities could no longer take an active part in the operations used to aid the cause as watchmen, spies or dressers of food. It was owing to their thorough organisation, the secrecy and security with which they went to work, but chiefly to the religious garb in which they shrouded their murders, that they could continue for centuries to practise their craft. The extraordinary fact was that Thugee was regarded as a regular profession by the Indian Rulers both Hindu and Mahomedans. The Thugs paid taxes to the State and the State left them unmolested.

It was not until the British became rulers of the country that any attempt was made to suppress the Thugs. By 1835, 382 Thugs were hanged and 986 were transported or imprisoned for life. Even as late as 1879 the number of registered Thugs was 344 and the Thuggee and the Dacoity department of the Government of India continued to exist until 1904 when its place was taken by the Central Criminal Intelligence

Department. While these open and professional criminals have been suppressed and are no more to exact their toll and disturb the peace, there are still in India communities whose occupation is crime and who are listed by Government as Criminal Tribes.

The Criminal Tribes live in the plains in close proximity, if not in the midst of, civilized life. Because they subsist by organised robbery and dacoity, they are for this reason proscribed by the Government of India as Criminal Tribes. Hollius in his "Criminal Tribes of the United Provinces" gives an account of their activities. They live entirely by crime. A few may be ostensibly engaged in agriculture but this is only to cover up their real activities. Their nefarious practices found most scope in dacoity or robbery by violence, but being a community organised for crime nothing came amiss to them. On deciding to commit a dacoity in any particular locality, spies would be sent out to select a suitable victim, study the general habits of the villagers and the distance from any effective aid, and enumerate the number of men and firearms.

The raid usually took place at midnight. Acting on the information given by the spies, men would be posted at various points in the village and by firing off their guns, attract attention from the main gang which would attack the particular house or houses previously appointed. The gang would usually consist of 30 to 40 men. It is essential to emphasise the great part played by crime in the general life of these peoples. A boy is initiated into crime as soon as he is able to walk and talk. No doubt the motive is practical to a great extent in so far as it is always better to risk a child in petty theft, who if he were caught, would probably be cuffed, while an adult would immediately be arrested. An important part is also played by women, who, although they do riot participate in the actual raids, have many heavy responsibilities. Besides disposing of most of the stolen property, they are also expert shoplifters.

Like the Criminal Tribes the Untouchables also live in the midst of civilized Hindu Society and possess a degree of culture and morality which completely separate them from the Primitive Tribes and the Criminal Tribes. The Untouchables have the culture of the Hindu Community. They observe the religious rites of the Hindu Community. They recognise the sacred as well as the secular laws of the Hindus. They celebrate the

Hindu festivities. But they derive no benefit from this. On the contrary they are segregated and shunned because their physical contact is held by the Hindus to cause pollution. There is therefore an interdict on all social intercourse with them except for unavoidable purposes. They live on the outskirts of a village and not in the midst of it. Every village has its Untouchable quarters, they are attached to the village but are not a part of the village. Segregated from the rest of the Hindu population they are bound down to a code of behaviour, which is appropriate to a servile state. According to this code, an Untouchable may not do anything, which raise him above his appointed station in life. He should not dress in style superior to that of his status, nor should the untouchable woman adorn herself with ornaments after the fashion of the higher class Hindu women. He should not have a house better or bigger than the houses of the rest of the Hindus in the village. In any case he must not have a tiled roof over his house. An Untouchable must not sit in the presence of a Hindu and must always salute him first. An Untouchable must not wear clean clothes, must not use brass or copper pots and must not wear gold or silver ornaments.

When some one dies in the family of a Hindu, an Untouchable must go miles to convey the message of the death to the relatives of the family, no matter how far away they might be living, because a Hindu in a village feels disgraced in the eyes of his relatives if he has to communicate such messages by postal communication. An Untouchable must accompany the women folk of the Hindus on their journey from their homes to their parents and *vice versa*. Their dignity requires that they should have a retinue and the Untouchable is the only available class from which such a retinue can be drawn without any cost. At every ceremony at the house of a Hindu, the Untouchables must come and do menial work. An Untouchable must not own and cultivate land and lead an independent life.

For his livelihood he must depend upon stale remnants of food left over by the Hindu households and upon meat of cattle that die in the village. These remnants of food he must collect from door to door. For he must go on his begging round every evening. Similarly an Untouchable must carry the dead animals out of the village. Indeed he alone must carry them because no Hindu will agree to do scavenging. An Untouchable should not take to such services as would give him authority and power over caste Hindus. He must be humble and must not ask for more than his lot under this code. It is true that some of the Untouchables have risen above the low status prescribed by this customary code of conduct and have acquired high place, but the majority of them are still socially in the most servile position and economically in abject poverty.

Such is the condition of the 791/2 millions of people. The problem of these deadened, if not dead, souls is no small problem. The total population of these three classes comes to over 60% of the population of the United States but exceeds the population of the whites in the British Empire by 91/2 millions. It also exceeds the population of Japan by 91/2 millions. It exceeds the population of Italy by 37 millions. It exceeds the population of Germany by 131/2 millions and of France by 371/2 millions. It is ten times the population of Belgium and twenty times the population of Denmark. What a colossal total of sunken humanity?

The saddening and if, one may say, annoying part of the story is that the state of these unfortunate human beings should be what it is although they are surrounded and fed by a high civilisation. But it must strike any impartial observer that there must be something very radically wrong with a civilisation, which has failed to elevate to their manhood 791/2 millions of human beings.

Civilisation as comprising and accumulated store of knowledge of man and nature, of arts and crafts, an ethical code regulating the conduct of man towards his fellows, a social code laying down the forms and conventions to be observed by individuals, a civil code prescribing the rights and duties of the rulers and the ruled and a religious creed relating the natural to the supernatural—is a rare prize. It has not been the good fortune of all races to develop it in all its fullness. Many have stood where they were at the start. Many took one or two steps and have been at a halt. Others have only revolved round and round. The primitive races of Australia and Polenasia, when they were first discovered a few generations ago, were found to have developed articulate speech and to know how to make fire. They had not advanced beyond the middle stage of savagery.

The Alliapascous, a Primitive Tribe of the Hudson Bay Territory and the Indians of the valley of Columbia had not gone beyond the stage of the Bow and the Arrow. They knew nothing of pottery, domestication of animals or of the smelting of iron. The civilization of Egypt, Babylonia, Assyria and even of Rome and Greece had only been a revolving civilization. Their progress and achievements are only the elaboration of the details of methods and intentions handed down by man when he was in a Barbaric state. They added nothing revolutionary to the sum total of civilization to which they were heirs. They merely did better what used to be done crudely by their predecessors. Nor have the stages of advancement followed in quick succession. That man was for long ages a savage before he made sufficient progress to be called a Barbarian admits of no doubt. Equally little in doubt is it that other long ages of Barbarism have preceded the final ascent to the lowest stage of civilization. The precise period of time covered by these successive 'ages' is of course only conjectural; but something like one hundred thousand years may perhaps be taken as a safe minimum estimate.

Civilization is indeed no easy gain. But civilization is a very vital thing, not for one gereration but also for the next. The civilization of one generation, when inherited becomes the equipment of the next. This social heritage is absolutely essential for each generation. All progress will die out if this social heritage is destroyed. As has been well put, "If the earth were struck by one of Mr. Wells' comets, and if in consequence every human being now alive were to lose all the knowledge and habits which he had acquired from preceding generations (though retaining unchanged all his own powers of invention and memory, and habituation) nine-tenths of the inhabitants would be dead in a month and 99 per cent of the remaining tenth would be dead in six months.

They would have no language to express their thoughts but vague reverie. They would not read notices or drive motor cars or horses. They would wander about, led by the inarticulate cries of a few naturally dominant individuals, drowning themselves, as thirst came on, in hundreds at the riverside landing places. Men could not invent in time to preserve their lives, methods of growing food or taming animals or making fire or clothing themselves. Life would have to be begun over again from the primitive stage. Like the primitive races a generation which has lost its social heritage would have to begin life on wild fruits and worms until they had accumulated a new social heritage. After some thousands of generations they would probably possess some thing which would be recognised as language, and perhaps some art of taming animals and cultivating land. They might or might not have created what we should call a religion or a few of our simpler mechanical inventions and political expedients. They might or might not have such general ideas as law, liberty, and justice. This is the difference, which social heritage makes and the difference is no doubt vast.

It is true that civilisation is not the privilege of all and even to those who are fortunate to have it, it is a matter of slow growth marked by long and monotonous halts. But it is also true that to those who are possessed of civilisation, their civilisation may be a hindrance rather than a help. It might have gone on a wrong track, it might have based itself on false values and false premises. Such a civilisation might easily cause stagnation of the Community and the stunting of the individual. It would be better to be without civilisation than to be burdened and unshackled by such a civilisation.

It is the boast of every patriotic Hindu that the Hindu or the Vedic Civilisation is the oldest in the world. One often hears with fire some repetitions a Hindu stating with a certain degree of malicious pride that India had reached a very high degree of civilisation when other people were leading a primitive life and moving naked.

One also hears a Hindu say that his civilisation has inherent strength because it has survived while all other ancient civilisation such as Egypt, Babylon, Judea, Rome and Greece have vanished. Such a view however legitimate misses the main point. The main point is not whether the civilisation is ancient and whether it has survived. The main point is what are the merits of a civilization? What is its worth, if it has survived, on what plain? In other words the principal question is, is this Hindu civilization, the social heritage a burden or a benefit? What does it offer by way of growth and expansion to classes and to individuals?

What is the contribution of Hindu Civilization to the knowledge of man and nature? Many patriotic Hindus like to believe that the knowledge of man and nature began with the Hindus. Granting that it is so it certainly did not advance beyond the most rudimentary stage. Can any Hindu doubt that the Hindu Philology, right or wrong, has remained where Panini and Katyayana left it? Can he deny that Philosophy right or wrong has remained where Kapila and Gautama left it? Can he doubt that literature remained where Vyasa and Valmiki left it. In Metaphysics the Hindus are said to have reached the stage of perfection. This is what Prof. Har Dayal has to say of Hindu Metaphysics:

"Metaphysics has been the curse of India. It has blighted her history and compassed her ruin. It has converted her great men into miserable quibblers, and led them into useless channels of inquiry and effort. It has been the dangerous will-o'-the-wisp of Indian intellect during many centuries. It has elevated sophistry to the rank of an Art, and substituted vain fancies for a knowledge. It has condemned Indians intellect to run in the same old roove for hundreds of years. It has blinded her seers and led them to mistake phantoms for realities..... Arrogant, pretentious, verbose and purblind, it has taken its cackling for an oracle and its fantastic word towers for solid piles of thought masonry....."

The Upanishads claim to expound 'that by knowing which every thing is known'. This mediaeval quest for 'the absolute' is the basis of all the superior metaphysics of India. The treatises are full of absurd conceits, quaint fancies, and chaotic speculations. And we have not yet learned that they are worthless. "Samadhi" or trance is regarded as the acme of spiritual progress!

How strange it is that a capacity for swooning away should be considered the mark of wisdom! It is very easy to lose consciousness if one has strong emotions and a feeble intellect. That is why ladies faint so often on the slightest provocation. But in India Samadhi is the eighth stage of Yoga, which only '*paramahans*' can reach. These be thy Gods, O, Israel! To look upon an abnormal psychological condition produced by artificial means as the sign of enlightenment was a folly reserved for Indian Philosophers."

In the domain of science. Arts and crafts the contribution of the Hindu Civilization is of the most primitive character. Except in some spheres such as weaving, spinning, etc., the Hindu Civilization has not evolved any technical equipment which can aid man in his struggle against nature to make a bare living that can be said to be higher than that of the brute. It is because of the complete absence of scientific and technical equipment and with all the transcendental nonsense that is being perpetrated that famines are desolating the land in all ages. Ignorance, superstition and disease which affect the mind, malaria and plague diseases which affect the body, have hung like a pall over the country throughout the ages.

In the field of Religion and Ethics the Hindus have made their greatest efforts. Of their contributions, these are the most elaborately developed. They are undoubtedly the most vital to man for the simple reason that they help to install in man the springs of thought and action. They are responsible for the outlook which man has on life. They are responsible for the attitude one holds towards his fellow man. They prescribe principles which govern conduct, mould character and implant in man that mysterious thing called conscience which acts as his sentinel and prevents him from going wrong.

It is when one comes to examine this Hindu Civilisation in the matter of its religious content, the way of life it prescribes, that one begins to doubt whether this Hindu Civilisation is at all an advantage to the generations who are fated to inherit it. What does this civilisation offer to the 25 millions of Primitive Tribes who are living on its frontiers? What does it offer to the 5 millions of Criminal Tribes who are living in the midst of that civilisation? What does it offer to the 50 millions of Untouchables who are not only living in the midst of that civilisation but are required to sustain it? What would the Primitive Tribes say of a civilisation which has made no effort to adopt them in its fold? What would the Criminal Tribes say of a civilisation which has driven them to take to criminal ways for earning their livelihood? Would it be unjust if they said that this is not Civilisation, this is infamy?

As to the Untouchables, theirs has been a fate of degradation and destitution in the past and for whom under the Hindu Civilisation there seems to be no escape in the future. Even

Indians do not seem to realise the extent of degradation and destitution that is involved in this system of Untouchability. The observations of the Committee appointed by the Government of Bombay to inquire into the grievances of the Depressed Classes and Aboriginal Tribes in 1928 are very pertinent. It said.

"There is nothing strange in the idea that an unclean person or thing causes repulsion which underlies the idea of pollution. But what is regrettable about it as applied to the (UNTOUCHABLES), is its irrationality. It stamps an individual as untouchable by the mere accident of his birth. A person born Untouchable, remains Untouchable however superior he may be in personal cleanliness to the so-called touchable, and there is no way open to him by which he can escape his fate. What is surprising in all this is that an Orthodox Hindu, notwithstanding the differences between his religious notions and mode of living and outlook in life and those of the Mahomedans, Parsis and Christians treat them as touchables.

This has resulted in further aggravating the position of the (Untouchables). For this unjust discrimination on the part of the Orthodox Hindus, in some cases being influenced by the Orthodox Hindus especially in villages, even the Mahomedans, Parsis and Christians observe untouchability towards the (Untouchables) though their religions teach contrariwise. What we are concerned most to point out are the evils attributable to it in so far as Untouchability includes isolation and inferiority. But there are evils specifically attributable to untouchability as such. Pressed to its logical limit, in an Orthodox Hindu Society it would prevent the (Untouchables) from obtaining entry into a public school though it is maintained at the expense of the state, it would prevent them from entering the public services though they may be qualified for it, except for the services customarily allotted to them. It would also prevent them from taking water from the public watering places maintained out of public funds.

Looked at from this point of view untouchability is not merely a social problem. It is a problem of the highest political importance and affects the fundamental question of the civic rights of the subjects of the state." This states the hardships only of the Untouchables. But untouchables are not the only people who are subjected to this life of ignominy. There are classes who are placed in a worse position. Untouchables are those who cause pollution only by a physical touch. There are people who cause pollution if they come within a certain distance. They are known as unapproachable. Again there are people who are in a worse position than the unapproachable. They cause pollution if they come within sight. They are known as unseeable. It is said of the Nayadis —a people who fall into the category of the unapproachable, "that they are the lowest caste among the Hindus— the dogeaters. They are the most persistent in their clamour for charity, and will follow at a respectful distance, for miles together any person walking, driving or boating. If any thing is given to them, it must be laid down, and after the person offering it has proceeded a sufficient distance, the recipient comes timidly forward, and removes it." Of the same people Mr. Thurston says "The subject (*i.e.* the Nayadis) whom I examined and measured at Shoranur, though living only about three miles off had, by reason of the pollution which they traditionally carry with them to avoid walking over the long bridge which spans the river, and follow a circuitous route of many miles".

In the Tinnevalley District of the Madras Presidency, there is a class of unseeables called Purada Vannas. Of them it is said, "that they are not allowed to come out during day time because their sight is enough to cause pollution. These unfortunate people are 'compelled' to follow the nocturnal habits, leaving their dens after dark and scuttling home at the false dawn like the badger, hyaena, aordvark." What must be the hardships of the unapproachables and unseeables?

How must they be passing their lives? If their sight or their approach even is not tolerated, what work can they obtain? What else can they do except to beg and live on dog's meat? Surely no civilisation can be guilty of greater cruelty! It is indeed a great mercy that the population of the unapproachables and of the unseeables is so small. But are 50 millions of Untouchables entitled to any civilisation? An Untouchable cannot escape his fate for he cannot pass off as a Touchable. In the village where he resides he is of course known and there is no room for impersonation while he is there. If he leaves his village and comes to a town there is a chance for him to pass off as Touchable. But he knows what would be his fate if he were discovered. The following incident, which was reported in the papers, will give some idea of the risk involved in any attempt to impersonate:

***Orthodoxy Run Mad:*** Alleged Barbarious Treatment of "Untouchables" : Crime of being Mahars.

Mr. Keshavji Ranchhodji Vaghela from Ahmedabad has informed Dr. B. R. Ambedkar, President, Bahishkrit Hitkarani Sabha as follows:

One Bapoorao Laxman and his brother Kaurao have been residents of Ahmedabad during the last six years. They used to mix with some people from the Deccan belonging to Maratha caste. Kaurao's two sons, *viz.* Damoo and Laxman, used to take part in the Bhajan parties of the Marathas. The latter, however, recently came to know that the brothers Damoo and Laxman were Mahars by caste and in order to ascertain this, two Mahars employed in the parcel train between Surat and Ahmedabad were specially called to identify Damoo and Laxman. After it was ascertained that Damoo and Laxman were Mahars they were called at a Bhajan party at Kalupur, Bhandari Pole, at midnight on the 11th instant. Asked as to what caste they belonged to, Damoo and Laxman replied that they were Somavanshis. This reply enraged the Marathas, who freely abused them for having defiled their persons and places. The Mahar brothers were assaulted by the Marathas. One of the brothers had a gold ring on his person. It was forcibly taken away from him and sold for Rs. 11. Out of this amount Rs. 6 was paid to the Mahar who had been called from Surat toidentify the brothers. Damoo and Laxman entreated and Marathas were requested to allow them to return to their homes, but the latter refused to do so unless a fine of Rs. 500 was paid.

On the Mahar brothers Bombay Chronicle 25th Feb. 1938, pleading their inability to pay such a heavy sum, one of the Marathas suggested that the Mahar brothers should be fined only Rs. 125. But then one of the Marathas opposed the proposal for fine saying that they should not be satisfied with fine, but should punish the Mahars severely for their crime of concealing their caste. Having decided upon the course, the Mahar brothers were detained and at about 9 O'clock in the morning they were subjected to barbarous indignities, their moustaches in the left side and eyebrows on the right side were shaved, their bodies besmeared with soot mixed in oil and also with dirt, garlands made of old shoes were put around their necks, and one of them was asked to hold a broom in his hand and the other to hold a placard on which it was written that the punishment was meted out to the culprits for venturing to touch high caste people.

The Mahar brothers were taken in procession consisting of about 75 people, a drum being beaten in the front. A complaint has been lodged with the Police by the said two Mahar brothers. The accused in their statement have admitted that Damoo and Laxman were treated in the alleged manner, but pleaded that the complainants had willingly agreed to undergo the punishment. Obviously Damoo and Laxman were helpless when they were abused, assaulted and threatened with severe punishment and actually subjected to barbarous indignities. This case has created a great sensation among the people belonging to the so called Untouchables castes, and efforts are being made to give proper legal aid to the complainants.

But the rules of this Hindu Civilisation are so meticulous in regard to untouchability as to leave no possibility for an Untouchable to pose as a Touchable. Consequently there exist rules in certain areas where Untouchables are required to bear a black thread so as to be easily identifiable and to proclaim by word of mouth that he is an Untouchable to prevent a Touchable touching him in ignorance and thereby getting himself polluted. In the town of Dwarka (in the Bombay Presidency) which is famous as being the shrine of the great Hindu God Krishna it is a rule that every Untouchable while walking in the streets has to clap his hands and say "Post, Post "so as to proclaim the fact that he is an Untouchable and let the Touchables beware of him. The following is recorded of the Cherumans of the Madras Presidency:

*"Very low is indeed the social position of these miserable beings. When a Cheruman meets a person of superior caste he must stand at a distance of thirty feet. If he comes within this prohibited distance, his approach is to cause pollution, which is removed only by bathing in water. A Cheruman cannot approach a Brahmin village or temple or tank. If he does so, purification becomes*

*necessary. Even while using the public road, if he sees his lord and master, he has to leave the ordinary way and walk, it may be in the mud, to avoid his displeasure by accidentally polluting him. To avoid polluting the passer-by, he repeats the unpleasant sound, "O,.Oh, O" In some places i.e. Palghat, one may see a Cheruman with a dirty piece of cloth spread on the road side, and yelling in a shrill voice, "Ambrane, Ambrane, give me some pice and throw them on the cloth ". His position is intolerable in the Native States of Cochin and Travancore, where the Brahaman influence is in the ascendant, while in the Palghat Taluka the Cherumans cannot, even to this day enter the bazaar. In Malabar it is stated that "The man of high caste shouts occasionally as he goes along, so that the low caste man can go off the road, and allow him to pass unpolluted. And those of the lowest castes shout, as they go, to give notice of their Pollution bearing presence, and learning the command of the man of high caste, move away from the road. It is common to see people of inferior caste travelling parallel to the road, but not daring to go along it".*

What a degradation for these unfortunate souls who have been turned by this Hindu Civilisation into social lepers! To be called an Untouchable is enough of a misfortune. But to require an Untouchable to proclaim by his own mouth his shame that he is an Untouchable is a cruelty to which in my opinion there is no parallel. What would an Untouchable say of this Hindu Civilisation? Would it be wrong if he said that it is felony and not civilisation?

That the condition of the Primitive Tribes, of the Criminal Tribes and of the Untouchables is the result of fundamental doctrines of Hindu Civilisation there can be no manner of doubt. Why have there been no missions to bring these Primitive Tribes into the Hindu fold? Why has crime become an occupation for certain tribes? Why have certain classes been treated as unfit for human association, as Untouchables?

The answer to each of these questions will have reference to some basic principle of the Hindu Civilisation. To the first question the answer is that the caste system prevents the

Hindu Religion from becoming a missionary religion and caste is a fundamental part of the Hindu Civilisation. To the second question the answer is that the system of Chaturvarna limits the opportunities which a person can have for earning an honourable living. All learned are the preserve of the Brahmins; all warlike services are the monopoly Thurston—Tribes and castes of Southern India, Vol. 5, p. 196. of the Kshatriya class; trade is open only to Vaishya, services to the Sudras. Those outside, there being nothing honourable left, have been driven to dishonourable and criminal ways of earning a livelihood. This is the result of Chaturvarna and Chaturvarna is again a fundamental part of Hindu Civilisation.

To the third question the answer is that untouchability is part of the Hindu law as contained in the Smritis which are again a fundamental part of the Hindu Civilisation. It is true that as for the past the state of degradation has been the common fate of all the three categories of this 791/2 millions of India's population. But it cannot be said that their future destiny will also be common to them. That is because although their condition is apparently similar, their position is essentially different.

The first thing to note is that the Primitive Tribes and the Criminal Tribes are not afflicted by this system of untouchability. To a Hindu they do not cause pollution. Indeed these Primitive and Criminal Tribes observe untouchability towards the Untouchables. The situation is full of humour when one sees members of these Primitive and Criminal Tribes feeling that they would be polluted if they would touch an Untouchable. They are poor, filthy, superstitious, ignorant, far more than the Untouchables yet they pride themselves as socially superior to the Untouchables. This of course is the result of the contagion, which they have from the Hindus. But the point to note is that the Hindu does not treat them as Untouchable.

That is an advantage which they have over the Untouchables and which makes their future assured. If the Primitive Tribes have no opportunities for advancement it is because they choose to live in isolation. But once they come out of their forest recesses and take part in civilisation. There is nothing that will stand in their way. Similarly the Criminal Tribes have their future assured. Government has established settlements where these Criminal Tribes are kept and taught useful trades. There is no doubt that in a very short time they will be completely weaned from their vicious habits.

The case of the Untouchables stands on quite a different footing altogether. Their disabilities are imposed upon them. Their isolation is really segregation which is enforced upon them. The problem of the Untouchables is different from the problem of the Primitive Tribes because in their case the evils of segregation are aggravated by the fact of untouchability and the result is that while in the case of the Primitive Tribes the problem is due to geographical isolation combined with lack of desire to avail themselves of the opportunities for betterment, in the case of the Untouchables the problem is due to positive denial of opportunities.

There does not seem to be much hope for the emancipation of the Untouchables, at any rate their emancipation is far more problematical and distant than the emancipation of the Primitive Tribes. The problem of the slaves was one of denial of political or economic rights. If the problem of the Untouchables was one of denial of political and economic rights, it could be solved by legal and constitutional methods. The denial of political and economic rights is the result of the social psychology of the Hindus. The problem for the Untouchables arises directly out of the social behaviour of the Hindus. Untouchability will vanish only when Hindus will change their mentality. The problem is how to make the Hindus unlearn their way of life. It is no small matter to make a whole nation give up its accustomed way of life. Besides the way of life the Hindus are accustomed to, is a way which is sanctified by their religion, at any rate they believe it to be so. To change their way of life is almost to change their religion.

How can this happen? Only when it is realised that what is tragedy for the Untouchables is the crime of the Hindus. How long shall the Untouchables have to wait for this revolution in the religious psychology of the Hindus? Let those who have a gift for prophecy answer. In the meantime it would be desirable to describe their condition and to state the problems which they and their friends have to face.

## The House the Hindus have Built

Is there any thing peculiar in the social organisation of the Hindus? An unsophisticated Hindu who is unaware of investigations conducted by scholars will say that there is nothing peculiar, abnormal or unnatural in the organisation of the society to which he belongs. This is quite natural. People who live their lives in isolation are seldom conscious of the peculiarities of their ways and manners. People have gone on from generation to generation without stopping to give themselves a name. But how does the social organisation of the Hindu strike the outsiders, non-Hindus? Did it appear to them as normal and natural?

Megasthenese who came to India as the ambassador of the Greek King Seleukos Nickator to the Court of Chandragupta Maurya some time about the year 305 B.C. did feel that the social organisation of the Hindus was of a very strange sort. Otherwise he would not have taken such particular care to describe the peculiar features of the Hindu social organisation. He has recorded: "The population of India is divided into seven parts. The philosophers are first in rank, but form the smallest class in point of number. Their services are employed privately by persons who wish to offer sacrifices or perform other sacred rites, and also publicly by the kings at what is called the Great Synod, wherein at the beginning of the new year all the philosophers are gathered together before the King at the gates, when any philosopher who may have committed any useful suggestion to writing, or observed any means for improving the crops and the cattle, or for promoting the public interests, declares it publicly. If any one is detected giving false information thrice, the law condemns him to be silent for the rest of his life, but he who gives sound advice is exempted from paying any taxes or contributions.

The second caste consists of the husbandmen, who form the bulk of the population, and are in disposition most mild and gentle. They are exempted from military service, and cultivate their lands undisturbed by fear. They never go to town, either to take part in its tumults, or for any other purpose. It therefore not infrequently happens that at the same time, and in the same part of the country, men maybe seen drawn up in array of battle, and fighting at risk of their lives, while other men close at hand are ploughing and digging in perfect security, having these soldiers to protect them. The whole of the land is the property of the King, and the husbandmen till it on condition of receiving one-fourth of the produce.

The third caste consists of herdsmen and hunters, who alone are allowed to hunt, and to keep cattle, and to sell draught animals or let them out on hire. In return for clearing the land of wild beasts and fowls which devour the seeds sown in the fields, they receive an allowance of grain from the king. They lead a wandering life and live under tents.

The fourth class, after herdsmen and hunters, consists of those who work at trades, of those who vend wares, and of those who are employed in bodily labour. Some of these pay tribute, and render to the State certain prescribed services. But the armour-makers and shipbuilders receive wages and their victuals from the king, for whom alone they work. The general in command of the army supplies the soldiers with weapons, and the admiral of the fleet lets out ships on hire for the transport both of passengers and merchandise.

The fifth class consists of fighting men, who when not engaged in active service, pass their time in idleness and drinking. They are maintained at the King's expense, and hence they are always ready, when occasion calls, to take the field, for they carry nothing of their own with them but their own bodies.

The sixth class consists of the overseers, to whom is assigned the duty of watching all that goes on, and making reports secretly to the King. Some are entrusted with the inspection of the city, and others with that of the army. The former employs as their coadjutors the courtesans of the city, and the latter the courtesans of the camp. The ablest and most trustworthy men are appointed to fill these offices.

The seventh class consists of the councillors and assessors of the king. To them belong the highest posts of government, the tribunals of justice, and the general administration of public affairs. No one is allowed to marry out of his own caste, or to exchange one profession or trade for another, or to follow more than one business. An exception is made in favour of the philosopher, who for his virtue is allowed this privilege. Alberuni who wrote an account of his travels in India some time about 1030 A.D. must have been struck by the peculiarity of the Hindu Social Organisation. For he too has not omitted to make a note of it. He observed: The Hindus call their castes varna, *i.e.* colours, and from a genealogical point of view they call them jataka, *i.e.* births. These castes are from the very beginning only four.

I. The highest caste is the Brahmana, of whom the books of the Hindus tell that they were created from the head of Brahman. And a Brahman is only another name for the force called nature, and the head is the highest part of the animal body, the Brahmana are the choice part of the whole genus. Therefore the Hindus consider them as the very best mankind.

II. The next caste are the Kshatriya, who were created, as they say, from the shoulders and hands of Brahman. Their degree is not much below that of the Brahmana.

III. After them follow the Vaisya, who were created from the thigh of Brahman.

IV. The Sudra, who were created from his feet, "Between the latter two classes there is no very great distance. Much, however, as these classes differ from each other, they live together in the same towns and villages, mixed together in the same houses and lodgings.

After the Sudra follow the people called Antyaja, who render various kinds of services, who are not reckoned amongst any caste, but only as members of a certain craft or profession. There are eight classes of them who freely intermarry with each other, except the fuller, shoemaker and weaver, for no others would condescend to have anything to do with them. These eight guilds are the fuller, shoemaker, juggler, the basket and shield maker, the sailor, fisherman, the hunter of wild animals and of birds, and the weaver. The four castes do not live together with them in one and the same place. These guilds live near the villages and towns of the four castes, but outside them.

The people called Hadi, Doma (Domba), Candala and Badhatau (sic) are not reckoned amongst any caste or guild.

They are occupied with dirty work, like the cleansing of the villages and other services. They are considered as one sole class, and distinguished only by their occupations. In fact, they are considered like illegitimate children; for according to general opinion they descend from a Sudra father and a Brahmani mother as the children of fornication; therefore they are degraded outcaste.

The Hindus give to every single man of the four castes characteristic names, according to their occupations and modes of life, *e.g.* the Brahman is in general called by this name as long as he does his work staying at home. When he is busy with the service of one fire, he is called Ishtin; if he serves three fires, he is called Agnihotrin; if he besides offers an offering to the fire, he is called Dikshita. And as it is with the Brahmana, so is it also with the other castes. Of the classes beneath the castes, the Hadi are the best spoken of, because they keep themselves free from everything unclean. Next follow the Doma, who play on the lute and sing. The still lower classes practise as a trade killing and the inflicting of judicial punishments. The worst of all are the Badhatau, who not only devour the flesh of dead animals, but even of dogs and other beasts.

Each of the four castes, when eating together, must form a group of themselves, one group not being allowed to comprise two men of different castes. If, further, in the group of the Brahmana there are two men who live at enmity with each other, and the seat of the one is by the side of the other, they make a barrier between the two seats by placing a board between them, or by spreading a piece of dress, or in some other way; and if there is only a line drawn between them, they are considered as separated. Since it is forbidden to eat the remains of a meal, every single man must have his own food for himself; for if any one of the party who are eating should take of the food from one and the same plate, that which remains in the plate becomes, after the first eater has taken part, to him who wants to take as the second, the remains of the meal, and such is forbidden. Alberuni did not merely content himself with recording what struck him as peculiar in the Hindu Social organisation. He went on to say:

*"Among the Hindus institutions of this kind abound. We Muslims, of course, stand entirely on the other side*

*of the question, considering all men as equal, except in piety; and this is the greatest obstacle which prevents any approach or understanding between Hindus and Muslims."*

Duarte Barbosa who was Portuguese official in the service of the Portuguese Government in India from 1500 to 1517 has left a record of his impressions of Hindu Society. This is what struck him:

> *"And before this kingdom of Guzerate fell into the hands of the Moors, a certain race of Heathen whom the Moors called Resbutos dwelt therein, who in those days were the knights and wardens of the land, and made war where so ever it was needful. These men kill and eat sheep and fish and all other kinds of food; in the mountains there are yet many of them, where they have great villages and obey not the king of Guzerate, but rather wage daily war against him: who, do what he may, is yet not able to prevail against them, nor will do so, for they are very fine horsemen, and good archers, and have besides divers other weapons to defend themselves withal against the Moors, on whom they make war without ceasing; yet have they no king nor lord over them."*

And in this kingdom there is another sort of Heathen whom they call Baneanes, who are great merchants and traders. They dwell among the Moors with whom they carry on all their trade. This people eat neither flesh nor fish, nor anything subject to death; they slay nothing, nor are they willing even to see the slaughter of any animal; and thus they maintain their idolatry and hold it so firmly that it is a terrible thing. For often it is so that the Moors take to them live insects or small birds, and make as though to kill them in their presence, and the Baneanes buy these and ransom them, paying much more than they are worth, so that they may save their lives and let them go. And if the King or a Governor of the land has any man condemned to death, for any crime, which he has committed, they gather themselves together and buy him from justice, if they are willing to sell him, that he may not die.

And divers Moorish mendicants as well, when they wish to obtain alms from this people, take great stones wherewith they beat upon their shoulders and bellies as though they would slay themselves before them, to hinder which they give them great alms that they may depart in peace. Others carry knives with which they slash their arms and legs, and to these too they give large alms that they may not kill themselves. Others go to their doors seeking to kill rats and snakes for them, and to them also they give much money that they may not do so. Thus they are much esteemed by the Moors!

When these Baneanes meet with a swarm of ants on the road they shrink back and seek for some way to pass without crushing them. And in their houses they sup by daylight, for neither by night nor by day will they light a lamp, by reason of certain little flies which perish in the flame thereof; and if there is any great need of a light by night they have a lantern of varnished paper or cloth, so that no living thing may find its way in, and die in the flame. And if these men breed many lice they kill them not, but when they trouble them too much they send for certain men, also Heathen, who live among them and whom they hold to be men of a holy life; they are like hermits living with great abstinence through devotion to their gods.

These men louse them, and as many lice as they catch they place on their own heads and breed them on their own flesh, by which they say they do great service to their Idol. Thus one and all they maintain with great self-restraint their law of not killing. On the other hand they are great usurers, falsifiers of weights and measures and many other goods and of coins; and great liars. These heathen are tawny men, tall and well looking, gaily attired, delicate and moderate in their food.

Their diet is of milk, butter, sugar and rice, and many conserves of divers sorts. They make much use of dishes of fruit and vegetables and potherbs in their food. Where so ever they dwell they have orchards and fruit gardens and many water tanks wherein they bathe twice a day, both men and women; and they say when they have finished bathing that they are clear of as many sins as they have committed up to that hour. These Baneanes grow very long hair, as women do with us, and wear it twisted up on the head and made into a knot, and over it a turban, that they may keep it always held together; and in their hair they put flowers and other sweet scented things.

They use to anoint themselves with white sandalwood mixed with saffron and other scents. They are very amorous people. They are clad in long cotton and silken shirts and are shod with pointed shoes of richly wrought cordwain; some of them wear short coats of silk and brocade. They carry no arms except certain very small knives ornamented with gold and silver, and this for two reasons: First, because they are men who make but little use of weapons; and secondly, because the Moors defend them.

***Bramenes:*** And there is here another class of Heathen whom they call Bramenes, who are priests among them, and persons who manage and rule their houses of prayers and idol-worship, which are of great size and have great revenues; and many of them also are maintained by alms. In these houses are great numbers of wooden Idols, and others of stone and copper and in these houses or monasteries they celebrate great ceremonies in honour of these idols, entertaining them with great store of candles and oil lamps, and with bells after our fashion. These Bramenes and Heathen have in their creed many resemblance to the Holy Trinity, and hold in great honour the relation of the Triune Three, and always make their prayers to God, whom they confess and adore as the true God, Creator and maker of all things, who is three persons and one God and they say that there are many other gods who are rulers under him, in whom also they believe. These Bramenes and heathen wheresoever they find our churches enter them and make prayers and adoration to our Images, always asking for Santa Maria, like men who have some knowledge and understanding of these matters; and they honour the Church as is our manner, saying that between them and us there is little difference. These men never eat anything subject to death, nor do they slay anything. Bathing they hold to be a great ceremony and they say that by it they are saved.

There is also in this same Kingdom of Calicut a caste of people called Bramenes who are priests among them (as are the clergy among us) of whom I have spoken in another place.

These all speak the same tongue, nor can any be a Bramene except he be the son of a Bramene. When they are seven years of age they put over their shoulder a strip of two fingers in breadth of untanned skin with the hair on it of a certain wild beast, which they call Cryvamergam, which resembles a wild ass. Then for seven years he must not eat betel for which time he continues to wear this strap. When he is fourteen years old they make him a Bramene, and taking off their leather strap they invest him with the cord of three strands which he wears for the rest of his life as a token that he is a Bramene. And this they do with great ceremonial and rejoicings, as we do here for a cleric when he sings his first mass. Thereafter he may eat betel, but not flesh or fish. They have great honour among the Indians and as I have already said, they suffer death for no cause whatsoever, their own headman gives them a mild chastisement.

They marry once only in our manner, and only the eldest son marries, he is treated like the head of an entailed estate. The other brothers remain single all their lives. These Bramenes keep their wives well guarded, and greatly honoured, so that no other men may sleep with them; if any of them die, they do not marry again, but if a woman wrongs her husband she is slain by poison. The brothers who remain bachelors sleep with the Nayre women, they hold it to be a great honour, and as they are Bramenes no woman refuses herself to them, yet they may not sleep with any woman older than themselves. They dwell in their own houses and cities, and serve as clergy in the houses of worship, whither they go to pray at certain hours of the day, performing their rituals and idolatries.

Some of these Bramenes serve the Kings in every manner except in arms. No man may prepare any food for the King except a Bramene or his own kin; they also serve as couriers to other countries with letters, money or merchandise, passing wherever they wish to go in safety, and none does them any ill, even when the Kings are at war. These Bramenes are learned in their idolatry, and possess many books thereof. The Kings hold them in high esteem.

I have already spoken many times of the Nayres, and yet I have not hitherto told you what manner of men they are. You are to know that in this land of Malbar there is another caste of people, called Nayres, and among them are noble men who have no other duty than to serve in war, and they always carry their arms whither so ever they go, some swords and shields, others bows and arrows, and yet others spears. They all live with the King, and the other great Lords; nevertheless all receive stipends from the King or from the great Lords with whom they dwell. None may become a Nayre, save only he who is of Nayre lineage. They are very free from stain in their nobility. They will not touch any one of low caste, nor eat, nor drink save in the house of a Nayre.

These men are not married, their nephews (sisters' sons) are their heirs. The Nayre women of good birth are very independent, and dispose of themselves as they please with Bramenes and Nayres, but they do not sleep with men of caste lower than their own under pain of death. When they reach the age of twelve years their mothers hold a great ceremony. When a mother perceives that her daughter has attained that age, she asks her kinsfolk and friends to make ready to honour her daughter, then she asks of the kindred and especially of one particular kinsman or great friend to marry her daughter; this he willingly promises and then he has a small jewel made, which would contain a half ducat of gold, long like a ribbon, with a hole through the middle which comes out on the other side, string on thread of white silk.

The mother then on a fixed day is present with her daughter gaily decked with many rich jewels, making great rejoicing with music and singing, and a great assembly of people. Then the Kinsman or friend comes bringing that jewel, and going through certain forms, throws it over the girl's neck. She wears it as a token all the rest of her life, and may then dispose of herself, as she will. The man departs without sleeping with her inasmuch as he is her kinsman; if he is not, he may sleep with her, but is not obliged to do so. Thenceforward the mother goes about searching and asking some young man to take her daughter's virginity; they must be Nayres and they regard it among themselves as a disgrace and a foul thing to take a woman's virginity. And when any one has once slept with her, she is fit for association with men.

Then the mother again goes about enquiring among other young Nayres if they wish to support her daughter, and take her as a Mistress so that three or four Nayres agree with her to keep her, and sleep with her, each paying her so much a day; the more lovers she has the greater is her honour. Each one of them passes a day with her from midday on one day, till midday on the next day and so they continue living quietly without any disturbance nor quarrels among them. If any of them wishes to leave her, he leaves her, and takes another, and she also if she is weary of a man, she tells him to go, and he does so, or makes terms with her.

Any children they may have stay with the mother who has to bring them up, for they hold them not to be the children of any man, even if they bear his likeness, and they do not consider them their children, nor are they heirs to their estates, for as I have already stated their heirs are their nephews, sons of their sisters, (which rule whosoever will consider inwardly in his mind will find that it was established with a greater and deeper meaning than the common folk think) for they say that the Kings of the Nayres instituted it in order that the Nayres should not be held back from their service by the burden and labour of rearing children.

In this Kingdom of Malabar there is also another caste of people whom they call Biabares, Indian Merchants, natives of the land. They were there ere foreign nations had sailed to India. They deal in goods of every kind both in the seaports and inland, where so ever their trade is of most profit. They gather to themselves all the pepper and ginger from the Nayres and husbandmen, and offtimes they buy the new crops beforehand in exchange for cotton clothes and other goods which they keep at the seaports. Afterwards they sell them again and gain much money thereby. Their privileges are such that the King of the country in which they dwell cannot execute them by legal process.

There is in this land yet another caste of folk known as Cuiavern. They do not differ from the Nayres, yet by reason of a fault which they committed, they remain separate from them. Their business is to make pottery and bricks for roofing the houses of the Kings and idols, which are roofed with bricks instead of tiles; only these, for as I have already said, other houses are thatched with branches. They have their own sort of idolatry, and their separate idols.

There is another Heathen caste which they call Mainatos, whose occupation is to wash clothes for the Kings, Bramenes and Nayres. By this they live, and may not take up any other. There is another lower caste than these which they call Caletis, who are weavers who have no other way of earning save by weaving of cotton and silk cloths, but they are low caste folk and have but little money, so that they clothe the lower races. They are apart by themselves and have their own idolatry.

Besides the castes mentioned above, there are eleven others lower than they within whom the others do not associate, nor do they touch them under pain of death; and there are great distinctions between one and another of them, preserving them from mixture with one another. The purest of all these low, simple folk they call Tuias. Their work is mainly that of tending the palm-groves, and gathering the fruit thereof, and carrying it away for wages on their backs, for there are no beasts of burden in the land.

There is another caste still lower than these whom they call Manen (Mancu in the printed text) who neither associate with others nor touch them, nor do the others touch them. They are washermen for the common people, and makers of sleeping mats, from which occupations all but they are barred; their sons must perforce follow the same trade; they have their own separate idolatry.

There is another caste in this land still lower whom they call Canaqus. Their trade is making buckles and umbrellas. They learn letters for purposes of astronomy, they are great astrologers, and foretell with great truth things that are to come; there are some lords who maintain them for this cause.

There is also another lower caste, also Heathens, called Ageres. They are masons, carpenters, smiths, metal workers and some are goldsmiths, all of whom are of a common descent, and a separate caste, and have their idols apart from other folk. They marry, and their sons inherit their property, and learn their fathers' trade.

There is another caste still lower in this country called Mogeres, they are almost the same as the Tuias, but they do not touch one another. They work as carriers of things belonging to the Royal State when it moves from one place to another, but there are very few of them in this land; they are a separate caste; they have no marriage law; the most of them gain their living on the sea, they are sailors, and some of them fishers; they have no idols. They are as well slaves of the Nayres.

There is another caste yet lower whom they call Monger, fishers who have no other work than fishing, yet some sail in the Moors' ships and in those of other heathens, and they are very expert seamen. This race is very rude. They are shameless thieves; they marry and their sons succeed them, their women are of loose character, they sleep with any one-so ever, and it is held no evil. They have their own idolatry.

In this land of Malabar there is another caste of Heathen even lower than these, whom they call Betunes. Their business is salt making and rice growing, they have no other livelihood.

They dwell in houses standing by themselves in the fields away from the roads, whither the gentlefolk do not walk. They have their own idolatry. They are slaves of the Kings and Nayres and pass their lives in poverty. The Nayres make them walk far away from them and speak to them from afar off. They hold no intercourse with any other caste.

There is another caste of Heathen, even lower and ruder, whom they call Paneens, who are great sorcerers, and live by no other means.

There is another caste lower and ruder than they, named Revoleens, a very poor folk, who live by carrying firewood and grass to the towns, they may touch none, nor may any touch them under pain of death. They go naked, covering only their private parts with scant and filthy rags, the more part of them indeed with leaves of certain trees. Their women wear many brass rings in their ears; and on their necks, arms and legs necklaces and bracelets of heads.

And there is yet another caste of Heathens lower than these whom they call Poleas, who among all the rest are held to be accursed and excommunicate; they dwell in the fields and open campaigns in secret lurking places, whither folk of good caste never go save by mischance, and live in huts very strait and mean. They are tillers of rice with buffaloes and oxen. They never speak to the Nayres save from off, shouting so that they may hear them, and when they go along the roads they utter loud cries, that they may be let past, and whosoever hears them leaves the road, and stands in the wood till they have passed by: and if any one, whether man or woman, touches them his kinsfolk slay them forthwith, and in vengeance therefore they slay Poleas until they are weary without suffering any punishment.

Yet another caste there is even lower and baser called Pareens, who dwell in the most desert places away from all other castes. They have no intercourse with any person nor any one with them they are held to be worse than devils, and to be damned. Even to see them is to be unclean and out-caste. They eat yams and other roots of wild plants. They cover their middles with leaves, they also eat the flesh of wild beasts.

With these end the distinctions between the castes of the Heathen, which are eighteen in all, each one separate and unable to touch others or marry with them; and besides these eighteen castes of the Heathen who are natives of Malabar, which I have now related to you, there are others of outlandish folk, merchants and traders in the land, where they possess houses and estates, living like the natives, yet with customs of their own.

These foreigners were not able to give a full and detailed picture of caste. This is understandable. For to every foreigner the private life of the Hindu is veiled and it is not possible for him to penetrate it. The social organism of India, the play of its motive forces, is moreover, regulated infinitely more by custom, varying according to locality and baffling in its complexity, than by any legal formula which can be picked out of a legal text book. But there is no doubt that caste did appear to the foreigners as the most singular and therefore the most distinguishing feature of Hindu Society. Otherwise they would not have noted its existence in the record they made of what they observed when they came to India.

Caste therefore is something special in the Hindu Social organization and marks off the Hindus from other peoples. Caste has been a growing institution. It has never been the same at all time. The shape and form of caste as it existed when Magasthenes wrote his account was very different from what the shape and form it has taken when Alberuni came and the appearance it gave to the Portuguese was different from what it was in the time of Alberuni. But to understand caste one must have more exact idea of its nature than these foreigners are able to give.

To follow the discussion of the subject of caste it is necessary to familiarise the readers with some basic conceptions, which underlie the Hindu Social organisation. The basic conception of social organisation which prevails among the Hindus starts with the rise of our classes or varnas into which Hindu society is believed to have become divided. These four classes were named: (1) Brahmins, the priestly and the educated class, (2) The Kshatriyas, the Military Class, (3) The Vaishyas, the trading class and, (4) The Sudras, the servant class. For a time these were merely classes. After a time what were only Classes (Varnas) became Castes (Jatis) and the four castes became four thousand. In this way the modern Caste System was only the evolution of the ancient Varna System.

No doubt the caste system is an evolution of the Varna System. But one can get no idea of the caste system by a study of the Varna System. Caste must be studied apart from Varna.

An old agnostic is said to have summed up his philosophy in the following words: "The only thing I know is that I know nothing; and I am not quite sure that I know that."

Sir Denzil Ibbetson undertaking to write about caste in the Punjab said that the words of these agnostic about his philosophy expressed very exactly his own feelings regarding caste. It is no doubt true that owing to local circumstances there does appear a certain diversity about caste matters and that it is very difficult to make any statement regarding any one of the castes absolutely true as it may be as regards one locality which will not be contradicted with equal truth as regards the same caste in some other area.

Although this may be true yet it cannot be difficult to separate the essential and fundamental features of caste from its nonessential superficial features. For easy approach to this to ascertain by asking what are the matters for which a person is liable to be excluded from caste. Mr. Bhattacharya has stated the following as causes for expulsion from caste: (1) Embracing Christianity or Islam, (2) Going to Europe or America, (3) Marrying a widow, (4) Publicly throwing the sacred thread, (5) Publicly eating beef, pork or foul, (6) Publicly eating *Kaccha* food prepared by a Mahomedan, Christian or low caste Hindu, (7) Officiating at the house of a very low caste Sudra, (8) By a female going away from home for immoral purposes and (9) By a widow becoming pregnant. This list is not exhaustive and omits the two most important causes which entail expulsion from caste. They are (10) intermarrying outside caste, (11) Interdining with persons of another caste, (12) Change of occupation. The second defect in the statement of Mr. Bhattacharya is that it does not make any distinction between essentials and (un) essentials. Of course when a person is expelled from his caste the penalty is uniform. His friends, relatives, and fellow men refuse to partake of his hospitality. He is not invited to entertainment in their houses. He cannot obtain brides or bridegrooms for his children. Even his married daughters cannot visit him without running the risk of being excluded from caste. His priest, his barber and washer man refuses to serve him. His fellow caste men sever their connection with him so completely that they refuse to assist him even at the funeral of a member of his household. In some cases the man excluded from caste is debarred access to public temples and to the cremation or burial ground.

These reasons for expulsion from caste indirectly show the rules and regulations of the caste. But all regulations are not fundamental. There are many which are unessential. Caste can exist even without them.

The essential and unessential can be distinguished by asking another question. When can a Hindu who has lost caste regain his caste. The Hindus have a system of *Prayaschitas* which are penances and which a man who has been expelled from caste must perform before he can be admitted to cast fellowship. With regard to these *Prayaschitas* or Penances certain points must be remembered. In the first place there are caste offences for which there is no *Prayaschita.* In the second place the *Prayaschitas* vary according to the offence. In some cases the *Prayaschita* involves a very small penalty. In other cases the penalty involved is a very severe one.

The existing of a *Prayaschita* and its absence have a significance which must be clearly understood. The absence of *Prayaschita* does not mean that any one may commit the offence with impunity. On the contrary it means that the offence is of an immeasurable magnitude and the offender once expelled is beyond reclamation. There is no re-entry for him in the caste from which he is expelled. The existence of a *Prayaschita* means that the offence is compoundable. The offender can take the prescribed *Prayaschita* and obtain admission in the caste from which he is expelled.

There are two offences for which there is no penance. These are (1) change from Hindu Religion to another religion, (2) Marriage with a person of another caste or another religion. It is obvious if a man loses. Caste for these offences he loses it permanently.

Of the other offences the *Prayaschitas* prescribed are of the severest kind are two: (1) Interdining with a person of another caste or a non-Hindu and (2) Taking to occupations which is not the occupation of the caste. In the case of the other offences the penalty is a light one almost nominal.

The surest clue to find out what are the fundamental rules of caste and what caste consists in is furnished by the rules regarding *Prayaschitas.* Those for the infringement of which there is no *Prayaschita* constitute the very soul of caste and those for the infringement of which the *Prayaschita* is of the severest kind make up the body of caste. It may therefore be said without any hesitation that there are four fundamental rules of caste. A caste may be defined as a social group having (a) belief in Hindu Religion and bound by certain regulations as to, (b) marriage, (c) food and (d) occupation. To this one more characteristic may be added namely a social group having a common name by which it is recognised.

In the matter of marriage the regulation lays down that the caste must be endogamous. There can be no intermarriage between members of different castes. This is the first and the most fundamental idea on which the whole fabric of the caste is built up.

In the matter of food the rule is that a person cannot take food from and dine with any person who does not belong to his caste. This means that only those who can intermarry can also interdine. Those who cannot intermarry cannot interdine. In other words caste is an endogamous unit and also a communal unit.

In the matter of occupation the regulation is that a person must follow the occupation which is the traditional occupation of his caste and if the caste has no occupation then he should follow the occupation of his father.

In the matter of status of a person it is fixed and is hereditary. It is fixed because a person's status is determined by the status of the caste to which he belongs. It is hereditary because a Hindu is stamped with the caste to which his parents belonged, a Hindu cannot change his status because he cannot change his caste. A Hindu is born in a caste and he dies a member of the caste in which he is born. A Hindu may lose his status if he loses caste. But he cannot acquire a new or a better or different status.

What is the significance of a common name for a caste? The significance of this will be clear if we ask two questions, which are very relevant, and a correct answer to each is necessary for a complete idea of this institution of caste. Social groups are either organised or unorganised. When the membership of the group and the process of joining and leaving the groups, are the subject of definite social regulations and involve certain duties and privileges in relation to other members of the group then the group is an organised group. A group is a voluntary group in which members enter with a full knowledge of what they are doing and the aims which the association is designed to fulfil. On the other hand there are groups of which an individual person becomes a member without any act of volition, and becomes subject to social regulation and traditions over which he has no control of any kind.

Now it is hardly necessary to say that caste is a highly organised social grouping. It is not a loose or a floating body. Similarly it is not necessary to say that caste is an involuntary grouping. A Hindu is born in a caste and he dies as a member of that caste. There is no Hindu without caste, cannot escape caste and being bounded by caste from birth to death he becomes subject to social regulations and traditions of the caste over which he has no control.

The significance of a separate name for a caste lies in this, namely it makes caste an organised and an involuntary grouping. A separate and a distinctive name for a caste make caste asking to a corporation with a perpetual existence and a seal of separate entity. The significance of separate names for separate castes has not been sufficiently realised by writers on caste. In doing that they have lost sight of a most distinctive feature of caste social groups there are and there are bound to be in every society. Many social groups in many countries can be equated to various castes in India and may be regarded as their equivalent. Potters, Washermen, Intellectuals, as social groups are every where. But in other countries they have remained as unorganised and voluntary groups while in India they have become organised and involuntary *i.e.* they have become castes is because in other countries the social groups were not given name while in India they did. It is the name which the caste bears which gives it fixate and continuity and individuality. It is the name which defines who are its members and in most cases a person born in a caste carries the name of the caste as apart of his surname. Again it is the name which makes it easy for the caste to enforce its rules and regulations. It makes it easy in two ways. In the first place, the name of the caste forming a surname of the individual prevents the offender in passing off as a person belonging to another caste and thus escape the jurisdiction of the caste. Secondly, it helps to identify the offending individual and the caste to whose jurisdiction he is subject so that he is easily handed up and punished for any breach of the caste rules.

This is what caste means. Now as to the caste system. This involves the study of the mutual relations between different castes. Looked at as a collection of caste the caste system presents several features, which at once strike the observer. In the first place there is no inter-connection between the various castes, which form a systems each caste is separate and distinct. It is independent and sovereign in the disposal of its internal affairs and the endorsement of caste Regulations. The castes touch but they do not interpenetrate. The second feature relates to the order in which one caste stands in relation to the other castes in the system. That order is vertical and not horizontal.

In other words castes are not equal in status. Their order is based on inequality. One caste is higher or lower in relation to another. Castes form an hierarchy in which one caste is at the top and is the highest, another at the bottom and it is the lowest and in between there are castes every one of which is at once above some caste and below some caste, The caste system is a system of gradation in which every caste except the highest and the lowest has a priority and precedence over some other caste:

How is this precedence or this superiority determined? This order of superiority and inferiority or this insubordination is determined by Rules (1) which are connected with religious rites and (2) which are connected with commonality.

Religion as a basis of Rules of precedence manifests itself in three ways. Firstly through religious ceremonies, secondly through incantations that accompany the religious ceremonies and thirdly through the position of the priest.

Beginning with the ceremonies as a source of rules of precedence it should be noted that the Hindu Scriptures prescribe sixteen religious ceremonies. Although those are Hindu ceremonies every Hindu Caste cannot by right claim to perform all the sixteen ceremonies. Few can claim the right to perform all. Some are allowed to perform certain ceremonies, some are not allowed to perform certain of the ceremonies. For instance take the ceremony of Upanayan, wearing the sacred thread. Some castes can't. Precedence follows this distinction in the matters of right to perform the ceremonies. A caste which can claim to perform all the ceremonies is higher in status than the caste which has a right to perform a few.

Turning to the Mantras it is another source for rules of precedence. According to the Hindu Religion the same ceremony can be performed in three different ways: (1) Vedokta, (2) Shastrokta and (3) Puranokta. In the Vedokta form the ceremony is performed with Mantras (incantations) from the Vedas. In the Shastrokta form the ceremony is performed with Mantras (incantations) from the Shastras. In the Puranokta form the ceremony is performed with Mantras (incantations) from the Puranas. Hindu Religious Scriptures fall into three distinct categories: (1) The Vedas which are four, (2) The Shastras which are six and (3) The Puranas which are eighteen. Although they are all respected as scriptures they do not all have the same sanctity. The Vedas have the highest sanctity. The Shastras stand next in order of sanctity and the Puranas have the lowest sanctity. The way the Mantras give rise to social precedence will be obvious if it is borne in mind that not every caste is entitled to have the ceremony performed in the Vedokta form. Three castes may well claim the right to the performance of one of the sixteen ceremonies. But it well be that one of it is entitled to perform it in the Vedokta form, another in the Shastrokta form and the third only in the Puranokta form. Precedence goes with the kind of Mantra that a caste is entitled to use in the performance of a religious ceremony. A caste which is entitled to use Vedic Mantra is superior to a caste which is entitled to use Shastrik Mantra and a caste which is entitled to use Shastrik Mantras is higher than a caste which is entitled to use only Puranokta Mantras.

Taking the priest as third source of precedence connected with Religion Hinduism requires the instrumentality of a priest for the derivation of the full benefit from the performance of a religious ceremony. The priest appointed by the scriptures is the Brahmin. A Brahmin therefore is indispensable. But the scriptures do not require that a Brahmin shall accept the invitation of any and every Hindu irrespective of his caste to officiate at a religious ceremony. The invitation of which caste he will accept and of which he will refuse is a matter left to the wishes of the Brahmin. By long and well-established custom it is now settled at which caste he will officiate and at which caste he will not. This fact has become the basis of precedence as between castes. The caste at which a Brahmin will officiate is held as superior to a caste at whose religious functions a Brahmin will not officiate.

The second source for rules of precedence is commonality. It will be noticed that rules of marriage have not given rise to rules of precedence as rules of commonality have. The reason lies in the distinction between the rules prohibiting intermarriage and interdining. That difference is obvious. The prohibition on intermarriage is such that it can not only be respected but it can be carried out quite strictly. But the prohibition of interdining creates difficulties. It cannot be carried out quite strictly in all places and under all circumstances. Man migrates and must migrate from place to place. In every place he happens to go he may not find his castemen. He may find himself landed in the midst of strangers. Marriage is not a matter of urgency but food is. He can wait for getting himself married till he returns to the society of his castemen. But he cannot wait for his food. He must find it from somewhere and from someone. Question arises from which caste he can take food if he has to. The rule is that he will take food from a caste above his but will not take food from a caste, which is below his. There is no way of finding how it came to be decided that a Hindu can take food from one caste and not from another. By long series of precedent every Hindu knows from what caste he can take food and from what caste he cannot. This is determined chiefly by the rule followed by the Brahmin. A caste is higher or lower according as the Brahmin takes from it food or not.

In this connection the Brahmin has a very elaborate set of rules in the matter of food and water. (1) He will take only water from some and not from others. (2) A Brahmin will not take food cooked in water by any caste. (3) He will take only food cooked in oil from some castes. Again he has as a set of rules in the matter of the vessel, in which he will accept food and water. He will take food or water in an earthen vessel from some caste, only in metallic vessel from some and only in glass vessel from others. This goes to determine the level of the caste. If he takes food cooked in oil from a caste its status is higher than the caste from which he will not. If he takes water from a caste it is higher than the caste from which he will not. If he takes water in a metallic vessel that caste is higher than the caste from which he will take water in an earthen vessel and the caste from which he will take water in an earthen vessel is higher than the caste from which he will take water in a glass vessel. Glass is a substance which is called *Nirlep* (which conserves no stain) therefore a Brahmin can take water in it even from the lowest. But other metals do conserve stains. Contaminating character of the stain depends upon the status of the person who has used it. That status depends upon the Brahmin's will to accept water in that vessel.

These are some of the factors which determine the place and status of a caste in this Hindu hierarchical system of castes.

Such is caste and such is caste system. Question is, is this enough to know the Hindu Social Organisation. For a static conception of the Hindu Social Organisation an idea of the caste and the caste system is enough. One need not trouble to remember more than the facts that the Hindus are divided into castes and that the castes form a system in which all hang on a thread which runs through the system in such a way that while encircling and separating one caste from another it holds them all as though as it was a string of tennis balls hanging one above the other. But this will not be enough to understand caste as a dynamic phenomenon. To follow the workings of caste in action it is necessary to note one other feature of caste besides the caste system, namely class-caste system.

The relationship between the ideas of caste and class has been a matter of lively controversy. Some say that caste is analogous to class. Others hold that the idea of caste is analogous to class and that there is no difference between the two. Others hold that the idea of caste is fundamentally opposed to that of class. This is an aspect of the subject of caste about which more will be said hereafter. For the present it is necessary to emphasis one feature of the caste system which has not been referred to here in before. It is this. Although caste is different from and opposed to the notion of class yet the caste-system as distinguished from caste recognises a class system which is somewhat different from the graded status referred to above. Just as the Hindus are divided into so many castes, castes are divided into different classes of castes.

The Hindu is caste conscious. He is also class conscious. Whether he is caste conscious or class conscious depends upon the caste with which he comes in conflict. If the caste with which he comes in conflict is a caste within the class to which he belongs he is caste conscious. If the caste is outside the class to which he belongs he is class conscious. Any one who needs any evidence on this point may study the Non-Brahmin Movement in the Madras and Bombay Presidency. Such a study will leave no doubt that to a Hindu caste periphery is as real as class periphery and caste consciousness is as real as class-consciousness.

Caste, it is said, is an evolution of the Varna System. I will show later on that this is nonsense. Caste is a perversion of Varna, at any rate it is an evolution in the opposite direction. But while Caste has completely perverted the Varna System it has borrowed the class system from the Varna System.

Indeed the Class-Caste System follows closely the class cleavages of the Varna System.

Looking at the caste system from this point of view one comes across several lines of class cleavage which run through this pyramid of castes dividing the pyramid into blocks of castes. The first line of cleavage follows the line of division noticeable in the ancient Chaturvarna system. The old system of Chaturvarna made a distinction between the first three Varnas, the Brahmins, Kshatriyas, Vaishyas, and the forth Varna namely the Sudras. The three former were classes as the Regenerate classes. The Sudra was held as the unregenerate class. This distinction was based upon the fact that the former were entitled to wear the sacred thread and study the Vedas. The Sudra was entitled to neither and that is why he was regarded as the unregenerate class. This line of cleavage is still in existence and forms the basis of the present day class division separating the castes which have grown out of the vast class of Sudras from those which have grown out of the three classes of Brahmins, the Kashatriyas and Vaishyas. This line of class cleavage is the one which is expressed by the terms High Castes and Low Castes and which are short forms for High Class Castes and Low Class Castes.

Next after this line of cleavage there runs through the pyramid a second line of class cleavage. It runs just below the Low Class Castes. It sets above all the castes born out of the four Varnas *i.e.* The High Castes as well as the Low Castes above the remaining Castes, which I will merely describe as the 'rest'. This line of class cleavage is again a real one and follows the well defined distinction which was a fundamental principle of the Chaturvarna System. The Chaturvarna System as is pointed out made a distinction between the four Varnas putting the three Varnas above the fourth. But it also made an equally clear distinction between those within the Chaturvarna and those outside the Chaturvarna. It had a terminology to express this distinction. Those within the Chaturvarna high or low. Brahmins or Sudras were called *Savarna i.e.* those with the stamp of the Varna. That outside the Chaturvarna were called Avarna *i.e.* those without the stamp of Varna. All the Castes, which have evolved out of the four Varnas, are called Savarna Hindus—which is rendered in

English by the term caste Hindus. The 'rest' are the *Avarnas* who in present parlance spoken of by Europeans as Non-Caste Hindus *i.e.* those who are outside the 4 original castes or Varnas.

Much that is written about the Caste System has reference mostly to the Caste-System, among the Savarna Hindus. Very little is known about the Avarna Hindus. Who are these Avarna Hindus, what is their position in Hindu Society, how are they related to the Savarna Hindus, are questions to which no attention has so far been paid. I am sure that without considering these questions no one can get a true picture of the social structure the Hindus have built. To leave out the Class cleavage between the Savarna Hindus and the Avarna Hindus is to relate Grimm's Fairy Tale which leaves out the witches, the goblins and the ogres.

The Avarna Hindus comprise three divisions: (1) Primitive Castes, (2) Criminal Castes and (3) The Untouchable Castes. The total population of persons comprising these three classes is by no means small. The population of the Primitive Tribes in India according to the Census of 1931 is stated to be about 25 millions. The total population of persons listed as Criminal is somewhere about 4 1/2 millions. The total population of Untouchables in 1931 was about 50 millions. The grand total of these three comes to 79 1/2 millions.

What is the relation of the Savarna Castes to the Avarna Castes? The cleavage between the Savarna Castes and the Avarna Castes is not uniform in its consequences with the result that the position created is not easy to grasp. The line of the cleavage running between the Savarna Castes and the Avarna Castes produces a relationship between the Savarna Castes and the two Avarna Castes—the Primitive and the Criminal Castes which is different from the relationship which it produces between the Savarna Castes and the last of the Avarna Castes namely the Untouchables. This line of cleavage between the Savarna Castes and the first two of the Avarna Castes is a cleavage between kindred and friends. It does not make intercourse on respectful terms between the two impossible. The cleavage between the Savarna Castes and the Untouchables is of a different kind. It is a cleavage between two non-kindred and hostile groups. There is no possibility of friendly intercourse on respectable terms. What is the significance of this line of cleavage? On what is it based? Although the cleavage is definite the basis of it has not been defined.

But it seems that the basis of cleavage is the same as that which exists between the Dwijas and the Sudras. Like the Sudras the Avarna Castes are composed of unregenerate people. They are not twice born and have no right to wear the sacred thread. This also brings out two facts which otherwise are lost sight of. The first fact is that the difference between the Sudra Castes of the Savarna division of cast's and the Primitive and the Criminal Castes of the Avarna division is very thin. Both are touchable and both are unregenerate. The difference is one of cultural development. But although the cultural difference between the two sections is great—as great as there is between a highly cultured and the unmitigated barbarian—from the point of view of the orthodox Hindu, the difference between them is one of degree. It is to mark this difference in culture that the Hindus invented a new terminology which recognised two classes of Sudras: (1) Sat-Sudras and (2) Sudras. Calling the old body of Sudras as Sat Sudras or cultured Sudras and using the term Sudras to those comprising the Primitive Castes who had come within the pale of Hindu Civilisation. The new terminology did not mean any difference in the rights and duties of Sudras. The distinction pointed out those Sudras who were fit for associated life with the Dwijas and those who were less fitted for it.

What is the relation of Avarna Castes to one another? Do they exist as mere collection of castes or have they any class cleavages? They are certainly mere collection of Castes. There are certainly lines of class cleavages running through this block of Avarna Castes. Whether there is a line of class cleavage running between the Primitive Castes and the Criminal Castes may be a matter of some doubt. Perhaps the line is faint. But there is no doubt that there is a very definite a very broad and a very emphatic line of cleavage between the Primitive Castes and the Criminal Castes and the Untouchables. The former two have a very clear notion that they are the higher classes and the Untouchables are the lower classes within this block of Avarna Castes.

The discussion carried on so far reveals three characteristic features of Hindu Social Organisation: (1) Caste, (2) A hierarchical System of Castes and (3) A Class System cutting into the Caste System. Undoubtedly the structure is a very complicated one and it is perhaps difficult for one who has not been woven into it to form a true mental picture of the same. Perhaps a diagrammatic presentation may be helpful. I give below one such representation which in my judgment is calculated to give the idea of this social structure of the Hindus.

| A Caste Hindus : C Caste Hindus | | : E | Non-Caste Hindus Avarna Castes ' | G Non-caste Hindus |
|---|---|---|---|---|
| Savarna Castes | Savarna Castes | | | |
| Class I | Class II | | Class III | Class IV |
| High Castes Dwijas—Castes evolved out of the three Varnas. Brahmins, Kshatriyas and Vaishas. | Low Caste : Shudras-' Castes evolved out of the 4th Varna namely Shudras. | 1 | Primitive Castes Criminal Castes | Untouchables |

This diagram presents a Class-Caste-System of the Hindus and is so drawn as to give a true and a complete picture of their social organisation. This diagram brings out several of its important features. It shows that there are two divisions of Hindus—(1) Savarna Hindus and (2) Avarna Hindus. It shows that within the first division there are two classes of Castes: (1) Dwijas and (2) Sudras and within the second division there are two Classes of castes: (1) Primitive and Criminal Castes and (2) The Untouchable Castes. The next thing to note is that each caste is enclosed and separated from the rest a fact which is not shown in the diagram each of the four classes of Castes is grouped together and placed within a class enclosure.

This enclosure segregates a class of a Caste and marks it off from another class. A class of Castes is not as organised as a Caste is. But a feeling of Class is there. The third thing to note is the nature of partitions used for the enclosures. They are of various strengths, some are permanent, some are temporary. The partition between the Dwijas Castes and the Sudras Castes is not a partition at all. It is only a curtain. It is not a partition at all. It is intended to keep them aloof. It is not intended to cut them as under. The line of cleavage between the Sudra Castes and the first two of the Avarna

Castes is a regular partition. But it is both thin and small. It can be jumped over. The partition separates but does not cause severance. But the partition between these three classes and the Untouchables is a real and irremovable partition.

It is a barbed wire fence and its intention is to mark a severance. To express the same thing in a different way the first three enclosures are so placed that they are one within the other. The first partition between the Dwijas and the Sudra Castes may be removed the two become the occupants of one enclosure instead of two separate enclosures. Similarly the second partition may be removed in which case the Castes which are Dwija, Sudra, Primitive and Criminal form one whole—if not a single whole—occupying one single enclosure. But the third partition can never be removed. Because all three Classes of Castes are united on one issue namely that they shall not be *one (This space is left blank in the typed copy of MS. The word 'one' is introduced by us.*—Ed.) with the Untouchables as one united body of people. There is a bar sinister, which serves the Untouchables from the rest and compels them to be apart and outside.

The diagram shows the different Classes of Castes one above the other. This is done to mark the hierarchy, which is an important feature of the Caste System. I have described the two classes of the Savarna Castes as High Class Castes and Low Class Castes. But I have not described the other two classes of Avarna Castes as lower Class Castes and lowest Class Castes. In a sense this would have been correct. In general social esteem they are no doubt lower and lowest in status.

But in another sense this would not be appropriate. The terminology of high, low, lower and lowest assumes that they are parts of one whole. But are the Avarna Castes and the Savarna Castes parts of one whole? They were not. The Primitive and the Criminal Castes were not in contemplation when the plan of the Varna System, the parent of the present caste system, was laid. Consequently nothing is said about their status and position in the rules of the Varna System. But that is not the case with the Untouchables. They were within the contemplation of the Varna System and the Rule of the Varna System with regard to the Untouchables is very clear and very definite. The rule as laid down by Manu the Hindu Law giver is that there are only four Varnas and that there is not to be a fifth Varna.

The reformers who are friends of Mr. Gandhi in his campaign for removal of Untouchability are endeavouring to give a new meaning to the statement of Manu. They say that Manu has been misunderstood. According to Manu there is no fifth Varna and therefore he intended to include the Untouchables into the 4th Varna namely the Sudras. But this is an obvious perversion. What Manu meant was there were originally four Varnas and four they must remain. He was not going to admit the Untouchables into the House the ancient Hindus had built by enlarging the Varna System to consist of five Varnas. That is what he meant when he said that there is not to be a fifth Varna. That he wanted the Untouchables to remain out of the Hindu social structure is clear from the name by which he describes the Untouchables. He speaks of them as Varna—Bahyas (those outside the Varna System). That is the difference between the Primitive and Criminal Castes and the Untouchables. There being no positive injunction against their admission in Hindu Society they may in course of time become members of it.

At present they are linked to Hindu Society and hereafter they may become integrated into it and become part of it. But the case of the Untouchables is different. There is positive injunction against their incorporation in Hindu Society. There is no room for reform. They must remain separate and segregated without being a part of the Hindu Society. The Untouchables are not a part of the Hindu Society. And if they are a part they are a part but not of the whole.

The idea showing the connection between the Hindus and the Untouchables was accurately expressed by Ainapure Shastri the leader of the orthodox Hindus at a Conference held in Bombay. He said that the Untouchables were related to the Hindus as a man is to his shoe. A man wears a shoe. In that sense it is attached to man and may be said to be a part of the man. But it is not part of the whole for two things that can be attached and detached can't be said to form parts of one whole. The analogy though is none the less accurate.

## The Rock on which it is Built

Hindu Society is a house of Castes. Hindus are not a people. They are the aggregates of groups of people formed into castes. This is its peculiarity. This is what has struck the stream of foreigners who have visited India in the course of history. Notwithstanding this there are however people who endeavour to say that there is nothing peculiar about caste. For instance Prof. Baines remarks:

"There is little in the system which is not to be found, or which has not at some time or other existed, in other countries, even of the West, though it has there been long ago worn away by other influences. The crystallisation of certain bodies into definite orders or classes, for instance, is a common, almost a universal, trait and among them the tendency to become hereditary and as exclusive or aspiring as circumstances allow may almost be called natural ". The argument may be strengthened by reference to the social organisation of Primitive peoples. In Primitive Society man is never found alone.

The commonest and therefore the most natural condition of men are to live in-groups. This social grouping has taken many forms in the course of history. The family is one such social group which is universal and which has survived. The group larger than the immediate family was the clan. In its lowest terms, the clan (which also called kin, Sept. or sib) was supposed to be a group of individuals related to one another either through the mother or through the father. Far distant cousins might be considered in the relationship, and were regarded as members of the group. Again, the relationship may be purely fictitious, but from the social point of view this was as real a bond as that made by common blood. The next larger division than the clan is a social grouping of the clans. When the clans are organised into two groups each group is called a moiety. When it is organised in more than two groups each is called a phratry. This dual system was not by any means world-wide in distribution and the functions which the phratry or the moiety was intended to perform are not quite definitely known. But there is no doubt that each moiety and phratry was a social grouping in which there was a feeling of brotherhood between the members of clans associated together.

The tribal groups come next. There were wide differences in the nature, character and structure of tribes. Tribes may be made up of village communities with no divisions into clans or moieties. They may have clans and no moieties, or moieties and no clans; or they may have both moieties and clans. Tribal consciousness was sometimes strong or some time weak. Although in the formation of tribal groups there was neither a definite rule nor a single line of evolution, there were certain common features present namely a common dialect, common customs, a more or less definite territory and some form of Government to which the whole tribe was present. Larger than the tribe was the confederacy or union of Tribes. But this was very uncommon. A loose and informal alliance to meet some specific danger may bring about a union of tribes. It is very seldom that a definite compact is found among the primitive peoples. The famous Iroquois confederacy is one of the exceptions.

These are social groups based either upon the idea of kindred or on that of locality. There were groups among primitive peoples, where the cleavage is along other lines. These other lines of grouping took as its basis sex, age or some other criteria. As a form of social grouping, there is nothing new or nothing peculiar in this institution of caste. A caste is like a clan and like the clan it is only a form of social grouping.

The analogy between caste and clan may be admitted although it must be strongly insisted that as to meaning and purpose, caste is antagonistic to clan. There is no clan system comparable to the caste system. There is no gradation of clans as there is no Class-Clan System to match the Class-Caste System. Indeed the clan organisation of the Primitive people is a complete antithesis of the caste organisation of the Hindus. I admit the analogy only to drive my point. To my mind the question whether the institution of caste is natural or unnatural, peculiar or common is no doubt an interesting and instructive. But it is not as important as the question I want to raise. That question is why has caste endured, remained in tact when similar social groupings which were existing in other countries have vanished with the growth of civilisation. The Romans had a Social organisation very similar to the Hindus. When all similar institutions have vanished why has caste alone endured?

Why do people obey its rules, what is the sanction for Caste? Obedience by men to rules of society is everywhere secured by means of four sanctions. They are (1) the natural, (2) popular, (3) legal and (4) religious. Which of these supports the caste system? But before going into that question it would be desirable to describe the manner each of these sanctions operates. The natural sanction operates through habit. When a person is habituated to act in a certain way nothing is required to force him to act in that way. He becomes automation and the regularity of the act is guaranteed as a matter of routine. Popular sanction works through public opinion. It was the sense of approbation and disapprobation prevalent in Society in relation to certain ways and practices. A certain way becomes folkway and Acts in conformity with an established folkway, receives approbation and an Act contrary to it is regarded with disapprobation.

There is nothing special either in the natural sanction or popular sanction. They are to be found everywhere and behind everything that is social in its import. Their native force is precarious and wherever it possesses more than its ordinary efficacy it is only when they are derived from either of the other two sanctions. Legal sanction and Religious sanction are the only two sanctions, which are capable of sustaining any given institution. There is no doubt that caste had the sanction of Hindu Law. Every Hindu Law Book has recognised Caste as a legal institution a breach of which was an offence and entailing punishment. The Law Book of Manu called Manav Dharma Shastra is the oldest and the most authoritative Law Book of the Hindus. It would be enough to quote from it texts showing that Caste was recognised by Law.

Manu, the Hindu Lawgiver gives legal recognition to the institution of the four Varnas. To lay down the law of the four Varnas seems to be the principal object of Manu's code. This is clear from the opening verses of the Code. They state that:

I.1. The great sages approached Manu, who was seated with a collected mind, and, having duly worshipped him spoke as follows:

I.2. "Deign, divine one, to declare to us precisely and in due order the sacred laws of each of the (four chief) castes (varna) and of the intermediate ones."

Not only he gives it his legal sanction, he makes it incumbent upon the King to uphold the institution:

VII.35. The king has been created (to be) the protector of the castes (varna) and orders, who, all according to their rank, discharge their several duties."

VIII.24. All castes (varna) would be corrupted (by intermixture), all barriers would be broken through, and all men would rage (against each other) in consequence of mistakes with respect to punishment."

Manu makes breach of Caste a sin and prescribes three different punishments to one who has become a Patit by loss of caste. The first punishment is punishment after death. Manu says:

"XII.60. He who has associated with outcasts, he who has approached the wives of other men, and he who has stolen the property of a Brahmana becomes Brahmarakshasa.". In this life the punishment which a Patit has to undergo was twofold. One was excommunication. The nature and character of excommunication prescribed by Manu has been prescribed by him in the following terms:

XI. 181. He who associates with an outcast, himself becomes an outcast after a year, not by sacrificing for him, teaching him, or forming a matrimonial alliance with him, but by using the same carriage or seat, or by eating with him.

XI. 182. He who associates with any one of those outcasts, must perform, in order to atone for (such) intercourse, the penance prescribed for that (sinner).

XI. 183. The Sapindas and Samanodakas of an outcast must offer (a libation of) water (to him, as if he were dead), outside (the village), on an inauspicious day, in the evening and in the presence of the relatives, officiating priests, and teachers.

XI. 184. A female slave shall upset with her foot a pot filled with water, as if it were for a dead person; (his Sapindas) as well as the Samanodakas shall be impure for a day and a night.

XI. 185. But thenceforward it shall be forbidden to converse with him, to sit with him, to give him a share of the inheritance, and to hold with him such intercourse as is usual among men. The other was disinheritance.

IX.201. Eunuchs and outcasts, (persons) born blind or deaf, the insane, idiots and the dumb, as well as those deficient in any organ (of action or sensation), receive no share.

XI. 186. And (if he be the eldest) his right of primogeniture shall be withheld and the additional share, due to the eldest son, and in his stead a younger brother, excelling in virtue, shall obtain the share of the eldest. The only way to avoid these two punishments of excommunication and disinheritance was to do penance in the prescribed form. Penance was the only remedy. Says Manu:

XI. 187. But when he has performed his penance, they shall bathe with him in a holy pool and throw down a new pot, filled with water.

XI. 188. But he shall throw that pot into water, enter his house and perform, as before, all the duties incumbent on a relative. There was a distinction between a male Patit and a female Patit. Neither was exempt. The Rule applies to both, for Manu says:

XI. 189. Let him follow the same rule in the case of female outcast; but clothes, food, and drink shall be given to them, and they shall live close to the (family) house". There can be no doubt that the legal sanction was powerful sanction. The punishment prescribed by law for breach of Caste was two folds. It involved excommunication and loss of right to inherit. How formidable these punishments were has been well described by Sir Thomas Strange in his treatise on Hindu Law. Referring to the subject he says:

It remains to consider one case, that may be said to be, with reference to personal delinquency, *instar omnium*—occurring in every enumeration on the subject as a cause of exclusion, namely: degradation, or the case of the outcaste. Accompanied with certain ceremonies, its effect is, to exclude him from all social intercourse, to suspend in him every civil function, to disqualify him for all the offices, and all the charities of life;—he is to be deserted by his connections, who are from the moment of the sentence attaching upon him, to desist from speaking to him, from sitting in his company, from delivering to him any inherited, or other property, and from every civil or usual attention, as inviting him on the first day of the year, or the like, so that a man under these circumstances, might as well be dead; which, indeed, the Hindu Law considers him to be, directing libations to be offered to Manes, as though he were naturally so.

This system of privations, mortifying as it must be, was enforced under the ancient law, by denouncing a similar fate to any one, by whose means they were endeavoured to be eluded; but this severity was moderated at the beginning of the present age, in which it is said "the sinner alone bears his guilt", the law deeming so seriously of nonintercourse, that if one who ought to associate at meals with another, refuses to do so, without sufficient cause, he is punishable. And, in the Bombay reports, there is an instance of an action of damages, for a malicious expulsion from caste.

The analogy between degradation by the Hindu law, and excommunication, as it prevailed formerly among us, holds, not merely in the general nature and effect of the proceeding, but in the peculiar circumstance of the one and the other being two-fold. As, with us, there was the less, and the greater excommunication, so, of offences considered with reference to their occasioning exclusion from inheritance among the Hindus, they may also be regarded in a two-fold point of view.

This we learn from a case that was before the Sudder Dewanny Adawlut of Bengal, in 1814, in which the official Pundits, having been referred to, distinguished between "those which involve partial and temporary degradation, and those which are followed by loss of caste", observing that "in the former state, that of partial degradation, when the offence which occasions it is expiated, the impediment to succession is removed; but in the latter, where the degradation is complete, although the sinfulness of the offence may be removed by expiatory penance, yet the impediment to succession still remains, because a person finally excluded from his tribe must ever continue to be an outcaste".

In the case alluded to, the party in question having been guilty of a series of profligate and abandoned conduct, having been shamefully addicted to spirituous liquors, having been in the habit of associating and eating with persons of the lowest description, and most infamous character; having wantonly attacked and wounded several people at different times; having openly cohabited with a woman of the Mahomedan persuation; and having set fire to the dwelling house of his adoptive mother, whom he had more than once attempted to destroy by other means", the Pundits declared that "of all the offences proved to have been committed by Sheannauth, one only, namely, that of cohabiting with a Mahomedan woman, was of such a nature, as to subject him to the penalty of expulsion from his tribe irrevocably," and of this opinion was the Court.

The power to degrade is, in the first instance, with the Castes themselves, assembled for the purpose, from whose sentence, if not acquiesced in, there lay an appeal to the King's Courts. In the case that has been cited, the question arose incidentally, upon a claim of inheritance, and that case shews that the power amounts to a species of Censorship, applicable to the morals of the people, in instances to which the law, strictly speaking, would not perhaps otherwise extend. The sentences can be inflicted only for offences committed by the delinquent in his existing state; and, where the offence is of an inferior nature, to justify it, it must have been repeated. What distinguishes degradation from other causes of exclusion is, that it extends its effects to the son, who is involved in his father's forfeiture, if born subsequent to the act occasioning it. Born before, he is entitled to inherit, and takes, as though his father were dead.

Whereas, in every other instance of exclusion, the son, if not actually in the same predicament with his father, succeeds, maintaining him; the same right extending as far as the great grandson. And, with regard to the father, or delinquent himself, where the exclusion from inheriting is not for natural defects, the cause must have arisen, previous to the division, or descent of the property; if it do not occur till after, the succession is not divested by it. Hence, adultery in the wife during coverture, bars her right of inheritance; divesting it also, after it has vested; the Hindu widow resembling, in this respect, the condition of ours in most instances of copyhold dower, and holding it, like her, *Dum casta fuerit* only; according to an opinion of great respectability, that for loss of caste, unexpiated by penance, and unredeemed by atonement, it is forfeited. In general, the law of disqualification applies alike to both sexes.

It appearing, then, that the incapacity to inherit, except in the instance of the outcaste, is personal merely; that one excluded may be said, in every case, to be entitled to be maintained; and that, in most, it is in his power, at any time, to restore himself to his rights; whatever may be thought of the wisdom of some of these provisions, it cannot be said that they are universally destitute of justice, or, in any instance, totally devoid of humanity. Nor, in comparing this part of the law with our own, ought we to forget, that the latter has made none, for preventing the absolute disinheriting of children by will.

It will appear, in a subsequent chapter, that, on entry into either of the two religious orders, the devotee (like the professed monk with us before the Reformation) becomes *Civiliter mortuus;* and the next heir succeeds, as though he were naturally deceased and, as the devotee himself, abdicating secular concerns, is incapacitated from inheriting, so is the religious pretender, and the eventual Apostate. Under the former term may be included Hypocrites and Impostors, used synonymously for those who, usurping sacred marks, practise austerities with an interested design.

The remaining cause of exclusion to be noticed, is, an Incompetent marriage; that is, where the husband and wife are descended from the same Stock. Such a marriage being incongruous, the issue of it cannot inherit, excepting among Sudras. And the consequence is the same, where the marriage has not been according to the order of Class.

"The heir, or heirs, under no disability, having succeeded to the inheritance, it is next to be seen, to what charge this is liable." Has Caste also a religious sanction? The Vedas recognise Caste. The Rig Vedas recognised Caste and also explains its origin in the following passage:

1. Purusha has a thousand heads, a thousand eyes, a thousand feet. On every side enveloping the earth, he overpassed (it) by a space of ten fingers.
2. Purusha himself is this whole (universe), whatever has been and whatever shall be. He is also the lord of immortality, since (or, when) by food he expands.
3. Such is his greatness, and Purusha is superior to this.

All existences are a quarter of him; and three fourths of him are that which is immortal sky.

4. With three-quarters Purusha mounted upwards. A quarter of him was again produced here. He was then diffused everywhere over things, which eat, and things, which do not eat.
5. From him was born Viraj, and from Viraj, Purusha. When born, he extended beyond the earth, both behind and before.
6. When the gods performed a sacrifice with Purusha as the oblation, the spring was its butter, the summer its fuel, and autumn its (accompanying) offering.
7. This victim, Purusha, born in the beginning, they immolated on the sacrificial grass. With him the gods, the Sadhyas, and the rishis sacrificed.
8. From that universal sacrifice were provided curds and butter. It formed those aerial (creatures) and animals both wild and tame.
9. From that universal sacrifice sprang the *rich* and *saman verses,* the *metres,* and *yajush.*
10. From it sprang horses, and all animals with two rows of teeth; kine sprang from it; from it goats and sheep.
11. When (the gods) divided Purusha, into how many parts did they cut him up? What was his mouth? What arms (had he)? What (two objects) are said (to have been) his thighs and feet?
12. The Brahman was his mouth; the Rajanya was his arms; the being (called) the Vaishya, he was his thighs, the Sudra sprang from his feet.
13. The moon sprang from his soul (manas), the sun from his eye, Indra and Agni from his mouth and Vayu from his breath.
14. From his navel arose the air, from his head the sky, from his feet the earth, from his ear the (four) quarters; in this manner (the gods) formed the worlds.
15. When the gods, performing sacrifice, bound Purusha as a victim, there were seven sticks (stuck up) for it (around the fire), and thrice seven pieces of fuel were made.

16. With sacrifice the gods performed the sacrifice. These were the earliest rites. These great powers have sought the sky, where are the former Sadhyas, gods."

The Brahmanas also recognise Caste. In the Satapatha-Brahmanas Caste is mentioned in the following terms:

23. Brahma (here, according to the commentator, existing in the form of Agni, and representing the Brahman caste was formerly this (universe), one only. Being one, it did not develop. It energetically created an excellent form, the Kshattra, *viz.*, those among the gods, who are powers (Kshattrani), Indra, Varuna, Soma, Rudra, Parjanya, Yama, Mrityu, Isana. Hence nothing is superior to the Kshattra. Therefore the Brahman sits below the Kshattriya at the rajasuya-sacrifice; he confers that glory on the Kshattra (the royal power). This, the Brahma, is the source of Kshattra. Hence, although the king attains supremacy, he at the end resorts to the Brahman as his source. Whoever destroys him (the Brahman) destroys his own source. He becomes most miserable, as one who has injured a superior.

24. He did not develop. He created the Vis.—*viz.*, those classes of gods who are designated by troops, Vasus, Rudras, Adityas, Visvedevas, Maruts.

25. He did not develop. He created the Sudra Class, Pushan. This earth is Pushan; for she nourishes all that exists.

26. He did not develop. He energetically created an excellent form, Justice (Dharma). This is the ruler (kshattra) of the ruler (kshattra), namely Justice. Hence nothing is superior to justice. Therefore the weaker seeks (to overcome) the stronger by justice, as by a king. This justice is truth. In consequence they say of a man who speaks truth, 'he speaks justice"; or of man who is uttering justice, 'he speaks truth'. For this are both of these.

27. This is the Brahma, Kshattra, Vis and Sudra. Through Agni it became Brahma among the gods, the Brahman among men, through the (divine) Kshattriya a (human) Kshattriya, through the (divine), Vaishya a (human) Vaisya, through the (divine) Sudra a (human) Sudra. Wherefore it is in Agni among the gods and in a Brahman among men, that they seek after an abode."

Taittiriya Brahmana, 1, 2, 6, 7. *daivyo vai varno brahmanh assuryyo sudrah.* "The Brahman caste is sprung from the gods;

the Sudra from the Ashuras." It must be admitted that the legal and the religious sanction were both powerful engines to keep caste going. But there is no doubt that the religious sanction was the primary sanction and caste has been maintained solely by the force of Religious Sanction. This is clear from two circumstances. That the legal sanction was very seldom invoked will have to be admitted. That means that the maintenance of caste was secured by other means. Secondly this legal sanction was in use only till 1850. It was lifted or rather done away with by the Caste Disabilities Removal Act passed in that year by the British Government. Although the legal sanction is withdrawn, caste has gone on without abatement. That could not have happened if caste had not in the Religious Sanction another and more powerful sanction independent of the legal sanction.

That the Religious Sanction is the highest sanction which an institution or a belief can have to support and sustain it, is beyond question. Its power is boundless in its measure and tremendous in its curb. But it is very seldom understood how and whence this Religious Sanction gets this high-grade horsepower. To appreciate this it is necessary to note that the sourpuss of authority behind the Religious Sanction is two-fold.

In the first place what is Religious is also social. To quote Prof. Durkheim.

The really religious beliefs are always common to a determined group, which makes profession of adhering to them and of practising the rites connected with them. They are not merely received individually by all the members of this group; they are something belonging to the group, and they make its unity. The individuals which compose it feel themselves united to each other by the simple fact that they have a common faith." In the second place what is Religious is Sacral. To quote Durkheim again:

> *"All known religious beliefs whether simple or complex, present one common characteristic; they presuppose a classification of all the things, real and ideal, of which men think, into two classes or, opposed groups, generally designated by two distinct terms-which are translated well enough by the* words profane *and* sacred..... *In all the history of human thought there exist no other example*

*of two categories of things so profoundly differentiated or so radically opposed to one another. The traditional opposition of good and bad is nothing besides this; for the good and the bad are only two opposed species of the same class, namely morals, just as sickness and health are two different aspects of the same order of facts, life, while the Sacred and the profane have always and everywhere been conceived by the human mind as two distinct classes, as two worlds between there is nothing in common. Religious beliefs are the representations which express the nature of sacred things and the relations which they sustain, either with each other or with profane things (while) rites are the rules of conduct which prescribe how a man should comfort himself in the presence of these Sacred objects."*

From this it will be clear that the Social, Religious and Sacral beliefs are closely knit. Religious is social though all that is social is not religious. Sacral is social though all that is social is not sacral. On the other hand the religious is both social and sacral.

One source of authority behind the religious sanction comes from the fact, that is, religion is social and the religious beliefs are social beliefs. Religious beliefs are enforced on the individual by the group in the same manner and for the same reasons which leads it to enforce its other non-religious and purely social beliefs.

The object is to maintain the integrity of the group and as the integrity of the group is more closely bound up with its religious beliefs, the strictness and severity with which a group punishes the breach of a religious belief is usually greater than the degree of strictness and severity it employs for the chastisement of a person guilty of a breach of a non-religious belief. Social force has an imperative authority before which the individual is often powerless. In the matter of a religious belief the imperative authority of the social force is tempered as steel is by the feeling that it is a breach of a graver kind and gives religious sanction a far greater force than a purely social sanction has.

The Sacral source of the authority behind religious sanction comes primarily from the individual and only secondarily from the group. That is the noteworthy peculiarity of the social source of religious sanction. It prepares the individual to uphold the religious beliefs. It dispenses with the necessity of the group using its social group. That is why the sacral source of its authority makes religious sanction of such high order as to supersede all other sanctions indeed to dispense with them. That is why the Religious sanction alone becomes sufficient to maintain the integrity of religious beliefs which even time and circumstances have proved powerless to affect. The way this happens is easy to follow. The Sacred inspires in the individual the sentiment of reverence and deference, which he certainly has not for the profane. To use the language of Durkheim,

> *"The simple defence inspired by men with high social functions is not different in nature from religious respect (for the sacred). It is expressed by the same movements: a man keeps at a distance from high personage; he approaches him only with precautions; in conversing with him, he used other gestures and language than that used with ordinary mortals."*

The Sacred creates the sentiment of Reverence. It also creates the sentiment that it is inviolate. When a belief becomes consecrated as a sacred thing, it is forbidden to touch it, to deny it or to contest it. There is a prohibition of criticism of the Sacred. The Sacred is 'untouchable and above discussion". When an individual is saturated with these sentiments, when these sentiments become a part of his being, he himself becomes an upholder and protector of what he is taught to regard as something sacred.

This is exactly what the Hindus have done in the matter of Caste. They have given caste a place in the Vedas. Caste has thereby become sacred because the Vedas are Sacred. It would be wrong to say that the Vedas are sacred because they are religious. The position is that they are religious because they are sacred.

It might appear that the Hindus have no name for the Veda directly expressing the feeling of sacredness, which the Hindu entertains towards the Vedas. Veda simply means knowledge. That may be so. But there can be no doubt that they regard the Vedas as sacred. Indeed the term they apply to Vedas expresses a far greater degree of reverence than the word sacred does. They call the Vedas *Shruti,* which means the word of God heard by (*i.e.* revealed to) man. In the primitive religion the Sacred is what man has made. In the Hindu religion the Sacred is what God has appointed it to be.

The Hindus regard the Vedas as the Sacred Book of their religion. They put the Vedas in a class by themselves. The Hindus hold that there are cycles of creations called *Kalpas.* At the end of every cycle there is a deluge and a new cycle of creation begins. At the end of a Kalpa, the Vedas are destroyed in the deluge. At the beginning of every Kalpa they are revealed by God. Accordingly the *Vedas* were destroyed in the deluge at the end of the last *Kalpa* and that the beginning of the present *Kalpa* commencing with the *Krita Yug,* they were revealed by God to the *Rishis.* The Vedas are regarded by the Hindus as *Nitya* (enternal) *Anadi* (beginningless) and *Apaurusheya* (not made by man), In short the Vedas are the words of God and constitute God's ordinances to man.

Even if the Vedas were not called *Shruti* they would have had the impressiveness of the 'Sacred'. Religions have been variously classified by Prof. Max Muller. Natural as against Revealed is one way of classifying them. Individual as against National is another way. The third way of classifying them is to call them Atheistic, Deistic, Dualistic, Polytheistic, Monotheistic, Henotheistic and Animistic. True and False is also another way of classifying Religions. Bookless Religions and Religions with books are two classes into which Religion could be grouped. This probably does not exhaust the ways of classifying Religions. For there remains one more distinction to be made, namely Religions which have founders and religions which have no founders.

These distinctions have social significance except two. They are the distinctions between Natural and Revealed and that between Bookless Religion and Book Religion. They differ in their function although that difference is not often noted.

The Book religion has a definite advantage over a Bookless religion. A Book religion is a Religion with a written constitution. A Bookless Religion is a Religion without a written constitution. A book religion creates the impression that it is true which a bookless religion cannot. By comparison with a book religion, a bookless religion wears the inferiority complex of being false. In the language of Max Muller Religions with books are alone "considered as real religions, and though they may contain false doctrines, they are looked upon as a kind of aristocracy to whom much may be forgiven, while the vulgar crowd of bookless or illiterate religions are altogether out of Court". It is easy to understand the superiority accorded to a religion with a book over a bookless religion. When 'black on white' has become synonymous with true, it may seem very natural that a religion which is written, which is something black on white is not false. The Book serves as the voucher for truth. A religion without a book has no voucher.

The social significance of a religion with a book lies in the fact that it controls the mind of the people by giving them the impression that the religion contained in the book is true. It gives Religion authority over people and induces willing obedience in them.

But however a Religion may appear to be true by reason of the fact that it is a book religion, such appearance cannot save Religion from going under, if beliefs and rites empirically erroneous have crept into it. Man may go wrong in theory but his practical instincts will seldom allow him to go after a wrong theory for a long time. Unless therefore the religious beliefs of a social group are true, practically Religion must in the long run give way.

Herein comes the social significance of the distinction between Natural Religion and Revealed Religion. A Revealed Religion has superiority over Natural Religion. Natural Religion is used by several writers to certain historical forms of religion. Something which has grown along with the growth of people as result of the interaction between the needs of the peoples and the environment in which they are placed. A natural religion is made by man. Its sanction is the sense of truth and the voice of conscience that is to be found in man. A Revealed Religion does not rest on the authority of man. It is not man-made, it is God-made. Its sanction is God who is absolute truth and absolute good. The function of Revealed Religion is to make religion sacred therefore inviolate and immune from criticism.

The Vedas have the characteristics of both. They have the advantage, which a Religion with a book has over the Bookless

Religion. They have the advantage, which a Revealed Religion has over Natural Religion.

This discussion is intended to enforce the conclusion that Caste being preached by the Vedas, it automatically gets the authority of the written book and the sanctity of the divine word. As a scheme propounded by the Veda it is doubly protected. Every one must accept Caste because it is divine truth and no body must attack it as an error without being guilty of sacrilege because it is sacred.

This is the Hindu view of Caste and the average Hindu is not impressed by the modern explanation of it by Risley with his racial theory, by Senart with his occupational theory, by Nesfield with his functional theory. He knows and he believes that Caste must have been created by God, because it is mentioned in the Vedas which is *Shruti* or the word of God. It is therefore eternal and true.

That Caste is divine, that caste is sacred and that caste must therefore remain eternal has been the line of defence adopted by the Brahmins whenever they have been called out to defend 'Caste' against the criticism of its opponents. This view of Caste comes out in its luminous colours in the controversy that once raged on the subject of Caste between Brahmins on the one hand and Buddha and his followers, on the other *i.e.*:

> *If the belief was once established, that not only the simple effusions of the Rishis, but the pointed doctrines of the Brahmanas also, emanated from a divine source and could not therefore be attacked by human reasoning, it is clear that every opposition to the privileges which the Brahmans claimed for themselves, on the sacred authority of the Veda, became heresy; and where the doctrines of the Brahmans were the religion of the people, or rather of the king, such opposition was amenable to the hierarchical laws of the state. The Brahmans themselves cared much more to see the divine authority of the Sruti as such implicitly acknowledged, than to maintain the doctrines of the Rishis in their original simplicity and purity. In philosophical discussions, they allowed the greatest possible freedom; and, although at first three philosophical systems only were admitted as*

*orthodox (the two Mimansas and the Nyaya), their number was soon raised to six, so as to include the Vaiseshika, Sankhya, and Yoga-schools. The most conflicting views on points of vital importance were tolerated as long as their advocates succeeded, no matter by what means, in bringing their doctrines into harmony with passages of the Veda, strained and twisted in every possible sense. If it was only admitted that besides the perception of the senses and the induction of reason, revelation also, as contained in the Veda, furnished a true basis for human knowledge, all other points seemed to be of minor importance. Philosophical minds were allowed to exhaust all possible views on the relation between the real and transcendental world, the Creator and the created, the divine and the human nature. It was not from such lucubrations that danger was likely to accrue to the caste of the Brahmans. Nor was the heresy of Buddha Sakya Muni found so much in his philosophical doctrines, many of which may be traced in the orthodox atheism of Kapila. His real crime lay in his opposition to the exclusive privileges and abuses of the Brahmans. These abuses were sanctioned by the divine authority of the Veda, and particularly of the Brahmans. In attacking the abuses, Buddha attacked the divine authority on which they were founded, and the argument was short: he is a heretic; anathema etc.*

Buddha was Kshatriya. He was of principal origin, and belonged to the nobility of the land. He was not the first of his caste who opposed the ambition of the Brahmans. Several centuries before Buddha, Vishvamitra, who, like Buddha, was a member of the royal caste, had to struggle against the exclusiveness of the priests. At that early time, however, the position of the Brahmans was not yet impregnable; and Vishvamitra, although a Kshatriya, succeeded in gaining for himself and his family the rights for which he struggled, and which the Brahmans had previously withheld from all but their own caste. King Janaka of Videha again, whose story is given in the Brahmanas, refused to submit to the hierarchical pretensions of the Brahmans, and asserted his right of performing sacrifices without the intercession of priests.

However great the difference may have been between the personal character of these two men and of Buddha, the first principle of their opposition was the same. All three were equally struggling against the over-wining pretensions of a selfish priesthood.

But while Vishvamitra contented himself with maintaining the rights of his tribe or family, and became reconciled as soon as he was allowed to share in the profits of the priestly power, while King Janaka expressed himself satisfied with the homage paid to him by Yajnavalkya and other Brahmans, while, in short, successive reformers as they appeared were either defeated or gained over to the cause of the Brahmans, the seeds of discontent were growing up in the minds of the people. There is a dark chapter in the history of India, the reported destruction of all the Kshatriyas by Parsurama. It marks the beginning of the hierarchical supremacy of the Brahmans. Though the Brahmans seem never to have aspired to the royal power, their caste, as far as we know the history and traditions of India, has always been in reality the ruling caste. Their ministry was courted as the only means of winning divine favour, their doctrines were admitted as infallible, their gods were worshipped as the only true gods, and their voice was powerful enough to stamp the simple strains of the Rishis, and the absurd lucubrations of the authors of the Brahmans, with a divine authority. After this last step, however, the triumph of Brahmanism was preparing its fall.

In India, less than in any other country, would people submit to a monopoly of truth; and the same millions who were patiently bearing the yoke of a political despotism threw off the fetters of an intellectual tyranny. In order to overthrow one of the oldest religions of the world, it was sufficient that one man should challenge the authority of the Brahmans, the gods of the earth (Bhudeva), and preach among the scorned and degraded creatures of God the simple truth that salvation was possible without the mediation of priests, and without a belief in books to which these very priests had given the title of revelation. This man was Buddha, a Sakya Muni. Now if we inquire how Buddha's doctrines were met by the Brahmans, it is true that here and there in their philosophical works, they have endeavoured to overthrow some of his metaphysical axioms by an appeal to reason. An attempt of this kind we have, for instance, in Vachaspati Misra's commentary on the Vedanta Sutras. In commenting on the tenets of Buddha, that "ideas like those of being, and not being, &c., do not admit of discussion", Vachaspati observes that the very fact of speaking of these ideas, includes the possibility of their conception; nay, that to affirm they do not admit of reasoning, involves an actual reasoning on them, and proves that the mind can conceive the idea of being as different from that of not-being.

Such, however, were not the usual weapons with which Brahmanism fought against Buddhism. The principal objection has always been, that Buddha's teaching could not be true, because it did not derive its sanction from Sruti or revelation. The Brahmans, as a caste, would readily have allowed being and not being, and the whole of Buddha's philosophy, as they did the Sankhya philosophy, which on the most important points is in open opposition to the Vedanta.

But while Kapila, the founder of the Sankhya school, conformed to the Brahmanic test by openly proclaiming the authority of revelation as paramount to reasoning and experience, Buddha would not submit to this, either for his philosophical (abhidharma), or for his much more important moral and religious doctrines (vinaya). No doubt it would have been easy for him to show how some of his doctrines harmonised with passages of the Veda, as in the Veda all possible shades of the human mind have found their natural reflection. If he had done so only for some of his precepts, such, for instance, as, "Thou shall not murder", "Thou shall not drink", "Thou shall eat standing", the Brahmans would readily have passed over other doctrines, even such as came into practice after Buddha's death, like "Who longs for heaven, shall worship the holy sepulchre", "He shall pull out his hair", &c. As he refused to do so, the line of argument taken by the Brahmans was simply confined to an appeal to revelation, in disproof of the possibility of the truth of Buddha's doctrines.

There must be something very tempting in this line of argument, for we see that in later times the Buddhists also endeavoured to claim the same divine character for their sacred writings which the Brahmans had established for the Veda. A curious instance of this is given in the following discussion, from Kumarila's Tantra-varttika. Here the opponent (purva-paksha) observes, that the same arguments which prove that the Veda is not the work of human authors, apply with equal force to Sakya's teaching. His authority, he says, cannot be questioned, because his precepts are clear and intelligible; and as Sakya is not the inventor, but only the teacher of these precepts, and no name of an author is given for Sakya's doctrines, the frailties inherent in human authors affect them as little as the Veda. Everything, in fact, he concludes, which has been brought forward by the Mimansakas to prove the authority of the Veda, proves in the same way the authority of Buddha's doctrine, Upon this, the orthodox Kumarila grows very wroth, and says: These Sakyas, Vaiseshikas, and other heretics who have been frightened out of their wits by the faithful Mimansakas, prattle away with our own words as if trying in lay hold of a shadow.

They say that their sacred works are eternal; but they are of empty minds, and only out of hatred they wish to deny that the Veda is the most ancient book. And these would-be logicians declare even, that some of their precepts (which they have stolen from us,) like that of universal benevolence, are not derived from the Veda, because most of Buddha's other sayings are altogether against the Veda. Wishing, therefore, to keep true on this point also, and seeing that no merely human precept could have any authority on moral and supernatural subjects, they try to veil their difficulty by aping our own argument for the eternal existence of the Veda. They know that the Mimansakas have proved that no sayings of men can have any authority on supernatural subjects; they know also that the authority of the Veda cannot be contradicted, because they can bring forward nothing against the proofs adduced for its divine origin, by which all supposition of a human source have been removed.

Therefore, their hearts being gnawed by their own words, which are like the smattering of children, and having themselves nothing to answer, because the deception of their illogical arguments has been destroyed, they begin to speak like a foolish suitor who came to ask for a bride, saying, 'My family is as good as your family'. In the same manner they now maintain the eternal existence of their books, aping the speeches of others. And if they are challenged and told that this is our argument, they brawl, and say that we, the Mimansakas have heard and stolen it from them. For a man who has lost all scheme, who can talk away without any sense, and tries to cheat his opponent, will never get tired, and will never be put down! "Towards the end of this harangue, Kumarila adds, what is more to the point, that the Buddhas, who ascribe to everything a merely temporary existence, have no business to talk of an eternal revelation."

From the foregoing discussion it will be seen that Caste is born in religion which has consecrated it and made it Sacred so that it can be rightly and truly said that Religion is the Rock on which the Hindus have built their social structure. Does this not show that Caste is a very peculiar institution not to be compared with other forms of social grouping? I venture to say that any one who maintains that there is nothing strange in caste simply does not know what Caste is. I repeat that Caste is Sacred, which is its distinguishing feature. Caste is Sacred, which is what makes it abiding.

Prof. Max Muller makes some very instructive observations on the effects of Religion with Sacred books on the progress of Society. Says Max Muller:

History, however, teaches us another lesson, namely that codes of law are apt to become a kind of fetish, requiring an implicit and unquestioning submission, that their historical or natural origin is often completely forgotten, and that the old ideas of what is right and just are almost absorbed, nay, almost annihilated, in the one idea of what is written and legal.

The study of Eastern religions teaches us the same lesson. Sacred books often become a kind of fetish, requiring an implicit and unquestioning faith; their historical or natural origin is often completely forgotten, and the old ideas of what is true and divine are almost absorbed in the one idea of what is written and orthodox.

And there is a third lesson which history teaches us. The sense of responsibility of every citizen for the law under which he lives is in great danger of becoming deadened, when law becomes a profession and is administered with mechanical exactness rather than with a strong human perception of what is right and what is wrong. Nor can it be denied that the responsibility of every believer for the religion under which he lives is in the same danger of becoming deadened, when religion becomes a profession, and is administered with ceremonial exactness rather than with a strong human perception of what is true and what is false.

My object, however, is not to show the dangers which arise from sacred books, but rather to protest against the prejudice which prevails so widely against religions which have no sacred books.

There is great difference between book-religions and bookless religions, and the difference offers, from an historical point of view, a very true ground of division. But because the book-religions have certain advantages, we must not imagine that the bookless religions are mere outcasts. They have their disadvantages, no doubt; but they have a few advantages also.

A Blackfoot Indian, when arguing with a Christian missionary, described the difference between his own religion and that of the white man in the following words:

*'There were two religions given by the Great Spirit, one in a book for the guidance of the white men who, by following its teachings, will reach the white man's heaven; the other is in the hands of the Indians, in the sky, rocks, rivers, and mountains. And the red men who listen to God in nature will hear his voice, and find at last the heaven beyond.'*

*"Now that religion which is in the head and in the heart, and in the sky, the rocks, the rivers and the mountains is what we call Natural Religion. It has its roots in nature, in human nature, and in that external nature which to us is at the same time the veil and the revelation of the Divine. It is free, it grows with the growth of the human mind, and adapts itself to the requirements of every age. It does not say, 'Thou shall, but rather, 'I will'. These natural or bookless religions are not entirely without settled doctrines and established customs. They generally have some kind of priesthood to exercise authority in matters of faith, morality, and ceremonial. But there is nothing hard and unchangeable*

*in them, nothing to fetter permanently the growth of thought. Errors when discovered, can be surrendered, a new truth, if clearly seen and vigorously defended, can be accepted. If, however, there is once a book, something black on white, the temptation is great, is almost irresistible, to invest it with a more than human authority in order to appeal to it as infallible, and as beyond the reach of human reasoning. We can well understand what the ancient poets of the Veda meant by calling their hymns God-given, or by speaking of them as what they had seen or heard, not what they had elaborated themselves. But a new generation gave a new meaning to these expressions, and ended by representing every thought and word and letter of the Veda as 'God-given,' or revealed. This was the deathblow given to the Vedic religion, for whatever cannot grow and change must die. From this danger the bookless religion are exempt."*

Similar observations are made by Sir William Muir. Speaking of Islam he has given powerful expression to the dangers arising from Sacred Codes of Religion. Sir William Muir says:

*"From the stiff and rigid shroud in which it is thus swathed, the religion of Mahomed cannot emerge. It has no plastic power beyond that exercised in its earliest days. Hardened now and inelastic, it can neither adapt itself, nor yet shape its votaries, nor even suffer them to shape themselves, to the varying circumstances, the wants and developments of mankind". (Quoted by E de Bunsen in an article in the Asiatic Quarterly Review, April, 1889, Mahomed's Place in the Church, p. 287.)*

Every one who is interested in the progress of humanity cannot fail to echo these sentiments regarding the social consequences of Sacred Codes of Religion. But it seems to me that a further distinction is possible within the Class of Religion with Sacred Codes. It is a pity that Prof. Max Muller did not pursue the matter further. But it is worth pursuing because it discloses a difference which is very real which marks off the Hindus as a people with a Sacred Code of Religion from other people also possessing a Sacred Code of Religion. The difference will be clear if one begins to examine the different religions to find out what are the objects which religions have sought to consecrate.

Such an examination will show that there are instances where Society has consecrated inanimate things and inculcated on the minds of its members the religious belief that they are sacred. There are cases where stones, rivers, trees are made gods and goddesses. There are instances where Society has consecrated living things and inculcated on the minds of its members the religious belief that they are sacred. There are cases of animals which have become clan totems. There are instances where Society has consecrated human beings and inculcated the religious beliefs that they are sacred.

But there are no instances where a particular Social Order has been consecrated by Religion and made Sacred. The primitive world had its clan order and its tribal order. But the clan or the tribal order was only a social order and was never consecrated by religion and made sacred and inviolate. The ancient world countries like Egypt, Persia, Rome, Greece etc., each had its social order in which some were free and some were slaves, some were citizens, some were aliens, some of one race, some of another. This class order again was only a social order and was never consecrated by religion and made sacred and inviolate. The modern world has its order, in some it is Democracy, in some Fascism, in some Nazism and in some Bolshevism. But here again the order is only Social order. It is not consecrated by religion and made sacred and inviolate.

Nowhere has Society consecrated its occupations, the ways of getting a living. Economic activity has always remained outside the sanctity of religion. Hunting society was not without religion. But hunting as an occupation was not consecrated by religion and made sacred. Pastrol Society was not without religion. But pasturage was not consecrated by religion and made sacred. Farming as an occupation did not become consecrated by religion and made sacred. Feudalism with its gradations, with its Lords, villains and serfs was a purely social in character. There was nothing sacred about it.

The Hindus are the only people in the world whose Social order the relation of man to man is consecrated by religion and made sacred eternal and inviolate. The Hindus are the only people in the world whose economic order the relation of workman to workman is consecrated by religion and made sacred, eternal and inviolate. It is not therefore enough to say that the Hindus are a people with a sacred code of Religion. So are the Zoroastrians, Israelites, Christians and Muslims. All these have sacred codes. They consecrate beliefs and rites and make them sacred. They do not prescribe, nor do they consecrate a particular form of social structure the relationship between man and man in a concrete form and make it sacred inviolate. The Hindus are singular in this respect. This is what has given caste its abiding strength to defy the ravages of time and the onslaughts of time.

There is one other respect in which Hindus differ from other folk possessing codified religions similar to that of the Hindus. The Hindu Code of Religion is a revelation from God. That is why the Vedas are called Shruti (what is heard). So are the Codes of Religions accepted by the Zoroastrians, Jews, Christians and Muslims. Ask to whom this God's word sent to the Zoroastrian, Jews, Christians, and Muslims was revealed, who heard this word of God? The Zoroastrian will say that the word of God contained in their Religious Code was heard by Zoroaster. The Jews will say it was heard by Moses, Christians will say it was heard by Jesus and Muslims will say it was heard by Muhammad. Now ask the Hindu who heard the word of God contained in the Vedas, to whom was it revealed.

The Hindu has no answer. He cannot name the person who heard this word of God. Now the Mantras contained in the Vedas have their authors mentioned in the Vedas themselves. But the Hindus will not say that these are the persons who heard the word of God, which is contained in the Vedas. This difference goes a great way to protect the sacred character of the Vedas. For the Bible as a Sacred Book can be attacked by attacking the character of Moses or Jesus. Similarly, the Quran as a Sacred Book can be attacked by attacking the character of Mahommed. But the Veda cannot be attacked by attacking the character of the messenger or the founder. For the simple reason that there is none.

As I have said Religion is the Rock on which the Hindus have built their house. It will now be seen that it is not an ordinary sort of hard Rock. It is granite.

## Touchables v/s Untouchables

A relationship of touchables against untouchables may cause surprise. Such a surprise will not be altogether without reason. The touchables are not one uniform body of people. They are themselves divided into innumerable castes. Each Hindu is conscious of the caste to which he belongs. Given this heterogeneity it does seem that to include all the touchable castes into one group and put them as forming a block against the untouchables is to create a division which can have no meaning. But although this division of touchables against untouchables may require explanation, the division so far as modern India is concerned is real and substantial.

The explanation of how the touchables have now become one block and are conscious of their being different from the untouchables means nothing but recounting the mutual relationship of the four Varnas.

At the outset it must be borne in mind that those who like Mr. Gandhi accept the Chaturvarna as an ideal form of society, either do not know the history of the mutual relations of the four Varnas or are cherishing an illusion or conjuring up a vision for purposes which they are out to serve. For, the fact is that the four Varnas never formed a society based on loving brotherhood or on economic organisation based on cooperative effort. The four Varnas were animated by nothing but a spirit of animosity towards one another. There would not be the slightest exaggeration to say that the social history of the Hindus is a history not merely of class struggle but class war fought with such bitterness that even the Marxist will find it difficult to cite parallel cases to match.

It seems that the first class struggle took place between the Brahmins, Kshatriyas and Vaishyas on the one hand and the Sudras on the other.

In Katyayana's Srauta Sutras, it is said, that men with the exception of those whose members are defective, who have not read the Veda, eunuchs, and Sudras, have a right to sacrifice. It is Brahmanas, Rajanyas and Vaishyas (only who) according to the Veda (possess this privilege)".

We are told by Manu that *(Quotation not given in the MS.)*. Manu also says that *(Quotation not given in the MS.)*. Compare with this the following instances and statements relating to the status of the Sudra occurring in the Vedic literature of a period earlier than Manu and even earlier than Katyayana.

Prof. Max Muller calls attention to two instances showing that Sudras were admitted to great sacrifices such as *"gavedhukacharu"*. One is that of Rathakara and the other of Nishadasthapati, both Sudras.

It might however be supposed that this was a concession made to the exceptional men from the Sudras. That it was not a mere concession but a right enjoyed by the Sudras is beyond question. In the Satapatha Brahmana which is a part of the Veda, the formula for the Brahmin Priest to call the sacrificer to come and make the oblation is given. He is asked to say *ehi,* come, in the case of a Brahman; *Agahi* 'come hither', in the case of a Vaishya; *Adrava,* 'hasten hither' in the case of a Kshatriya and *Adhava,* 'run hither' in the case of a Sudra. This passage is of very great importance. It shows that the Sudra had at one time the right to sacrifice. Otherwise a form of address for a Sudra sacrificer could not have found a place in the Vedic precept. If the Sudra had a right to sacrifice, they also must have had a right to study the Vedas.

For, according to Katyayana, only those who had the right to read the Vedas were entitled to perform the sacrifice. That the Sudras were at one time entitled to read the Vedas is a fact which is well supported by tradition which is referred to in the Shanti Parva of the Mahabharata, where the sage Bhrigu answers the question "How is Varna to be determined?" in the following terms:

> *"There is no difference of castes; this world, having been at first created by Brahma entirely Brahmanic, became (afterwards) separated into castes in consequence of works. 6940. Those Brahmans (lit. twice born men), who were fond of sensual pleasure, fiery, irascible, prone to violence, who had forsaken their duty, and were red-limbed, fell into the condition of Kshatriyas. Those Brahmans, who derived their livelihood from kine, who were yellow, who subsisted by agriculture, and who neglected to practise their duties, entered into the state of Vaisyas. Those Brahmans, who were addicted to mischief and falsehood, who were covetous, who lived*

*by all kinds of works, who were black and had fallen from purity, sank into the condition of Sudras. Being separated from each other by these works, the Brahmans became divided into different castes. Duty and the rites of sacrifice have not been always forbidden to (any of) them. Such are four classes for whom the Brahmanic Sarasvati was at first designed by Brahma, but who through their cupidity fell into ignorance."*

Interpreting the word "Brahmanic" Sarasvati the Commentator says:

*"Sarasvati, consisting of the Veda, was formerly designed by Brahma for all the four castes; but the Sudras having through cupidity fallen into 'ignorance i.e. of darkness,' lost their right to the Veda."*

After the Sudra was reduced came the turn of the Vaishya. The bitterest class war took place between the Brahmins and the Kashatriyas. The classical literature of the Hindus abounds in reference to class wars between these two Varnas. First was the conflict between the Brahmins and King Vena.

*"There was formerly a Prajapati (lord of creatures), a protector of righteousness, called Anga, of the race of Atri, and resembling him in power. His son was the Prajapati Vena, who was but indifferently skilled in duty, and was born of Sunitha, the daughter of Mritya. This son of the daughter of Kala (death), owing to the taint derived from his maternal grandfather, threw his duties behind his back and lived in covetousness under the influence of desire. This king established an irreligious system of conduct; transgressing the ordinances of the Veda, he was devoted to lawlessness. In his reign men lived without study of the sacred books and without the vashatkara, and the gods had no Soma-libations to drink at sacrifices. 'I', he declared, 'am the object, and the performer of sacrifice, and the sacrifice itself, it is to me that sacrifice should be presented, and oblations offered. 'This transgressor of the rules of duty, who arrogated to himself what was not his due, was then addressed by all the great rishis, headed by Marichi: 'We are about to consecrate ourselves for a ceremony which shall last for many years, practice not*

*unrighteousness, o Vena; this is not the eternal rule of duty. Thou art in very deed a Prajapati of Atri's race, and thou hast engaged to protect thy subjects. 'The foolish Vena, ignorant of what was right, laughingly answered those great rishis who had so addressed him: 'Who but myself is the ordainer of duty? Or who ought I to obey? Who on earth equals me in sacred knowledge, in prowess, in austere fervour, in truth? Yet who are deluded and senseless know not that I am the source of all beings and duties. Hesitate not to believe that I, if I willed, could burn up the earth, or deluge it with water, or close up heaven and earth'. When owing to his delusion and arrogance Vena could not be governed, then the mighty rishis becoming incensed, seized the vigorous and struggling king, and rubbed his left thigh. From this thigh, so rubbed, was produced a black man, very short in stature, who, being alarmed, stood with joined hands. Seeing that he was agitated, Atri said to him 'Sit down" (nishida). He became the founder of the race of the Nishadas, and also progenitor of the Dhivaras (fisherman), who sprang from the corruption of Vena. So too were produced from him the other inhabitants of the Vindhya range, the Tukharas and Turnburas, who are prone to lawlessness. Then the mighty sages, excited and incensed, again rubbed the right hand of Vena, as men do the Arani wood, and from it arose Pritha, respondent in body, glowing like the manifested Agni."*

*"The son of Vena (Prithu) then, with joined hands, addressed the great rishis: 'A very slender understanding for perceiving the principles of duty has been given to me by nature; tell me truly how I must employ it. Doubt not that I shall perform whatever you shall declare to me as my duty, and its object.' Then those gods and great rishis said to him: 'Whatever duty is enjoined perform it, without hesitation, disregarding what thou may est like or dislike, looking on all creatures with an equal eye, putting far from the lust, anger, cupidity, and pride. Restrain by the strength of thin arm all those men who swerve from righteousness, having a constant regard*

*to duty. And in thought, act, and word take upon thyself, and continually renew, the engagement to protect the terrestrial Brahman (Veda or Brahmans?)...... And promise that thou wilt exempt the Brahmans from punishment, and preserve society from the confusion of Castes'. The son of Vena then replied to the gods, headed by the rishis: 'The great Brahmans, the chief of men, shall be reverenced by me'. 'So be it,' rejoined those declares of the Veda. Sukra, the depository of divine knowledge, became his purohita: the Balakhilyas and Sarasvetyas his ministers; and the venerable Garga, the great rishi, his astrologer. "The second conflict took place between the Brahmins and the Kshatriya king Pururavas. A brief reference to it occurs in the Adiparva of the Mahabharata.*

*"Subsequently the wise Pururavas was born of 11, who, as we have heard, was both his father and his mother. Ruling over thirteen islands of the ocean, and surrounded by being who were all superhuman, himself a man of great renown, Pururavas, intoxicated by his prowess, engaged in a conflict with the Brahmans, and robbed them of their jewels, although they loudly remonstrated. Sanatkumara came from Brahma's heaven, and addressed to him an admonition, which, however, he did not regard. Being then straightway cursed by the incensed rishis, he perished, this covetous monarch, who, through pride of power, had lost his understanding. This glorious being (virat), accompanied by Urvasi, brought down for the performance of sacred rites the fires which existed in the heaven of the Gandharvas, properly distributed into three."*

A third collision is reported to have occurred between the Brahmins and King Nahusha. The story is given in great details in the Udyogaparva of the Mahabharata. It is there recorded:

*"After his slaughter of the demon Vrittra, Indra became alarmed at the idea of having taken the life of a Brahmin (for Vrittra was regarded as such), and hid himself in waters. In consequence of the disappearance of the king of gods, all affairs, celestial as well as terrestrial, fell*

*into confusion. The rishis and gods then applied to Nahusha to be their king. After at first excusing himself on the plea of want of power, Nahusha at length, in compliance with their solicitations, accepted the high function. Up to the period of his elevation he had led a virtuous life, but he now became addicted to amusement and sensual pleasure; and even aspired to the possession of Indrani, Indra's wife, whom he had happened to see. The queen resorted to the Angiras Vrihaspati, the preceptor of the gods, who engaged to protect her. Nahusha was greatly incensed on hearing of this interference; but the gods endeavoured to pacify him, and pointed out the immorality of—appropriating another person's wife. Nahusha, however, would listen to no remonstrance, and insisted that in his adulterous designs he was no worse than Indra himself; 373. The renowned Ahalya, a rishi's wife, was formerly corrupted by Indra in her husband's lifetime; Why was he not prevented by you? 374. And many barbarous acts, and unrighteous deeds, and frauds, were perpetrated of old by Indra; Why was he not prevented by you? The gods, urged by Nahusha, then went to bring Indrani; but Vrihaspati would not give her up. At his recommendation, however, she solicited Nahusha for some delay, till she should ascertain what had become of her husband. This request was granted. The gods next applied to Vishnu on behalf of Indra; and Vishnu promised that if Indra would sacrifice to him, he should be purged from his guilt, and recovers his dominion, while Nahusha would be destroyed. Indra sacrificed accordingly: and the result is thus told; "Having divided the guilt of Brahmanicide among trees, rivers, mountains, the earth, women, and the elements, Vasava (Indra), lord of the gods, became freed from suffering and sin, and self-governed." Nahusha was by this means, shaken from his place. But (unless this is said by way of prelepsis, or there is some confusion in the narrative) he must have speedily regained his position, as we are told that Indra was again ruined,, and became invisible. Indrani now went in search of her husband; and by the help of Upasruti (the goddess of night and reveller of secrets) discovered him existing in a very subtle form in the stem of a lotus growing in a lake situated in a continent within an ocean north of the Himalaya. She made known to him the wicked intention of Nahusha, and entreated him to exert his power, rescue her from danger, and resume his dominion. Indra declined any immediate interposition on the plea of Nahusha's superior strength; but suggested to his wife a device by which the usurper might be hurled from his position. She was recommended to say to Nahusha that "if he would visit her on a celestial vehicle borne by rishis, she would with pleasure submit herself to him". The question of the gods accordingly went to Nahusha, by whom she was graciously received, and made this proposal: "I desire for thee, king of the gods, a vehicle hitherto unknown, such as neither Vishnu, nor Rudra, nor the ashuras, nor the rakshases employ. Let the eminent rishis, all united, bear thee, lord, in a car: this idea pleases me". Nahusha receives favourably this appeal to his vanity, and in the course of his reply thus gives utterance to his self-congratulation: "He is a personage of no mean prowess who makes the munis his bearers. I am a fervid devotee of great might, lord of the past, the future and the present. If I were angry the world would no longer stand; on me everything depends.... Wherefore, O goddess, I shall, without doubt, carry out what you propose. The seven rishis, and all the Brahman-rishis, shall carry me. Behold beautiful goddess, my majesty, and my prosperity." The narrative goes on: "Accordingly this wicked being, irreligious, violent, intoxicated by the force of conceit, and arbitrary in his conduct, attached to his car the rishis, who submitted to his commands, and compelled them to bear him ". Indrani then again resorts to Vrihaspati, who assures her that vengeance will soon overtake Nahusha for his presumption: and promises that he will himself perform a sacrifice with a view to the destruction of the oppressor, and the discovery of Indra's lurking place. Agni is then sent to discover and bring Indra to Vrihaspati; and the latter, on Indra's arrival, informs him of all that had occurred during his absence. While Indra with Kuvera, Yama, Soma, and Varuna, was devising means for the destruction of Nahusha, the sage Agastya came up, congratulated Indra on the fall of his rival, and proceeded to relate how it had occurred. Wearied with carrying the sinner Nahusha, the eminent divine rishis, and the spotless brahman-rishis asked that divine personage Nahusha (to solve) a difficulty; "Dost thou, a Vasava, most excellent of conquerors, regard as authoritative or not those Brahmana texts which are recited at the immolation of kine?' 'No', replied Nahusha, whose understanding was enveloped in darkness. The rishis rejoined: 'Engaged in unrighteousness, thou attainest not unto righteousness: these texts, which were formerly uttered by great rishis, are regarded by us as authoritative.' The (proceeds Agastya) disputing with the munis, Nahusha, impelled by unrighteousness, touched me on the head with his foot. In consequence of this the king's glory was smitten and his prosperity departed. When he had instantly become agitated and oppressed with fear, I said to him, 'Since thou, O fool, contemnest that sacred text, always held in honour, which has been composed by former sages, and employed by brahman-rishis, and has touched my head with thy foot, and employest the Brahma—like and irresistible rishis as bearers to carry thee, therefore, shorn of thy lustre and all thy merit exhausted, sink down, sinner, degraded from heaven to earth. For then thousand years thou shalt crawl in the form of a huge serpent. When that period is completed, thou shalt again ascend to heaven'. So fell that wicked wretch from the sovereignty of the gods."*

Next there is reference to the conflict between King Nimi and the Brahmins. The Vishnu Puran relates the story as follows:

*"Nimi had requested the Brahman-rishi Vashishtha to officiate at a sacrifice, which was to last a thousand years, Vashishtha in reply pleaded a pre-engagement to Indra for five hundred years, but promised to return at*

*the end of that period. The king made no remark, and Vashishtha went away, supposing that he had assented to this arrangement. On his return, however, the priest discovered that Nimi had retained Gautama (who was, equally with Vashishtha a Brahman-rishi) and others to perform the sacrifice; and being incensed at the neglect to give him notice of what was intended, he cursed the king, who was then asleep, to lose his corporeal form. When Nimi awoke and learnt that he had been cursed without any previous warning, he retorted, by uttering a similar curse on Vashishtha, and then died. "In consequence of this curse "(proceeds Vishnu Purana, iv. 5, 6)" the vigour of Vashishtha entered into the vigour of Mitra and Varuna. Vashishtha, however, received from them another body when their seed had fallen from them at the sight of Urvashi". Nimi's body was embalmed. At the close of the sacrifice which he had begun, the gods were willing, on the intercession of the priests, to restore him to life, but he declined the offer, and was placed by the deities, according to his desire, in the eyes of all living creatures. It is in consequence of this fact that they are always opening the shutting (Nimishas means "the twinkling of the eye")".*

Manu mentions another conflict between the Brahmins and King Sumukha. But of this no details are available. These are instances of conflict between the Brahmins and the Kshatriya Kings. From this it must not be supposed that the Brahmins and the Kshatriyas as two classes did not clash. That there were clashes between these two classes as distinguished from conflicts with kings is abundantly proved by material the historic value of which cannot be doubted. Reference may be made to three events.

First is the contest between the Vishvamitra the Kshatriya and Vashishtha the Brahmin. The issue between the two was whether a Kshatriya can claim Brahminhood. The story is told in Ramayana and is as follows:

*"There was formerly, we are told, a king called Kusa, son of Prajapati, who had a son called Kushanabha, who was father of Gadhi, the father of Vishvamitra. The latter ruled the earth for many thousand years. On one*

> *occasion, when he was making a circuit of the earth, he came to Vashishtha's hermitage, the pleasant abode of many saints, sages, and holy devotees, where, after at first declining he allowed himself to be hospitably entertained with his followers by the son of Brahma. Vishvamitra, however, coveting the wondrous cow, which had supplied all the dainties of the feast, first of all asked that she should be given to him in exchange for a hundred thousand common cows, adding that "she was a gem, that gems were the property of the king, and that, therefore, the cow was his by right". On this price being refused the king advances immensely in his offers, but all without effect. He then proceeds-very ungratefully and tyrannically, it must be allowed to have the cow removed by force, but she breaks away from his attendants, and rushes back to her master, complaining that he was deserting her. He replies that he was not deserting her, but that the king was much more powerful than he. She answers, "Men do not ascribe strength to a Kshatriya: the Brahmans are stronger. The Strength of Brahmans is divine, and superior to that of Kshatriya. Thy strength is immeasurable. Vishvamitra, though of great vigour, is not more powerful than thou. Thy energy is invincible. Commission me, who have been acquired by thy Brahmanical power, and I will destroy the pride, and force, and attempt of this wicked prince". She accordingly by her bellowing creates hundreds of Pahalvas, who destroy the entire host of Vishvamitra, but are slain by him in their turn. Sakas and Yavans, of great power and valour, and well armed, were then produced, who consumed the king's soldiers, but were routed by him."*

The cow then calls into existence by her bellowing, and from different parts of her body, other warriors of various tribes, who again destroyed Vishvamitra's entire army, foot soldiers, elephants, horses, chariots, and all.

A hundred of the monarch's sons, armed with various weapons, then rushed in great fury on Vashishtha, but were all reduced to ashes in a moment by the blast of that sage's mouth. Vishvamitra, being thus utterly vanquished and humbled, appointed one of his son to be regent, and travelled to the Himalaya, where he betook himself to austerities, and thereby obtained a vision of Mahadeva, who at his desire revealed to him the science of arms in all its branches, and gave him celestial weapons with which, elated and full of pride, he consumed the hermitage of Vashishtha, and put its inhabitants to flight.

Vashishtha then threatens Vishvamitra and uplifts his Brahmanical mace. Vishvamitra too, raises his fiery weapon and calls out to his adversary to stand. Vashishtha bids him to show his strength, and boasts that he will soon humble his pride. He asks: "What comparison is there between a Kshatriya's might, and the great might of a Brahman? Behold, thou contemptible Kshatriya, my divine Brahmanical power. The dreadful fiery weapon uplifted by the son of Gadhi was then quenched by the rod of the Brahman, as fire is by water." Many and various other celestial missiles, as the nooses of Brahma, Kala (time), and Varuna, the discuss of Vishnu, and the trident of Shiva, were hurled by Vishvamitra at his antagonist, but the son of Brahma swallowed them up in his all-devouring mace. Finally, to the intense consternation of all the gods, the warrior shot off the terrific weapon of Brahma (brahmastra): but this was equally ineffectual against the Brahmanical sage.

Vashishtha had now assumed a direful appearance: "Jets of fire mingled with smoke darted from the pores of his body; the Brahmanical mace blazed in his hand like a smokeless mundane conflagration, or a second sceptre of Yama." Being appeased, however by the munis, who proclaimed his superiority to his rival, the sage stayed his vengeance; and Vishvamitra exclaimed with a groan: "Shame on a Kshatriya's strength: the strength of a Brahman's might alone is strength: by the single Brahmanical mace all my weapons have been destroyed." No alternative now remains, to the humiliated monarch, but either to acquiesce in this helpless inferiority, or to work out his own elevation to the Brahmanical order. He embraces the latter alternative: "Having pondered well this defeat, I shall betake myself, with composed senses and mind, to strenuous austere fervour, which shall exalt me to the rank of a Brahman".

Intensely vexed and mortified, groaning and full of hatred against his enemy, he travelled with his queen to the south, and carried his resolution into effect; and we are first of all told that three sons Havishyanda, Madhusyanda, and Dridhanetra were born to him. At the end of a thousands years Brahma appeared, and announced that he had conquered the heaven of royal sages (rajarshis); and, in consequence of his austere fervour, he was recognised as having attained that rank. Vishvamitra, however, was ashamed, grieved, and incensed at the offer of so very inadequate a reward, and exclaimed; "I have practised intense austerity, and the gods and rishis regard me only as a rajarshi.

Austerities, it appears, are altogether fruitless". Notwithstanding this disappointment, he had ascended one grade, and forthwith recommenced his work of mortification. "At this point of time his austerities were interrupted by the following occurrences: King Trisanku, one of Ikshvaku's descendants, had conceived the design of celebrating a sacrifice by virtue of which he should ascend bodily to heaven. As Vashishtha, on being summoned, declared that the thing was impossible (asakyam), Trisanku travelled to the south, where the sage's hundred sons were engaged in austerities, and applied to them to do what their father had declined.

Though he addressed them with the greatest reverence and humility, and added that "the Ikshvaku regarded their family-priests as their highest resource in difficulties, and that, after their father, he himself looked to them as his tutelary deities "he received from the haughty priests the following rebuke for his presumption: "Asakyam" "Fool, thou hast been refused by thy truth speaking preceptor. How is it that, disregarding his authority, thou has resorted to another school (sakha).

The family priest is the highest oracle of all the Ikshvakus; and the command of those veracious personages cannot be transgressed. Vashishtha, the divine rishi, has declared that 'the thing cannot be'; and how can we undertake thy sacrifice? Thou art foolish king; return to thy capital. The divine (Vashishtha) is competent to act as priest of the three worlds; how can we shew him disrespect?" Trisanku then gave them to understand that as his preceptor and "his preceptor's sons had declined compliance with his requests, he should think of some other expedient."

In consequence of his venturing to express this presumptuous intention, they condemned him by their imprecation to become a Chandala. As this curse soon took effect, and the unhappy king's form was changed into that of a degraded outcast, he resorted to Vishvamitra (who, as we have seen, was also dwelling at this period in the south), enlarging on his own virtues and piety, and bewailing his fate. Vishvamitra commiserated his condition, and promised to sacrifice on his behalf, and exalt him to heaven in the same Chandala-form to which he had been condemned by his preceptor's curse. "Heaven is now as good as in thy possession, since thou hast resorted to the son of Kusika".

He then directed that preparations should be made for the sacrifice, and that all the rishis, including the family of Vashishtha, should be invited to the ceremony. The disciples of Vishvamitra, who had conveyed his message, reported the result on their return in these words: "Having heard your message, all the Brahmans are assembling in all the countries, and have arrived, excepting Mahodaya (Vashishtha). Hear what dreadful words those hundred Vashishthas, their voices quivering with rage, have uttered: 'How can the gods and rishis consume the oblation at the sacrifice of that man, especially if he be a Chandala, for whom a Kshatriya is officiating priest? How can illustrious Brahmans ascend to heaven, after eating the food of a Chandala, and being entertained by Vishvamitra?"

These ruthless words all Vashishthas, together with Mahodaya, uttered, their eyes inflamed with anger. Vishvamitra, who was greatly incensed on receiving this message, by a curse doomed the sons of Vashishtha to be reduced to ashes, and reborn as degraded outcasts (mritapah) for seven hundred births, and Mahodaya to become a Nishada. Knowing that this curse had taken effect, Vishvamitra thereafter eulogizing Trisanku, proposed to the assembled rishis that the sacrifice should be celebrated. To this they assented, being actuated by fear of the terrible sage's wrath.

Vishvamitra himself officiated at the sacrifice as yajakas; and the other rishis as priests (ritvijah) with other functions) performed all the ceremonies. Vishvamitra next invited the gods to partake of the oblations: "When, however, the deities did not come to receive their portions, Vishvamitra became full of wrath, and raising aloft the sacrificial ladle, thus addressed Trisanku: 'Behold, O monarch, the power of austere fervour acquired by my own efforts. I myself, by my own energy, will conduct thee to heaven. Ascend to that celestial region which is so arduous to attain in an earthly body. I have surely earned some reward of my austerity' "Trisanku ascended instantly to heaven in the sight of munis. Indra, however, ordered him to be gone, as person who, having incurred the curse of his spiritual preceptors, was unfit for the abode of the celestials; and to fall down headlong to earth. He accordingly began to descend, invoking loudly, as he fell the help of his spiritual patron.

Vishvamitra, greatly incensed, called out to him to stop: "Then by the power of his divine knowledge and austere fervour created, like another Prajapati, other Seven Rishis (a constellation so called) in the southern part of the sky. Having proceeded to this quarter of the heavens, the renowned sage, in the midst of the rishis, formed another garland of stars, being overcome with fury. Exclaiming, 'I will create another Indra, or the world shall have no Indra at all,' he began, in his rage, to call gods also into being. The rishis, gods (Suras), and Ashuras now became seriously alarmed and said to Vishvamitra, in a conciliatory tone, that Trisanku, "as he had been cursed by his preceptors, should not be admitted bodily into heaven, until he had undergone some lustration".

The sage replied that he had given a promise to Trisanku, and appealed to the gods to permit his protege to remain bodily in heaven and the newly created stars to retain their places in perpetuity. The gods agreed that "these numerous stars should remain, but beyond the Sun's path, and that Trisanku, like an immortal, with his head downwards should shine among them, and be followed by them," adding "that his object would be thus attained, and his renown secured, and he would be like a dweller in heaven". Thus was this great dispute adjusted by a compromise, which Vishvamitra accepted.

This story of Trisanku, it will have been observed, differs materially from the one quoted above from the Harivarnsa; but brings out more distinctly the character of the conflict between Vashishtha and Vishvamitra. "When all the gods and rishis had departed at the conclusion of the sacrifice, Vishvamitra said to his attendant devotees; "This has been a great interruption (to our austerities) which has occurred in the southern region: we must proceed in another direction to continue our penances". He accordingly went to a forest in the west, and began his austerities anew. Here the narrative is again interrupted by the introduction of another story, that of king Ambarisha, king of Ayodhya, who was, according to the Ramayana, the twentyeighth in descent from Ikshvaku, and the twentysecond from Trisanku.

Vishvamitra is nevertheless represented as flourishing contemporaneously with both of these princes. The story relates that Ambarisha was engaged in performing a sacrifice, when Indra carried away the victim. The priest said that this ill-omened event had occurred owing to the king's bad administration; and would call for a great expiation, unless a human victim could be produced. After a long search the royal rishi (Ambarisha) came upon the Brahman-rishi Richika, a descendant of Bhrigu, and asked him to sell one of his sons for a victim, at the price of a hundred thousand cows. Richika answered that he would not sell his eldest son; and his wife added that she would not sell the youngest: "eldest sons," she observed, "being generally the favourites of their fathers, and youngest sons of their mothers". The second son, Sunassepa, then said that in that case he regarded himself as the one who was to be sold, and desired the king to remove him. The hundred thousand cows, with the millions of gold-pieces and heaps of jewels, were paid down, and Sunassepa carried away.

As they were passing through Puskara Sunassepa beheld his maternal uncle Vishvamitra who was engaged in austerities there with other rishis, threw himself into his arms, and implored his assistance, urging his orphan, friendless, and helpless state, as claims on the sage's benevolence. Vishvamitra soothed him; and pressed his own sons to offer themselves as victims in the room of Sunassepa. This proposition met with no favour from Madhushyanda and the other sons of the royal hermit, who answered with haughtiness and derision: "How is it that thou sacrifices thine own sons, and seeks to rescue those of others? We look upon this as wrong, and like the eating of one's own flesh". The sage was exceedingly wroth at this disregard of his injunction, and doomed his sons to be born in the most degraded classes, like Vasishtha's sons, and to eat dog's flesh, for a thousand years. He then said to Sunassepa: "When thou art bound with hallowed cords decked with a red garland, and anointed with ungents, and fastened to the sacrificial post of Vishnu, then address thyself to Agni, and sing these two divine verses (gathas), at the sacrifice of Ambarisha; then shall thou attain the fulfilment (of thy desire)". Being furnished with the two gathas, Sunassepa proposed at once to king Ambarisha that they should set out for their destination. When bound at the stake to be immolated, dressed in a red garment, "he celebrated the two gods, Indra and his younger brother (Vishnu), with the excellent verses. The thousand-eyed (Indra) was pleased with the secret hymn, and bestowed long life on Sunassepa". King Ambarisha also received great benefits from this sacrifice. Vishvamitra meanwhile proceeded with his austerities, which he prolonged for a thousand years. At the end of this time the gods came to allot his reward; and Brahma announced that he had attained the rank of a rishi, thus apparently advancing an additional step. Dissatisfied, as it would seem, with this, the sage commenced his task of penance anew. After a length of time he beheld the nymph (Apsara) Menka, who had come to bathe in the lake of Pushkara. She flashed on his view, unequalled in her radiant beauty, like lightning in a cloud. He was smitten by her charms, invited her to be his companion in his hermitage, and for ten years remained a slave to her witchery, to the great prejudice of his austerities. At length he became ashamed of this ignoble subjection, and full of indignation at what he believed to be a device of the gods to disturb his devotion; and, dismissing the nymph with gentle accents, he departed for the northern mountains, where he practised severe austerities for a thousand years on the banks of the Kausiki river.

The gods became alarmed at the progress he was making, and decided that he should be dignified with the appellation of great rishi (maharshi); and Brahma, giving effect to the general opinion of the deities, announced that he had conferred that rank upon him. Joining his hands and bowing his head, Visvamitra replied that he should consider himself to have indeed completely subdued his senses, if the incomparable title of Brahman-rishi were conferred upon him. Brahma informed him in answer, that he had not yet acquired the power of perfectly controlling his senses; but should make further efforts with that view. The sage then began to put himself through a yet more rigorous course of austerities, standing with his arms erect, without support, feeding on air, in summer exposed to five fires (*i.e.* one on each of four sides, and the sun overhead), in the rainy season remaining unsheltered from the wet, and in winter lying on a watery couch night and day. This he continued for a thousand years. At last Indra and the other deities became greatly distressed at the idea of the merit he was storing up, and the power which he was thereby acquiring; and the chief of the celestials desired the nymph Rambha to go and bewitch him by her blandishments.

She expressed great reluctance to expose herself to the wrath of the formidable muni, but obeyed the repeated injunction of Indra, who promised that he and Kandarpa (the god of love) should stand by her, and assumed her most attractive aspect with the view of overcoming the sage's impassability. He, however, suspected this design, and becoming greatly incensed, he dommed the nymph by a curse to be turned into stone and to continue in that state for a thousand years. The curse took effect, and Kandarpa and Indra slunk away. In this way, though he resisted the allurements of sensual love, he lost the whole fruit of his austerities by yielding to anger; and had to begin his work over again. He resolved to check his irascibility, to remain silent, not even to breathe for hundreds of years; to dry up his body; and to fast and stop his breath till he had obtained the coveted character of a Brahman.

He then left the Himalaya and travelled to the east, where he underwent a dreadful exercise, unequalled in the whole history of austerities, maintaining silence, according to a vow, for a thousand years. At the end of this time he had attained to perfection, and although thwarted by many obstacles, he remained unmoved by anger. On the expiration of this course of austerity, he prepared some food to eat; which Indra, coming in the form of a Brahman, begged that he would give him. Visvarnitra did so, and though he had none left for himself, and was obliged to remain fasting, he said nothing to the Brahman, on account of his vow of silence. As he continued to suspend his breath, smoke issued from his head, to the great consternation and distress of the three worlds.

The gods, rishis, etc., then addressed Brahma: "The great muni Vishvamitra has been allured and provoked in various ways, but still advances in his sanctity. If his wish is not conceded, he will destroy the three worlds by the force of his austerity. All the regions of the universe are confounded, no light anywhere shines; all the oceans are tossed, and the mountains crumble, the earth quakes, and the wind blows confusedly. We cannot, O Brahma, guarantee that mankind shall not become atheistic..... Before the great and glorious sage of fiery form resolves to destroy (everything) let him be propitiated." The gods, headed by Brahma, then addressed Vishvamitra: "Hail Brahman rishi, we are gratified by thy austerities; O Kausika, thou hast, through their intesity, attained to Brahmanhood. I, O Brahman, associated with the Maruts, confer on thee long life. May every blessing attend thee; depart wherever thou wilt.' The sage, delighted, made his obeisance to the gods, and said: 'If I have obtained Brahmanhood, and long life, then let the mystic monosyllable (omkara) and the sacrificial formula (vashatkara) and the Vedas recognise me in that capacity.

And let Vashishtha, the son of Brahma, the most eminent of those who are skilled in the Kshattra-veda, and the Brahma-veda (the knowledge of the Kshatriya and the Brahmanical disciplines), address me similarly.'..... Accordingly Vashishtha, being propitiated by the gods, became reconciled to Vishvamitra, and recognised his claim to all the prerogatives of a Brahman rishi..... Vishvamitra, too, having attained the Brahmanical rank, paid all honour to Vashishtha." The second event has reference to the slaughter of the Brahmins by the Kshatriyas. It is related in the Adiparva of the Mahabharata from which the following account is taken:

> *There was a king named Kritvirya, by whose liberality the Bhrigus, learned in the Vedas, who officiated as his priests, had been greatly enriched with corn and money. After he had gone to heaven, his descendants were in want of money, and came to beg for a supply from the Bhrigus, of whose wealth they were aware. Some of the latter hid their money under ground, others bestowed it on Brahmans, being afraid of the Kshatriyas, while others again gave these last what they wanted. It*

*happened, however, that a Kshatriya, while digging the ground, discovered some money buried in the house of a Bhrigu. The Kshatriyas then assembled and saw this treasure, and, being incensed, slew in consequence all the Bhrigus, whom they regarded with contempt, down to the children in the womb. The widows, however, fled to the Himalaya mountains. One of them concealed her unborn child in her thigh. The Kshatriyas, hearing of its existence from a Brahmani informant, sought to kill it; but it issued forth from its mother's thigh with lustre, and blinded the persecutors. After wandering about bewildered among the mountains for a time, they humbly supplicated the mother of the child for the restoration of their sight; but she referred them to her wonderful infant Aurva into whom the whole Veda, with its Veda Vyas had entered, as the person who (in requisition of the slaughter of his relatives) had robbed them of their eyesight, and who alone could restore it.*

They accordingly had recourse to him, and their eyesight was restored. Aurva, however, meditated the destruction of all living creatures, in revenge for the slaughter of the Bhrigus, and entered on a course of austerities which alarmed both gods, ashuras, and men; but his progenitors (Pitris) themselves appeared, and sought to turn him from his purpose by saying that they had no desire to be revenged on the Kshatriyas: "It was not from weakness that the devout Bhrigus overlooked the massacre perpetrated by the murderous Kshatriyas. When we became distressed by old age, we ourselves desired to be slaughtered by them.

The money which was buried by some one in a Bhrigu's house was placed there for the purpose of exciting hatred, by those who wished to provoke the Kshatriyas. For what had me, who were desiring heaven, to do with money?" They added that they hit upon this device because they did not wish to be guilty of suicide, and concluded by calling upon Aurva to restrain his wrath; and abstain from the sin he was meditating: "Destroy not the Kshatriyas, O son, nor the seven worlds. Suppress thy kindled anger which nullifies the power of austere-fervour." Aurva, however, replies that he cannot allow his threat to remain unexecuted. His anger, unless wreaked upon some other object, will, he says, consume himself. And he argues on grounds of justice, expediency, and duty, against the clemency, which his progenitors recommend. He is, however, persuaded by the Pitris to throw the fire of his anger into the sea, where they say it will find exercise in assailing the watery element, and in this way his threat will be fulfilled." The third event has reference to the slaughter of the Kshatriyas by the Brahmins. This story is told in several places in the Mahabharata.

The magnificent and mighty Kartavirya, possessing a thousand arms, was lord of this whole world, living in Mahishmati. This Haihaya of unquestioned valour ruled over the whole sea-girt earth, with its oceans and continents". He obtained boons from the muni Dattatreya, a thousand arms whenever he should go into battle power to make the conquest of the whole earth, a disposition to rule it with justice and the promise of instruction from the virtuous in the event of his going astray.

"Then ascending his chariot glorious as the resplendent sun, he exclaimed in the intoxication of his prowess, 'Who is like me in fortitude, courage, fame, heroism, energy, and vigour?' At the end of this speech a bodiless voice in the sky addressed him: 'Thou knowest not, O fool, that a Brahman is better than a Kshatriya. It is with the help of the Brahman that the Kshatriya rules his subjects.' Arjuna answers: 'If I am pleased, I can create, or, if displeased, annihilate, living beings; and no Brahman is superior to me in act, thought or word.

The first proposition is that the Brahmans are superior; the second that the Kshatriyas are superior; both of these thou hast stated with their grounds, but there is a difference between them (in point of force). The Brahmans are dependent on the Kshatriyas and not the Kshatriyas are beaten up by the Brahmans, who wait upon them, and only make the Vedas a pretence. Justice, the protection of the people, has its seat in the Kshatriyas. From them the Brahmans derived their livelihood; how then can the latter be superior? I always keep in subjection to myself those Brahmans, the chief of all beings, who subsist on alms, and who have a high opinion of them selves. For truth was spoken by that female the Gayatri in the sky. I shall subdue all those unruly Brahmans clad in hides.

No one in the three worlds, god or man can hurl me from my royal authority; wherefore I am superior to any Brahman. Now shall I turn the world in which Brahmans have the upper hand into a place where Kshatriyas shall have the upper hand; for no one dares to encounter my force in battle.' Hearing this speech of Arjuna, the female roving in the night became alarmed. Then Vayu hovering in the air, said to Arjuna: 'Abandon this sinful disposition, and do obeisance to the Brahmans. If thou shalt do them wrong, thy kingdom shall be convulsed.

They will subdue thee: those powerful men will humble thee, and expel thee from thy country." The king asks him, 'Who art thou?' Vayu replies, 'I am Vayu, the messenger of the gods, and tell thee what is for thy benefit.' Arjuna rejoins, 'Oh, thou displayest today a great warmth of devotion to the Brahmans. But say that a Brahman is like (any other) earth-born creature." This king came into conflict with Parashuram the son of a Brahman sage Jamadagni. The history of this conflict is as follows:

> *"There lived a king of Kanyakubja, called Gadhi, who had a daughter named Satyavati. The marriage of this princess to the rishi Richika, and the birth of Jamadagni, are then told in nearly the same way as above narrated. Jamadagni and Satyavati had five sons, the youngest of whom was the redoubtable Parashuram. By his father's command he kills his mother (who, by the indulgence of impure desire, had fallen from her previous sanctity), after the four elder sons had refused this matricidal offence, and had in consequence been deprived of reason by their father's curse. At Parashuram's desire, however, his mother is restored by his father to life, and his brothers to reason; and he himself is absolved from all the guilt of murder; and obtains the boon of invincibility and long life from his father. His history now begins to be connected with that of king Arjuna (or Kartavirya). The latter had come to Jamadagni's hermitage, and had been respectfully received by his wife; but he had requited this honour by carrying away by force the calf of the sage's sacrificial cow, and breaking down his lofty trees. On being informed of this violence, Parasurama was filled with indignation, attacked*

*Arjuna, cut off his thousand arms, and slew him. Arjuna's sons, in return, slew the peaceful sage Jamadagni, in the absence of Parasurama."*

*"Rama, after performing, on his return, his father's funeral obsequies, vowed to destroy the whole Kshatriya race; and executed his threat by killing first Arjuna's sons and their followers. Twenty one times did he sweep away all the Kshatriyas from the earth, and formed five lakes of blood in Samantapanchaka; in which he satiated the manes of the Bhrigus, and beheld face to face (his grandfather), Richika, who addressed himself to Rama. The latter gratified Indra by offering to him a grand sacrifice, and gave the earth to the officiating priests. He bestowed also a golden altar, ten fathoms long and nine highs, on the mighty Kasyapa. This, by his permission, the Brahmans divided among themselves, deriving thence the name of Khandavavanas. Having given away the earth to Kasyapa, Parasurama himself dwells on the mountain Mahendra. Thus did enmity arise between him and Kshatriyas, and thus was the earth conquered by Rama of boundless might."*

The Kshatriyas who were slain by Parashuram are described in the Dronaparvan of the Mahabharata as of various provinces, *viz.*, Kasmiras, Darads, Kuntis, Ksudrakas, Malavas, Angas, Vangas, Kalingas, Videhas, Tamraliptakas, Marttikavatas, Sivis and other Rajanyas. The means by which the Kshattriya race was restored is also told as part of this story of annihilation of the Kshatriyas by the Brahmins. It is said:

"Having one and twenty times swept away all the Kshatriyas from the earth, the son of Jamadagni engaged in austerities on Mahendra the most excellent of mountains. After he had cleared the world of Kshatriyas, their widows came to the Brahmans, praying for offspring. The religious Brahmans, free from any impulse of lust, cohabited at the proper seasons with these women, who in consequence became pregnant, and brought forth-valiant Kshatriya boys and girls, to continue the Kshatriya stock. Thus was the Kshatriya race virtuously begotten by Brahmans on Kshatriya women, and became multiplied and long-lived. Thence there arose four castes inferior to the Brahmans."

# 2

# Ambedkar and Grievances of the Scheduled Castes

This Memorandum sets out the grievances of the Scheduled Castes in British India and suggests the measures that are necessary for redressing them. In listing the grievances I have taken note of such grievances only as the Central Government alone can remedy.

The grievances listed in this memorandum are divided into three categories (1) Political, (2) Educational and (3) Other Grievances, and are discussed separately. Part I deals with Political grievances. Part II with Educational grievances, and Part III with Other grievances. To this I have added Part IV in which I have ventured to speak of the duty which every Government must assume towards those who are living in a life of perpetual distress, in the hope that the Government of India will recognise it and do what they are bound to do to the Scheduled Castes. I have thought it advisable to give below a table divided into Parts. This table, it will be seen serves two purposes. It gives at the start the contents of this memorandum, and secondly it helps to convey at the outset a general idea of what these grievances are.

## Political Grievances

### *Inadequate Representation in the Central Legislature*

1. As at present constituted the Central Assembly consists of 141 members. Of these 102 are elected and 39 nominated. Of the nominated members 19 are non-

Officials and 20 are Officials. Of this total of 141 there are two who belong to the Scheduled Castes. Consider as against this the population of the Scheduled Castes. The census in India has become a political affair; and the Hindus, Muslims and the Sikhs have been attempting to cook up the census so as to show a rise in their numbers. This is done mostly at the cost of the untouchables. It is therefore difficult to get a correct figure of their population. Whatever estimate the census gives, it is bound to be an underestimate. However, taking the figure of 40 millions which is the figure given in the census of 1940 there can be no doubt that the representation of the Scheduled Castes in the central Legislature is ridiculously low.

2. To make the position clear, I give below two tables, which have a bearing on this question:

***Population in British India***

| *Communities* | *Total of each community in 1941* | *Order of importance in terms of population* | *% to total population ill* |
|---|---|---|---|
| *1* | *2* | *3* | *4* |
| Total | 295,808,722 | | |
| Hindus | 150,890,146 | 1 | 50.0 |
| Muslims | 79,398,503 | 2 | 23.6 |
| Scheduled Castes | 39,920,807 | 3 | 13.5 |
| Tribal | 16,713,256 | 4 | 5.7 |
| Sikhs | 4,165,097 | 5 | 1.3 |
| Indian | 3,245,706 | 6 | 1.0 |
| Europeans | 122,788 | 7 | |
| Anglo-Indians | 113,936 | 8 | |
| Parsis | 101.968 | 9 | |

***Note:*** In this table only the population of those communities whose position is relevant to the purpose of this Memorandum is given.

3. This table throws a flood of light on extent of representation, which the different communities in the Central Legislature have at present. Figures in column 5 give the total representation each community has, with the percentage ratio for some of them. I do not,

however, wish to lay stress on them. They include figure for Nominated Officials. They are intended primarily to represent Government and not the communities to whom they belong. Secondly, the communal composition of the Nominated Official Block is variable and not fixed. But I do wish to invite attention to figures in other columns. I will begin with column 6. It gives the total extent of the representation which different communities have secured through election as well as nomination. More striking are the figures given in column 3. It shows that the Hindus have been allowed 54.9% by election. In addition they are given 21% out of the quota reserved for nomination. The Muslims have got 33.5% by election. This is great deal in excess of what they are entitled to on the basis of their population. In addition they are allowed the benefit of 37% out of the quota reserved for nomination. The same is the case with the Sikhs and the Parsis. Both of them have representation through election much beyond what their numbers would justify. Yet each is allowed to have the benefit of 10.5% out of the quota for nomination. As against this, there is the naked fact that the Scheduled Castes who number 40 millions and who form the third largest community in India have no seat by election, and only one by nomination.

**_Communal Composition of the Central Assembly_**

| *Community* | *Elected Members* | | *Nominated* | | *Nominated* | | *Total including* | | *Total excluding* | |
|---|---|---|---|---|---|---|---|---|---|---|
| | | | *Non-Official Members* | | *Official Members* | | *Official Members* | | *Official Members* | |
| | *No.* | *%* | *No.* | *%* | *No.* | *%* | *No.* | *%* | *No.* | *%* |
| *1* | *2* | | *3* | | *4* | | *5* | | *6* | |
| Hindus | 56 | 54.9 | 4 | 21 | 8 | | 68 | 60 | 60 | 49.5 |
| Muslims | 34 | 33.5 | 7 | 37 | 3 | | 44 | 41 | 41 | 33.8 |
| Sikhs | 2 | | 2 | 10.5 | | | 4 | 4 | 4 | 3.3 |
| Parsis | 1 | | 2 | 10.5 | 1 | | 4 | 3 | 3 | 2.4 |
| Europeans | 8 | 7.8 | 1 | | 7 | | 16 | 9 | 9 | 7.4 |
| Indian Christians | | | 1 | | | | 1 | 1 | 1 | |
| Anglo-Indians | | | 1 | | | | 1 | 1 | 1 | |
| Scheduled Castes | | | 1 | | 1 | | 2 | 1 | 1 | |
| Vacant | 1 | | | | | | 1 | 1 | 1 | |
| Total | 102 | | 19 | | 20 | | 141 | | 121 | |

4. Given these facts two comments become quite in order. In the first place, the Legislature is quite an unbalanced body. It suffers from both the evils from over-representation of some communities and under-

representation of other communities. The evil exists in its most aggravated form. For the over-representation is of communities which are strong and powerful, and the under-representation is of communities, which are weak and poor. The second comment relates to the wrong use of the power of nomination. The power of nomination was reserved under the Constitution to rectify the inequalities of representation. To put it in different language, it was intended to give these communities, which did not secure enough representation, by election, sufficient representation through nomination.

There is no principle, which seems to govern either the election or the nomination in so far as they relate to the composition of the central Legislature. If at all there is any principle, it is to give Peter more than Paul and then to rob Paul who has almost nothing to enrich Peter who has almost everything.

5. There is no justification for so grave a wrong done to the Scheduled Castes in the matter of representation. In a legislature in which the Muslims and the Hindus are waging a war against each other for rights and privileges and in which both are careful not to lose anything to a third party like the Scheduled Castes what support can a single representative of the Scheduled Caste in a House of 141 get in his right for the rights of the Scheduled Castes? It was the view of the Southborough Committee, on the recommendations of which the present structure of the Central Legislature is reared, that the nominated officials may be expected to bear in mind the interests of the Scheduled Castes. It is a matter of some considerable interest that the then Government of India refused to accept this view. In their Dispatch on the Report of the Southborough Committee, the Government of India said: "But that arrangement is not, in our opinion, what the (Montague-Chelmsford) Report on Reforms aims at. The authors slated that the Depressed Classes should also learn the lesson of self-protection. It is surely fanciful to hope that this result can be expected from including a single

member of the community in an assembly where there are 60 to 90 Caste Hindus. To make good the principles of paras 151, 152 and 155 of the Report we must treat the outcastes more generously......"

Unfortunately no generosity was shown by the Government of India to the Scheduled Castes in making its proposal for the composition of the Central Legislative Assembly. They gave them one seat by nomination, and it has continued to be one since 1921.

6. The result of this meagre representation has been quite deplorable. A single representative of the scheduled castes in an Assembly of 141 cannot but feel the utter helplessness of his position. He has to contend against a vast volume of anti-Scheduled Caste prejudices arising from the Hindu side of the House. He cannot depend upon the support either of the Muslim block who are fighting their battle to advance their interests. Nor can he depend upon the Official Block, which has been more careful to preserve its good relations with the major Hindu and Muslim blocks than to support the just interests of the Scheduled Castes. It is not even possible for the single and solitary representative of the Scheduled Castes in the assembly to ventilate the grievances of the Scheduled Castes. I am informed that under the rules made by the President of the Legislative Assembly, the President gives the first chance to speak to those Hon'ble members who belong to a recognised party. I also understand that the President does not recognise a party unless it has the minimum strength of ten members. This means that ordinarily the representative of the Scheduled Castes has no chance of speaking in the House unless he chooses to join a party. For a representative of the Scheduled Castes to be faced with this kind of situation is not a very happy tiling. To join a party means for him to subordinate the interests of the Scheduled Castes to that of a party, the principles and interests of which may be quite inconsistent with the principles and interests of the Scheduled Castes. On the other hand, not to join a party means to lose altogether the right to speak. If one

may refer to what happened in the Assembly session (September 1942) in the debate that took place on the present political situation in India, the Hon'ble Rao Baliadur N. Sivaraj, the representative of the Scheduled Castes in the Central Assembly, found it difficult to obtain a chance to speak on behalf of the Scheduled Castes, although 5 or 6 Muslim members could easily speak for the Muslims.

7. It is, therefore, greatly necessary that the representation of the Scheduled Castes in the Assembly should be augmented. Of course this can be done only when vacancies occur in nominated non-official seals. When they do occur, justice requires that such vacancies should go to increase the representation of the Scheduled Castes in the Assembly.

## Inadequate Representation in the Central Executive

8. The Government of India has been very tardy in recognising the right of the Scheduled Castes for representation in the Central Executive. This has been a very sure point with the Scheduled Castes. For thy hold that whatever may have been their political status in the past, since the Round Table Conference their political status had become equal to the status of that of the Muslims, and if the Muslims have a right to representation in the Central Executive, so have the Scheduled Castes. There is no doubt that their contention is well founded. At the Round Table Conference it was the demand of the Scheduled Castes, and not merely of the Muslims, that provision for the adequate representation of the Scheduled Castes should be made by law. The Hindu point of view was not opposed to this demand. All that the Hindus said was that it should be left to convention. Ultimately a compromise was arrived at and it was agreed that the instrument of Instructions to the Governors of the Provinces and the Governor-General of India should contain a specific clause imposing upon them the obligation to endeavour to include representatives of

important minority communities. Although the communities were not specified, there could be no doubt that the phrase "important minorities "was intended to include the Scheduled Castes. At long last the Government of India has recognised this obligation to give representation to the Scheduled Castes in the Cabinet.

9. It must, however, be said that this delay in the recognition of their right has lost much of its virtue by reason of the delay and has not removed this grievance. For the Scheduled Castes feel that their representation in the cabinet is very inadequate. In a Cabinet of 15, there is only 1 Member of the Scheduled Castes while the Muslims have 3 Members. The grievances arise by reason of the great contrast between the representation granted to the various communities and their needs and their numbers. If population alone was the criterion there is no doubt that the Scheduled Castes are very near to the Muslims in the matter of population. It is therefore only fair to say that if the Muslims have three, the Scheduled Castes should at least have two in a Cabinet of fifteen. As it is, the communal formation of the Cabinet seems to be governed by no principle. The Sikhs who number only millions and the Untouchables who number 40 millions are placed on the same fooling.

10. The position of the Scheduled Castes in Indian politics needs a great deal of stabilisation, and there can be no doubt that the only effective remedy of stabilising their position in Indian politics is to give them representation in the Cabinet which is demanded by their numbers and their needs. I am sure I am not disclosing any secrets when I say that in the course of the interview that I had with Sir Stafford Cripps when he came to India he told me that one of the principal objects of His Majesty's Government was to stabilise the position of the Scheduled Castes by their inclusion in the Central Executive which was to be formed during the interim period, so that the Constituent Assembly which under his proposals was to meet to draft the new constitution

will find their positions established beyond challenge. I request that this policy should be given effect to when the next step in the direction of the Indianisation of the Executive Council takes place.

## Absence of Representation in the Public Services'

11. No greater injustice has been done to the Scheduled Castes than in the matter of their employment in Public Services. Having regard to the scope of this Memorandum I can deal only with those Services with which the Central Government is particularly concerned. They fall into two classes:— (a) The I. C. S. (b) The Central Services— (i) Those recruited on an all-India basis, and (ii) those recruited locally.

12. Any one who examines the communal composition of these services can have no manner of doubt that the Scheduled Castes have been rigorously excluded from both these Services. To give an idea of the rigorous exclusion of the Scheduled Castes from these Services, I like to present the following facts. I will first lake the position as it stands in the Indian Civil Service. The communal composition of the I.C.S. as it stands at present (1942) is as follows:

***Communal Composition of the I.C.S.***

| Community | Number in the I.C.S. |
|---|---|
| 1. Europeans | 488 |
| 2. Hindus | 363 |
| 3. Muslims | 109 |
| 4. Indian Christians | 23 |
| 5. Anglo-Indians | 9 |
| 6. Parsis | 9 |
| 7. Sikhs | 11 |
| 8. Scheduled Castes | 1 |
| 9. Others | 43 |
| Total | 1056 |

Out of 1,056 men in the I.C.S. there is only I from the Scheduled Castes. Such is the slate of affairs so far as the I.C.S. is concerned. In the matter of their recruitment to the central services the condition of the Scheduled Castes is equally bad. I do not propose to quote any figures. It is quite unnecessary to overburden this Memorandum with facts. For there is a clear admission on the part of the Home Department of the Government of India relating to this question. In one of their Office Memoranda relating to the recruitment of the different communities the Home Department say:

"This Department are much concerned at the almost total lack of progress in the recruitment of the members of the Depressed Classes as revealed by the information available."

The Memorandum from which the above statement is quoted is No. 4/5/38 Ests(s) and is dated 1st June 1939 and records a state of affairs as it existed on that date.

13. How is it that other communities have found a place in the services controlled by the Government of India? What are the reasons for the exclusion of the Scheduled Castes? As will be seen the reasons are to be found in the difference in the principles and methods for securing communal representation which the Government of India has adopted towards the Scheduled Castes and the other minority communities in India.

14. The principle of communal representation in the services centrally controlled came into operation in 1925 when the Government of India accepted a Resolution of Mr. Nair on the need of Communal Representation in Public Services moved in the Central Assembly on 10th March 1923 in which he complained that the Public Service was entirely monopolised by the Hindus, and particularly by the Brahmins, and that the other communities had found it extremely difficult to secure a footing. In pursuance of this Resolution the method adopted by the Government of India was to reserve one-third of all permanent vacancies for direct recruitment for the redress' 'of 'communal inequalities.

15. This method of giving effect to the policy of Communal Representation in Public Services did not satisfy the non-Hindu communities. The matter was taken up at the Round Table Conference and a demand was made for devising a more effective method of gaining the object. This demand was accepted by the Secretary of State and by the Government of India and given effect to in Home Department Resolution No. F. 14-17-8-33 of 4th July 1934.

***Proportions Fixed by the Resolution of 4th July 1934***

| *Minorities* | *I.C.S. Central and Subordinate services Recruited on All India Basis.* | *Railways and Customs* | *Posts and Telegraphs* | *Appraising Department and preventive services* |
|---|---|---|---|---|
| Muslims | 25% | 25% | 25% | This service is excluded from the operation of the Resolution, apparently to reserve recruitment for Anglo-Indians only on the ground that the Service requires special qualifications. |
| Anglo-Indians | | 8% | 5% | |
| Indian Christians Sikhs Parsis | *81/3% | 6% | 31/2% | |

***Note:** Para 7 (iii) of the said Resolution says—If communities obtain less than their reserved percentage and duly qualified candidates are not available, the residue of 81/2% will be available for Muslims.

16. It is this resolution which is now in operation and constitutes the Magna Charta securing justice to all communities in the Public Services of the country. A reference to the provisions of this Resolution is very necessary. It will show why the other minority communities have been so well represented in the Public Services and why the Scheduled Castes have not been represented at all. The Resolution has two fundamental provisions and which, as compared with the old resolution of 1923, are quite new:

(1) It declares what communities are to be treated as minorities for the purposes of recruitment to Public Services.

(2) It defines a fixed proportion of annual vacancies, which are to be allotted to the communities declared as minorities.

17. These are the provisions laid down by the Resolution of 1934 for securing representation to the various communities. Coming to particulars the Resolution in the first place defines the following communities as minorities: (1) Muslims, (2) Anglo-Indians, (3) Indian Christians, (4) Sikhs, (5) Parsis.

In the second place, the Resolution fixes the following proportion of annual vacancies to be filled by members belonging to the above mentioned minorities.

18. What is the provision, which this resolution makes to safeguard the position of the Scheduled Castes? I give below the two relevant provisions of the Resolution. In paragraph 3 the Resolution states that:

"No useful purpose will be served by reserving for them (Depressed Classes) a definite percentage of vacancies out of the number available for Hindus as a whole, but they hope to ensure that duly qualified candidates from the Depressed Classes are not deprived of fair opportunities of appointment.

The way in which Government hoped to ensure to the Scheduled Castes a fair share of representation in the Public Services is specified in para 7 (1) (vi) of the Resolution, which reads as follows: "In order to secure fair representation for the Depressed Classes duly qualified members of these classes may be nominated to a Public Service even though recruitment to that service is being made by competition". A perusal of these proposals brings out two facts:

(i) The Resolution does not declare the Scheduled Castes to be a minority.

(ii) The Resolution does not allot to the Scheduled Castes any fixed proportion of the annual vacancies. It goes without saying that there is a striking contrast between the provisions made by the Government of India for securing the recruitment of the Scheduled Castes and for the other minor communities to the Public Services. This contrast can be expressed in one sentence. The recruitment of the other communities is owing to the Resolution, not left to be a matter of discretion. It has been made a matter of obligation. The recruiting authority must fill in vacancy by recruiting a person, belonging to the community for which the vacancy is reserved. The recruitment of the Scheduled Castes on the other hand has been made a mere matter of discretion. The recruiting authority may fill an unreserved vacancy by appointing a person from the Scheduled Castes.

19. It is owing to this difference between must and may that the Muslims and other communities have been so well represented in the Public Services and the Scheduled castes so completely excluded. No better result is possible so long as the Government of India leaves the matter of recruitment of the Scheduled Castes in public services to the discretion and goodwill of the appointing officers. These officers are either Europeans, Hindus or Muslims. The European is blissfully ignorant of the Scheduled Castes, and he has never made the protection of the interests of the Scheduled Castes his special concern. So long as his general authority is maintained he is prepared to follow the advice of his Hindu or Muslim subordinates. The Muslims are naturally striving to strengthen their own position. They are concerned to sec that as many vacancies as possible should go to the Muslims: at any rate all those, which are reserved, to them. The Hindus who had so far the monopoly in the public service and who never know how to share the good things of life with others want to keep the balance to themselves. With their self-interest combined with their age-old prejudices against the Scheduled Castes the Hindus will never be fair to them. It is a sheer delusion to leave to the discretion of such officers the question of the recruitment of the Scheduled Castes and to hope that the Scheduled

Castes will as a result of it secure a fair share of representation.

20. The question of entry into the Public Service is an important question for all minority communities. But to the Scheduled Castes it is a vital question, a question of life and death. There are many reasons why this must be so. In the first place, it is a question of opening up a career for young men from the Scheduled Castes. This is an aspect of the question which the Scheduled Castes, and even the Government of India, cannot ignore. Trade and Industry, as openings for a career, are all blocked to young men of the Scheduled Castes. It is only in Government service that they can find a career. While this is an important aspect, it is not the only aspect, which makes this question so vital. For there is another aspect which is calculated to invest it with such importance. That aspect relates to the effect which the bestowal of Government patronage has in encouraging the spread of education in a community. The case of the Hindu community is quite in point. The rapid progress, which the Hindu community has made, is of course very striking. But it is very seldom realised that the reason why education has taken such deep root in the Hindu society is entirely due to the assurance that education opens up a career by entry in Government service. Such assurance of career is absolutely necessary in the case of the Scheduled Castes who are so backward in education. There is a third argument far more weighty that the two which have been referred to above. It relates to the interest of the general population of the Scheduled Caste people as distinguished from the interests of the educated classes from the Scheduled Castes. This will be clear if it is realised how important public administration is from the point of view of public welfare. In the first place, power of administration now a days includes the power to legislate. No Statute in modem days is complete and exhaustive. Most allow the administration the statutory power to make rules to carry into effect the purposes of the Act. Secondly,

whether the law is beneficial or not depends upon how efficaciously and how justly it is carried out. Good administration is therefore far more important than good laws. Good laws may prove of no avail if the administration is bad. Administration is therefore a vital question for the Scheduled Castes who are more interested in good administration than in good laws. Is the present administration good administration? What do the Scheduled Castes think of the present day administration? There can be no doubt that the view universally held is that the whole administration is hostile, unjust, and perverse in its attitude towards the Scheduled Castes all over India. Indeed much of the suffering and harassment of the Scheduled Caste population arises from the fact that the discretion vested in public servants is in almost all cases exercised against the interests of the Scheduled Castes and with the object of keeping them down. This is as it must be given the mentality of the Hindu and Muslim officers, towards the Scheduled Castes. This will continue to be so as long as the personnel of the administration is drawn from classes who have been opposed to the Scheduled Castes and who believe in their suppression. There cannot be a more powerful argument than that of the advantage and welfare of the general population of the Scheduled Castes to show that the entry of the Scheduled Castes in the Public Service must be regarded as a most vital consideration.

21. Certain facts are beyond doubt. The source of mischief is evident. How vital is the service interest of the Scheduled Castes is also clear. How serious is the mischief done to this vital interest by the discrimination, which Government has in its resolution of 4th July, 1934 made against the Scheduled Castes as compared with the other communities nobody can dispute.

How disastrous have been the consequences to the Scheduled Castes will be apparent from the figures given in the following table relating to the communal composition to the I.C.S.

## *Communal Proportion in the I.C.S. in 1942*

| *Community* | *Total* | *Percentage of Total of 1056 including Europeans* | *Percentage of Total of 568 excluding Europeans* |
|---|---|---|---|
| 1. Europeans | 488 | 42.4 | |
| 2. Hindus | 363 | 34.4 | 63.2 |
| 3. Muslims | 109 | 10.3 | 19.2 |
| 4. Indian Christians | 23 | 2.2 | 4.0 |
| 5. Anglo-Indians | 9 | .9 | 1.5 |
| 6. Parsis | 9 | .9 | 1.5 |
| 7. Sikhs | 11 | 1.0 | 2.0 |
| 8. Scheduled Castes | 1 | Nil | Nil |
| 9. Others | 43 | 3.9 | 8.0 |
| **Total** | 1,056 | | |

## *I.C.S. through Competition and Nomination*

| *Community* | *Through Competition* | *Through Nomination* | *Total* |
|---|---|---|---|
| 1. Europeans | 336 | 152 | 488 |
| 2. Hindus | 332 | 31 | 363 |
| 3. Muslims | 35 | 74 | 109 |
| 4. Indian Christians | 19 | 4 | 23 |
| 5. Anglo Indians | 8 | 1 | 9 |
| 6. Parsis | 8 | 1 | 9 |
| 7. Sikhs | 5 | 6 | 11 |
| 8. Scheduled Castes | | 1 | 1 |
| 9. Others | 28 | 15 | 43 |

## *Population Ratio as Compared with Ratio in the I.C.S.*

| *Community* | *Actual Ratio in the I.C.S. excluding Europeans* | *Population Ratio* | *Excess + Deficiency of Service Ratio as compared With Population Ratio* |
|---|---|---|---|
| 1. Hindus | 63.2 | 50.0 | + 13.2 |
| 2. Muslims | 19.2 | 23.6 | - 4.4 |
| 3. Indian Christians | 4.0 | 1.0 | +3.0 |
| 4. Anglo-Indians | 1.5 | .03 | + 1.47 |
| 5. Parsis | 1.5 | 0.3 | + 1.47 |
| 6. Sikhs | 2.0 | 1.3 | + 0.7 |
| 7. Scheduled Castes | | 13.5 | - 13.5 |
| 8. Others | 8.0 | | |

22. From these tables the following conclusions stand out as incontrovertible facts:

(1) All communities have made a fair degree of progress towards getting their apportioned share of representation in the I.C.S. The only exception is the unfortunate community of the Scheduled Castes who have made no progress at all.

(2) Some communities have secured a degree of representation in the I.C.S. much in excess of their population ratio. This is noticeable in the case of the Hindus. Excluding the share of the Europeans which is 50% and which must be excluded for comparing the relative position of the Indians the Hindus have got 63% of the I.C.S. appointments when the ratio of their population to the total population is only 50%. They are enjoying an excess of 13%.

(3) Nomination was intended only to correct the inequities of competition. Yet some communities have been given the benefit of nomination although it has been able to secure a very large of the I.C.S. appointments by competition and who do not need and cannot claim the benefit of nomination. This is undoubtedly the case with the Hindus. Between 1920-1942 the Hindus were able to secure 332 out of 435 that were filled by Indians by competition, and yet they were given 31 seats by nomination. The Muslims got only 35 appointments to the I.C.S. by competition between 1920-1942. But they were given 74 by nomination. The Sikhs have got only 5 by competition. But they got 6 by nomination. The Scheduled Castes who got none by competition get only one by nomination. All this shows how the position of the Scheduled Castes has remained deplorable and how Government which is striving to be considerate to other communities by not even trying to be correct towards the Scheduled Castes, is responsible for this result. 23. The condition of the Scheduled Castes is not only deplorable, but it is also intolerable. This is the result of the present

policy of the Government of India under which the quantum of recruitment of the Scheduled Castes in the Public Services instead of fixed by rule as is done in the case of the other minorities is left to the discretion "Of the appointing authorities, The appointing authorities are mostly caste Hindus and it is not possible to expect them to give the benefit of this discretion to the Scheduled Castes. I have no doubt that the interests of the Scheduled Castes will continue to be neglected and sacrificed to serve the interests of other communities so long as the present system continues. The Government of India should without further delay equalise the position of the Scheduled Castes and:

(a) declare that they are a minority for the purpose of services like the other communities.

(b) fix 13 1/2% as the proportion of annual vacancies in the I.C.S. and both in the Central Services that are recruited on an all India basis and that are recruited locally as the share to which they are entitled and which in equity and justice should be reserved for them. Unless this is done the Scheduled Castes will never get their due share in Public Services.

24. The difficulty lies in the Scheduled Castes not being declared a minority. It is essential that this obstacle in their way be removed. The reason is that under the resolution of 4th July 1934 it is only when a community is declared to be a minority that it becomes entitled to the benefit of reservation in the Public Services. A community as such does not get any such benefit. It is difficult to see what objection there can be to a declaration that the Scheduled Castes are a minority. The term minority is a political term and whatever may be its *de jure* definition its de facto definition can never be in doubt. The matter is settled by the terms of Communal Award so that any community, which is covered by the Communal Award of His Majesty's

Government, must be held to be a minority. Indeed that is the basis on which the Government of India could declare that the Muslims, Sikhs, Indian Christians, and Anglo-Indians are minorities. If these communities are minorities and they are minorities because they are covered by the Communal Award—then it is difficult to see how the claim of the Scheduled Castes to be declared a Minority be denied. For they too are covered by the same Award. Secondly, if Government is bound to declare them a minority then it follows as a natural consequence that Government is bound to define their share in the services and make it available by the same means and methods by which the share of other communities has been secured to them. Nor can anybody oppose the quantum of share to which they are entitled as the legitimate share of the Scheduled Castes. It has been shown that their population in British India is 13.6% and nothing more than a share of 13.6% in the services is claimed for them. This cannot injure the Hindus, for their population is 50% and they are getting 63% which is 13% more than is their due.

25. The opposition to this claim of the Scheduled Castes comes from very strange and unexpected quarters. It should come from the Hindus. But it cannot. The mutual rights of the Scheduled Castes and the Hindus are defined by the Poona Pact, which was made in 1932. It Is an agreement by which the Hindus have accepted that the Scheduled Castes are a minority and that they are entitled to adequate share in the Public services of the Country. It is true that the term ‘ adequate ‘ was not given a quantitative expression. That is because it was done in a hurry to save Mr. Gandhi from the hands of death. But there can be no doubt that ‘ adequate ‘ was never intended to be anything less than the population ratio. The Hindus therefore cannot oppose the claim of the Scheduled Castes and, as a matter of fact, they do not. The party opposing the claim of the Scheduled Castes is the Government of India and nobody else. In the debate on the question that took place in

the Central Legislative Assembly on March 1942 on a cut motion by Rao Bahadur N. Sivaraj, M.L.A. the claim of the Scheduled Castes for being declared a minority and for defining their share in services which was the subject matter of the Motion was supported by the Muslims, by the Europeans, Anglo-Indians and Sikhs. Except for one solitary individual, the Hindus did not oppose it. It was, however, opposed by the spokesmen of the Government of India. This is the most tragic part of the story. The Government of India has said that they were trustees for the welfare of the Scheduled Castes. As trustees, they should be more ready to safeguard the rights of the Scheduled Castes than to safeguard the rights of the other minorities. There would have been some excuse for the Government of India hesitating to allot to the Scheduled Castes their rights in the matter of recruitment to the Public Services if there was any obstacle placed in their way by the Hindus. But there is no such excuse. Would it be wrong if it was said that the enemies of the Scheduled Castes are not the Hindus and that their real enemy is the Government of India?

26. What is the reason, which the Government of India gives for opposing the claim of the Scheduled Castes? So far as the speech of the Hon'ble the Home Member made on the motion moved by the Hon'ble Rao Bahadur N. Sivaraj M.L.A., is an indication, the reason is that there are not enough educated men among the Scheduled Castes. It must be said that this is by no means a convincing reason. In the first place, this is the old reason given in 1934 in paragraph 3 of the Resolution. It takes no account of the progress that has been made during the last 8 years. In the second place, the statement was not true even for 1934. For 1942 it will be gross misstatement. As a matter of fact a census of college students of the Scheduled Castes was taken privately in about 1939-40, and the total number of graduates among the Scheduled Castes were found to number about 400 to 500. In the third place, this fact even if it were true cannot be a bar against declaring

the Scheduled Castes a minority and against fixing their proportion. For if the Scheduled Castes candidates with minimum qualification fall short in any one year of the annual proportion of vacancies reserved for them no body will be hurt because the unused vacancies will go to the Hindus. The difficulty anticipated by the Home Member cannot be said to arise only in the case of the Scheduled Castes. The condition of other minorities is not free from giving rise to the same difficulty. In fact when the government issued the resolution in 1934 they felt that such a difficulty might arise in their case also. But this did not stop Government from declaring them to be minorities and fixing their proportion. Government did declare them to be minorities and also fixed their proportion, and for the difficulty that duly qualified candidates may in any given year be less than the vacancies reserved, Government provided by paragraph 7(1) (iii) of the resolution that the residue of the vacancies will be available for the Muslims.

27. Surely the difficulties which can be overcome successfully in the case of the other minorities cannot be followed to stand in the way of the Scheduled Castes. If Government does that, it will be guilty of unjustly-defeating the just claims of the Scheduled Castes. It will be accused of using grounds which are not reasons but which are only excuses for sustaining its opposition to the claims of the Scheduled Castes.

28. Besides the two remedies suggested, namely (1) declaring them a minority and (2) fixing their proportion in the annual vacancies, it will be necessary to sanction other remedies to the Scheduled Castes for securing to them their fair share in the services. They are:

(1) Raising the Age bar,

(2) Reduction in examination fees, and

(3) Appointment of a Scheduled Caste officer to sec that the provisions made in the interests of the Scheduled Castes in this behalf are carried by all Departments concerned.

## Raising the Age Bar

29. Under the present rules for the I. C. S. and the Central Services the maximum age limit is 24. Generally this maximum age limit hits the Scheduled Castes very hard. For owing to their extreme poverty it is not possible for the Scheduled Caste boy to reach that level of education, which will enable him to compete with students from higher and well-to-do classes within the age limit. The children of the former have to suffer many breaks in their educational career and have no facilities at home either for tuition or even for study. The latter have all the facilities for rapid and continuous progress. Consequently the children of the Scheduled Castes by the time they reach the final stage of their education and are in a position to compete they become ineligible on account of age for recruitment in the Public Service. It is therefore, necessary to raise the age limit by at least 3 years. There is nothing very unreasonable in this demand and there will be nothing extraordinary if it was conceded by Government of India. In almost all Provincial Governments where a proportion in the services has been reserved this concession has been made and the age limit for the Scheduled Castes has been fixed at a pitch higher than what is fixed for others. In some Provinces the difference is of 2 and in some provinces it is of 3 years. In granting this concession the Government of India will be following a well-established principle.

## Reduction in Examination Fees

30. The I.C.S. Examination fee is Rs. 100/-, the Examination fee for the Indian Audit and Accounts Service is Rs. 82/8/-, and for other Ministerial services Examination (Assistant's Grade) the fee is Rs. 30/-. These fees are too heavy for the Scheduled Castes. They are really and truly a great handicap. Many a Scheduled Caste student after having spent time and energy in qualifying for an examination finds it difficult to appear at it because the

fees for the examination are beyond the means of their parents. This handicap needs to be removed. It is urged that the Scheduled Caste candidates should not be charged more than one-fourth of the fees chargeable for these examinations.

31. These two concessions if allowed will go a long way to assist the community of Scheduled Castes to compete on more equal terms with its competitors. But the assistance rendered by these steps will not be adequate. Something further must be done. That is, to appoint a Scheduled Caste Officer in the Government of India either in the Home Department or Labour Department whose duty it will be to see that effect is given to the claims of the Scheduled Castes in the matter of their entry in the Public Services. It is understood that such officers were at one time appointed by the Government of India in order to see that the rules framed by Government in the matter of communal representation in services were strictly followed. But even if that be not the case the necessity and urgency of appointing a Scheduled Castes Officer for protecting the service claims of the Scheduled Castes is beyond question. There is a great danger of such rules being set at naught as a result of the prejudices prevailing against the Scheduled Castes unless there was an officer charged with the duty of dealing with such cases. The only remedy is to have an independent officer charged with the duty to see that the rules are earned out.

## Absence of Representation of the Federal Public Service Commission

32. There are four members who at present constitute the Federal Public Service Commission. Of these, two are Europeans, one is a Hindu and one is a Mohammedan. The Scheduled Castes have been left out in framing the composition of the Federal Public Service Commission. There is no ground why they should be denied representation on the Federal Public Service Commission. There are three main sections of the people

in India. Of these the Scheduled Wastes form the third main section. The population of this section is measured in millions. Their interest in the service question is quite as important as those of the other two main sections of the populations. The danger to their interests is no less real than to the interests of the other two sections. And the necessity of warding off that danger is much greater than it is in the case of the other two. Judged by any test it is difficult to justify the refusal to give representation to the Scheduled Castes from the Federal Public Service Commission. The Federal Public Service Commission has definitely been given communal character. There can be only two conceivable reasons for doing this. In the first place it may be because it is desirable to have representatives of large sections of the people on the Commission. The second reason one can conceive of for giving communal composition to the Commission is to set off the communal bias of one community by the communal bias of the other community. Whichever way one looks at it, the omission to give representation to the Scheduled Castes on the Federal Public Service Commission is sheer injustice. The Scheduled Castes cannot have any confidence in a Public Service Commission which is infected by the point of view of the Hindus and the Muslims who with all their quarrels can very easily unite to distribute the loaves and fishes among themselves and to keep out the Scheduled Castes from getting their due share. It is difficult to prove that the Commission has been unjust to the Scheduled Castes though the fact remains that not a single Scheduled Caste candidate has so far been certified by the Commission to be fit. For no Commission can be convicted of partiality. It is open to every Commission to take shelter under that most elusive term "unsuitable ". That term far from giving an explanation is intended to cover a multitude of sins. Justice requires that the Scheduled castes should get representation on the Federal Public Service Commission, which is their due.

## Educational Grievances

### *Want of Assistance for Advanced Education*

33. Looking at the growth of Advanced Education among the Scheduled Caste boys, the following conclusions are deducible:
    (1) That education in Arts and Law is progressing satisfactorily.
    (2) That education in Science and Engineering has made no progress.
    (3) That Advanced Education in foreign Universities is a very far cry.
34. This sad situation needs to be properly appreciated. As was said in discussing the question of the entry of the Scheduled Castes in the public services the welfare of the Scheduled Castes depends entirely upon a sympathetic public service and that the public service if it is to be sympathetic must be representative of the different elements in the national life of the country, and particularly of the Scheduled Castes. To this it must be added that the representation of the Scheduled Castes if it is confined to ministerial posts will be of no consequence no matter how numerous are the posts they are permitted to occupy. This may be good from the standpoint of providing a career for educated young men. It cannot affect the condition of the Scheduled Castes. The status and condition of the Scheduled Castes will be improved only when the representatives of the Scheduled Castes come to occupy executive posts as distinguished from ministerial posts. Executive posts are strategic posts, posts from which a new direction can be given to the affairs of the State. The attainment of executive post it is obvious requires a high degree of education. Such posts will not be open except to those who have acquired advanced education.
35. Education in Arts and Law cannot be of much value to the Scheduled Castes either to the graduates themselves or to the people. It has not been of very high value even to Hindus. What will help the Scheduled Castes is

education of an advanced type in Science and Technology. But it is obvious that education in Science and Technology is beyond the means of the Scheduled Castes and this is why so many of them send their children to take up courses in Arts and Law. Without Government assistance, the field of Advanced Education in Science and Technology will never become open to the Scheduled Castes, and it is only just and proper that the Central Government should come forward to aid them in this connection.

36. This problem will be solved if the following proposals are accepted by the Government of India:

    (1) An annual grant of Rs. 2 lakhs for scholarships for Scheduled Caste students taking science and Technology courses tenable at the Universities or other Scientific and Technical Training Institutions in India.

    (2) An annual grant of one lakh of rupees to be spent on scholarships for the education of Scheduled Caste students for Science and Technology in foreign Universities in England, the Dominions, in Europe and in America.

37. There is nothing to prevent the Government of India from undertaking this responsibility. Education it is true is not a Central subject for legislative purposes. Still, section 150 (2) of the Government of India Act says that the Central Government may make grants for any purpose, notwithstanding that the purpose is not one with respect to which the Central Legislature may make laws. This power has been used by the Government of India to support Educational Institutions. Below is given a list of Educational Institutions outside the centrally Administered Areas, which receive grants-in-aid from the central revenues.

38. This does not include the annual subvention which the Government of India gives of Rs. 3 lakhs per annum to the Muslim University of Aligarh and of Rs. 3 lakhs per annum to the Hindu University of Benares. The claim made on behalf of the Scheduled Castes for help in the matter of advanced education at home and abroad

receives great support from the financial aid given by Central Government to these two Universities. The grant made to the Universities is really grant made to the Hindu and Muslim communities for supporting higher education. That being so, there is no reason why the Central Government should not undertake to make a similar grant of 3 lakhs of rupees annually to promote higher education among the Scheduled Castes. If the Government is interested in raising the status of the Scheduled Castes, which they have often proclaimed to be their duty, it is high time that a similar provision was made for them in the education budget of the Central Government.

| | *I. Educational Institutions* | *Amount per annum* |
|---|---|---|
| 1 | Indian Women's University Bombay | Two non-recurring grants of Rs.50000 were made to this Institution in 1937-38 and 1941-42 |
| | | Rs. |
| 2 | Visva-Bharti Santiniketan | 25000 |
| 3 | Inter-University Board India | 1000 |
| 4 | Inter-Provincial Board for Anglo-Indian and European Education | 3600 |
| | *II. Scientific Societies* | |
| 1 | Indian Association for the Cultivation of Science, Calcutta. | 18000 |
| 2 | Royal Asiatic Society of Bengal, Calcutta | 2500 |
| 3 | Indian Statistical Institute, Calcutta | 37000 |
| 4 | National Institute of Science of India, Calcutta | 6000 |
| 5 | Vishvesharanand Vedic Research Institute, Simla | 2500 |
| 6 | Indian Institute of Science, Bangalore | 150000 |
| 7 | Bhandarkar Oriental Research Institute, Poona | 4000 |
| 8 | Bose Research Institute, Calcutta | 45000 |
| | *III. Miscellaneous* | |
| 1 | Indian Olympic Association | 2000 |
| 2 | Girl Guides Association, India | 2500 |
| | Total of annual Recurring Grants | 299100 |

39. The scheme if it is given effect to will revolutionise the condition and status of the Scheduled Castes. The Scheduled Castes lay great store by it. They would even be prepared for the scheme being made a loan system rather than a system of grants. The Scheduled Caste boys who receive these scholarships shall be glad to take advantage of it even if they are required to refund the sums received by them when they are employed or they may be made to serve the Government for a term under a lower scale of salary. There can be no objection to Government accepting these proposals.

40. For the purpose of assisting Advanced Scientific and Technical Education among the Scheduled Caste students I am making two other proposals. One is to make: Provision for Scheduled Caste students in the School of Mines.

    The Government of India has under its control the Indian School of Mines, which is located at Dhanbad. The school provides high-grade instructions in Mine Engineering and in Geology. The training given in the Indian School of Mines is calculated to train men who can serve in the coal mining industry and other mineral industries in India. The number of students that are at present taking instructions in the Indian School of Mines are about 97. The school is open to students from all parts of India. From enquiries made it is established that out of the 97 students there is not a single one from the Scheduled Castes. It is very necessary that some special measures should be taken by the Government of India to see that the students belonging to the Scheduled castes are in a position to take advantage of the Indian School of Mines. To achieve this object it will be necessary: (a) To reserve a certain number of seats for the Scheduled Caste boys having the minimum standard of education required for admission. (b) The grant of free-ships. (c) The grant of scholarships.

    It will not be too much to claim that one-tenth of the total number of admissions should be reserved for the Scheduled Castes. This is a matter, which falls within the scope of the Labour Department. But it is a question, which concerns also the Finance Department in as much as the free-ships, and scholarships would mean the loss of revenue to the State. But the loss on account of these measures will not be very great. The annual fee on an average, which a student has to incur in the School of Mines, be about 60 rupees a month which would mean a monthly expense of Rs. 60 per student.

41. The other proposal, which I wish to make, is to give: *Representation to the Scheduled Castes on the Central Advisory Board of Education.*

42. The constitution of the Board consists of:

(1) The Honourable Member in charge of the Department of Education, Health and Lands (Chairman);

(2) The Educational Commissioner with the Government of India;

(3) Ten nominees of the Government of India, of whom one at least shall be a woman;

(4) One member of the Council of State elected by the Council of State;

(5) Two members of the Legislative Assembly elected by the Legislative Assembly.

(6) Three members of the Inter-University Board, India, nominated by the Inter-University Board of India.

(7) A representative of each local Government, who shall be either the Minister in charge of Education (or his deputy) or the Director of Public Instruction (or his deputy) or such other person as the Provincial Government may nominate in this behalf.

43. The functions of the Board are: (a) To advise on any educational question which may be referred to it by the Government of India or by local Government. (b) To call for information and advice regarding educational developments of special interest and value to India; to examine this information and to circulate it with recommendations to the Government of India and to local Governments.

44. From the functions of the Board it is quite clear that the board can study the educational problem of the Scheduled Castes as that of special interest and frame recommendations and advice Central and Provincial Governments in that connection. Such a thing can be of immense importance in focusing the attention of the Governments and the Universities on the spread of higher education among the Scheduled Castes.

45. It is, however, necessary in the first place to get the Board interested in the educational problem of specie classes like the Scheduled Castes. This can be done only by giving representation to members of the Scheduled Castes on the Board. It is therefore suggested that two representatives of the Scheduled Castes should be nominated on the board.

## Want of Facilities for Technical Training Technical Education

46. From the point of raising the economic condition, technical education for the Scheduled Castes is more important than literary education. But technical education is also very costly and it is not possible for children of the Scheduled Castes to take technical education, and without technical education their economic condition will not be improved. Owing to the social system of the Hindus, the Scheduled Castes occupy economically a very low place in the Indian economy. In times of prosperity he is last to be employed, and in times of depression he is first to be discharged. This, of course, is a result of the social prejudices of the Hindus, which operate against him. But there is also the other difficulty, which stands in his way and that are he is generally an unskilled labourer with no technical knowledge.

47. It seems to me that the Government of India can do a great deal to improve his lot by enabling him to acquire technical skill which he does not now possess and this can be easily done by introducing a system of apprenticeship for the Scheduled Caste boys in

undertakings run or controlled by the Government of India, in which the possibilities of giving such technical training do exist. I am referring only to two:— (1) *Apprenticeships in Government Printing Presses:* There are a number of Printing Presses which are maintained by the Government of India. There are so many skilled occupations, which are open to persons trained in a printing press— compositors, printers, binders, etc. There is no reason why the Government of India should not have a scheme whereby suitable boys from the Scheduled Castes should be taken as apprentices to learn the various occupations, which are related to the printing trade. (2) *Apprenticeships in Railway Workshops:* The Railways in India, most of which are owned by the Government of India, also maintain workshops where fitters, carpenters and other technicians are employed, and I do not know whether the Railway Department have schemes of taking apprentices to be trained as technicians to be subsequently employed on the Railways. But even if such a scheme was not in existence it is necessary to have one for the benefit of the Scheduled Castes.

48. I therefore suggest the scheme of apprenticeship whereby annually a good number of boys from the Scheduled Castes should be given training in the printing press and the Railway Workshops. The cost of it cannot be very great.

## Neglect in the Matter of Publicity

47. It is quite well known that the Government of India engages itself very largely in giving publicity to the saying and doings of different individuals and parties who represent the main forces operating in India. As an illustration of this I would refer to the Volume called "India and the Aggressor "(The Trend of Indian Opinion Between 1935-40) issued by the Bureau of Public Information of the Government of India. The name of the Volume is very misleading. It has nothing to do with the Aggressor. It is a collection of sayings and doings of the Political Parties and Politicians in the

country and presents a full resume of the views of the majority and minority in India.

48. Now the most annoying part of this volume is the complete neglect of the sayings and doings of the Scheduled Castes. Out of the 940 pages, 158 pages are given to the Congress, 85 pages are allotted to the Muslims. The Hindu Mahasabha and the Hindu League are given about 10 pages. The Liberal Federation has received 16 pages. The Sikhs are spread over 6 pages, Indian Christians over 2 pages and the Scheduled Castes are disposed of in about 3 pages and what is surprising is that in these 3 pages devoted to the Scheduled Castes the material which is included is of a trifling character. It omits altogether to take notice of some of the most important events that have taken place during this period and important pronouncements made by leading individuals from the Scheduled Castes. I may mention only one such event *viz.*, the movement for conversion. Beyond question it was a movement which shook the Hindu Society to its very foundations and attracted the notice of the whole world. To emphasise the trumpery sort of publicity given to the Scheduled Castes in this volume it is enough to say that the St. Mary's College, Kurscong, once undertook to give publicity to the cause of the Scheduled Castes and has as a result published material covering the same period and which fills a Volume of 507 pages. So vast have been the forces and movements affecting and emanating from the Scheduled Castes during this period of 1935-40. As to myself, I must have made many pronouncements touching the Scheduled Castes. Not one of them however finds a place in this Volume.

49. It is true that this Volume is intended for official use only. But in my opinion this fact does not alter the great value, which the compilation must necessarily have. It goes without saying that it is the mind of the Official, which is, to a large degree, responsible for determining the direction, which the affairs of the State will take. It also determines the value, which he ought to give to issues in which communal interests are

involved. It also goes without saying that the attitude and the mind of the Official is bound to be determined by the kind of material which is presented to him and on which he feeds in a Volume like this. Further, the degree of publicity given to a cause by Government in a Government publication may be treated by him as the value which government attaches to it and as a direction for him for evaluating the needs and claims of different communities. Looked at from this point of view this Volume is sure to give to the Officers working in the Central Secretariat as well as in the Provincial Governments and even to the Secretary of State the impression that the Government of India regards the Scheduled Castes as a negligible force not worth bothering about. That this is the effect, which this volume has produced, is evident from the speech delivered in Parliament by the Secretary of State where the references to the Muslims are emphatic and positive while the references to the Scheduled Castes are just of a parenthetical character. It is a grievous wrong done to the Scheduled Castes whose cause has received a setback at a most critical period in their struggle by reason of this unbalanced presentation of their case on the part of Government. I would press that the Bureau of Public Information be asked to prepare a supplement to the Volume which it has issued giving full space to movements carried on by the Scheduled Castes and the pronouncements their leaders have made.

50. Of course, Government may say that it is not bound to do publicity work for parties and communities, and that the parties and communities may do their own publicity. But that is not the case here. The Government of India, as I have shown, does engage itself very much in this work of publicity. And when a Government does it, it is bound to treat all parties on equal footing in the matter of publicity and give a true and correct picture of the movements and forces operating in the country.

## Closed-door in Government Contracts

51. A Good part of Government needs in Public Works is

carried out not departmentally but by contracts. This is so in normal times. In war times the work done for Government by the contract system has expanded several hundred fold. I can speak only of the Central Public Works Department. The list of approved contractors maintained, by the Central Public Works Department is 1,171. Of these, I am told, there is only one contractor belonging to the Scheduled Castes. The rest of them are Hindus, Sikhs and Muslims. It should be possible for Government to arrange things in such a manner as to make its contract system allow an open door to members of all communities to profit by it. There are many persons of the Scheduled Castes who could be trusted to carry out a Government contract. Already many members of the scheduled castes are working as employees of Hindus, Muslim or Sikh contractors. The result is that the Hindu, Muslim or Sikh contractors are taking profit while the Scheduled Caste men are working on a mere wage.

52. There is not much difficulty in getting a certain number of men from the Scheduled Castes put on the list of approved contractors. But what is important is to enable them to get a contract. There are two rules in the matter of Government contracts:

(1) That a contract is to be given generally to a contractor whose tender is the lowest;

(2) That Government is not bound to accept the lowest tender.

53. It is therefore, a matter of discretion, which is exercised by the Officer in charge whether a contract will go to a particular contractor or not. This discretion is not likely to be exercised in favour of a Scheduled Caste contractor. His tender may be the lowest but owing to communal prejudice he may not accept it and rely on the second rule "that he is not bound to accept the lowest ". If his tender is higher than the lowest, he will not accept it although he is free to do so. He will rely on the first of the two rules. Either way he will have his justification for rejecting the tender of the Scheduled Caste contractors.

54. There is of course, no remedy against communal basis. The only thing that strikes me that we can do is to amend the rule by saying that a tender of a Scheduled Caste contractor, if it is not higher than the lowest by 5 per cent, shall be deemed to be the lowest. This, of course, involves financial loss and the Finance Department will have to agree to it. I cannot give any idea of the approximate cost of such a concession. I am sure it will not be heavy as to break the camel's back.

## Duty of Government towards Distressed People

55. Some of the proposals submitted in this Memorandum on behalf of the Scheduled Castes, particularly those, which are put forth to remove political grievances, do not involve any financial burden on the public treasury. They are really not proposals so much as political demands which, by reason of their logic and their justice. Government must grant. The difficulty arises only with regard to the acceptance of those proposals, which involve a financial burden upon the revenues of the Central Government. Financial burden there is. But, it will not do to reject them merely on that account. For there can be no doubt that Government has a duty towards the Scheduled Castes, and if they accept their duty in this behalf they are bound to discharge it even if it involves a certain amount of financial burden on the public purse.

56. The policy of the British Government towards the Scheduled Castes has been one of complete and continuous neglect. It began from the very beginning when the British Government realised that its duty was not merely to maintain law and order, and extended to giving the people education and looking after their welfare. This will be clear from the following quotations from *the report of the Board of Education of the Bombay Presidency for the year 1850-51:*— Inquiry as to Upper Classes of India "*Paragraph 16. It being then demonstrated that only a small section of the population can be brought under the influence of Government education in India, and the Honourable Court having*

> *in effect decided that this section should consist of the ' upper classes ', it is essential* to *ascertain whom these latter consist of.*

## Upper Classes in India

*"Paragraph 17. The classes "who may be deemed to be influential and in so far the upper classes in India, may be ranked as follows:— 1st.—The landowners and jagirdars, representative of the former feudatories and persons in authorities under Native powers and who may be termed the Soldier class.*

2nd.—Those who have acquired wealth in trade or commerce or the commercial class. 3rd.—The higher employees of Government. 4th.—Brahmins with whom may be associated, though at long interval, those of higher castes of writers who live by the pen and as Parbhus and Seenvies in Bombay, Kayasthas in Bengal, provided they acquire a position either in learning or station.

## Brahmins the Most Influential

> *"Paragraph 18. Of these four classes incomparably the most influential, the most numerous and on the whole easiest to be worked on by the Government, are the latter. It is a well recognised fact throughout India that the ancient Jagirdars or soldier class is daily deteriorating under our rule.*
>
> *Nor among the commercial classes, with a few exceptions, is their much greater opening for the influences of superior education.*

Lastly the employees of the State, though they possess a great influence over the large numbers who come in contact with Government, have no influence, whatever, with the still larger numbers who are independent of Government;

## Poverty of Brahmins

*Paragraph 19. The above analysis, though it may appear lengthy is nevertheless, indispensable, for certain important conclusions deducible from it. First, it demonstrates that the influential class whom the Government is able to avail themselves of in diffusing the seeds of education are the Brahmins and other high castes Brahmans proximi.*

## Question as to Educating Low Castes

*"Paragraph 21. The practical conclusion to be drawn from these facts which years of experience have forced upon our notice, is that a very wide door should be opened to the children of the poor higher castes, who are willing to receive education at our hands. But here, again, another embarrassing question arises, which it is right to notice. If the children of the poor are admitted freely to Government Institutions what is there to prevent all the despised castes—the Dheds, Mahars, etc., from flocking in numbers to their walls?*

## Social Prejudices of the Hindus

*"Paragraph 22. There is little doubt that if a class of these latter were to reformed in Bombay they might be trained, under the guiding influence of such Professors and masters as are in the service of the Board, into men of superior intelligence to any in the community: and with such qualifications, as they would then possess, there would be nothing to prevent their aspiring to the highest offices open to Native talent—to Judgeships, the Grand Jury, Her Majesty's Commission of the Peace. Many benevolent men think it is the height of illiberality and weakness in the British Government to succumb to the prejudices which such appointments would excite into disgust amongst the Hindu community, and that an open attack should be made upon the barriers of caste.*

## Wise Observations of the Honourable Mount Stuart Elphinstone Cited

*"Paragraph 23. But herewith wise reflections of Mr. Elephinstone, the most liberal and large-minded administrator who has appeared this side of India, point out the true rule of action. ' It is observed, ' he says, ' that the missionaries find the lowest caste the best pupils; but we must be careful how we offer any special encouragement to men of that description; they are not only the most despised, but among the least numerous of the great divisions of society and it is to be feared that if our*

*system of education first took root among them, it would never spread further, and we might find ourselves at the head of a new class, superior to the rest in useful knowledge, but hated and despised by the castes to whom these new attainments would always induce us to prefer them. Such a state of things would be desirable, if we were contented to rest our power on our army or on the attachment of a part of the population but is inconsistent with every attempt to found it on a more extended basis!*

57. Such is the antagonism towards the Schedule Castes with, which began Government's policy of giving education to Indians. This policy was firmly applied. There is a case on record of a Mahar (Untouchable) boy who in 1856 petitioned to the Government of India for being admitted to a Government school in the Dharwar District. The following is the text of the resolution issued by the Government. *"The question discussed in the correspondence is one of very great practical difficulty."*

"1. There can be no doubt that the Mahar petitioner has abstract justice in his side; and Government trust that the prejudices which at present prevent him from availing himself of existing means of education in Dharwar may be ere long removed."

"2. But Government are obliged to keep in mind that to interfere prejudices of ages a summary manner, for the sake of one or few individuals, would probably do a great damage to the cause of education. The disadvantage under-which the petitioner labours is not one-which has originated-with this Government, and it is one which Government cannot summarily remove by interfering in his favour as he begs them to do."

58. In 1882 Government of India appointed the Hunter Commission to examine the Educational Policy. This Commission made a number of important proposals to spread education among Muslims. With regard to the Untouchables it did nothing. All that it did was to express an opinion that "Government should accept the principle that nobody be refused admission to Government College or School merely on the ground of

caste, "but qualified it by saying that the principle should "be applied with due caution!".

59. This antagonism when it passed away, its place was taken up by negligence and indifference. This negligence and indifference made its appearance not merely in the field of education. It also made its appearance in other fields, particularly in the Army. The whole Army of the East India Company consisted of the Depressed Classes. Indeed but for the Depressed Classes Army the British would never have been able to conquer India. The Untouchables continued to fill the Army till 1892. In 1892 their recruitment in the army was stopped all of a sudden and they were thrown in the street in utter distress with no education and no means to pursue other ways of honourable living.

60. Who can raise the Scheduled Castes from the distress in which they are now grovelling? It is certain they cannot do it by their own effort. Their resources are too scanty to afford them the means to raise themselves. They cannot depend upon the charity of the Hindus. The charity of the Hindus is beyond question communal in its scope and its benefits are confined to those who belong to the community of the donor. The Hindu donors are either businessmen or high State officials. The tragedy is that they make their money out of the general public. But when it comes to a question of doing charity they forget the public and remember their own castand their community. The Scheduled Castes have neither of these sources available to them and they are rigorously excluded from the charity founded by both. The only source therefore on which they can rely is financial aid from Government. I venture to say that it is the duty of the Central Government to come to the rescue of people who are in distress by no fault of theirs as is the case with the Scheduled Castes. The Central Government is bound to take steps to assist the Scheduled Castes to concede their just claims and to compete on more equal terms with their competitors. There is nothing extraordinary in asking the Central Government to pay special attention to improve the

condition of the Scheduled Castes. Let those who may think so consider the measures the Government of India has adopted for securing the welfare of the Anglo-Indian community. I will mention only a few of them.

(1) *Higher Salaries:* There was a time when the Anglo-Indian received a higher salary than the Indian. The extent of difference in the salary of the Anglo-Indian and the Indian will be obvious from the following table which gives figures for salaries on three Railways for a few posts selected at random for the sake of illustration:

| *Designation* | *Anglo-Indians* | *Indians* |
|---|---|---|
| North Western Railway | 625-25-675 | 475-25-500 |
| Permanent Way-Inspector | 550-25-600 | 400-25-450 |
| Drivers | 260-10-280 | Re. 1 to Rs. 1/14/a day |
| | | Special rate Rs. 2 a day |
| E. I. Railway | | |
| Train Examiners | 300-25-400 | 120-15-180 |
| | 200-20-280 | |
| G.P.I. Railway | | |
| Head Train Examiners | 275 | 125-275 |
| | 315 | |
| | 365 | |
| Washing Chargemen | 145 | 115 |

This difference in salary continued upto 1920. Thereafter it was abolished. One difference still remains and that is the Anglo-Indian gets a basic pay of Rs. 55 per month. He gets this even if he is employed as a peon in a State Railway, while an Indian chaprasi gets only Rs. 13-15. The cost of this favoured treatment to the Anglo-Indians which the Indian Exchequer has to bear annually is Rs. 10,000 in the Posts and Telegraph Department, Rs. 75,000 to the State Managed Railways and Rs. 75,000 to Company Managed Railways, in all Rs. 1,50,000.

(2) The reduction in the pass marks for the examination in the telegraph department from 50 per cent to 40 per cent in each subject and from 66 per cent to 60

per cent in the aggregate especially made to enable Anglo-Indians to compete successfully.

61. There are many other recommendations made by the Stewart Committee on the Anglo-Indians intended to give them special advantages over Indians. But I do not wish to burden this memorandum with them. I am only interested in showing the marked contrast between the treatment accorded to the Anglo-Indians and the Scheduled Castes. The care of the former and the neglect of the latter stand out in a marked contrast. What is it that can justify this contrast? In my opinion nothing, and the sooner the Central Government proceeds to assist the Scheduled Castes the better the Government will rank as a Government based on justice. A Government, which cheerfully bears the cost of Rs. 1,50,000 annually for the uplift of the Anglo-Indians, can, if it has the will, spend a few lakhs on the Scheduled Castes.

## The Untouchables and the Pax Britannica

Of the American Continent the objective of his voyage was reach India. Even this voyage of Columbus neglect of the Depressed Classes by the British Government which did not admit them as members of the Armed Forces. The manuscript, of which the first page is missing, was prepared by Dr. was not a sudden venture. It was a part of a plan of exploration of a sea route to India which he had received its first impetus from Prince Henry of Portugal, who was greatly interested in it and who in his reign of 42 years (1418—1460) helped it in every possible way.

What was the necessity for this quest for a direct sea route from Europe to India which impelled the Portuguese, the Dutch, the French and the English to come out of their seclusion. The coming of the English to India was not an adventure of a singular race. It was a concerted effort and there was so much eagerness on the part of each European nation that within this concert there was a competition for reaching India first. Because the Portuguese came first it does not follow that the rest were idle or indifferent. The English and the Dutch were under the belief that there was a shorter route to India than that of the

Cape of Good Hope and their delay in their coming to India was due to the fact that they were busy in finding out its possibilities. The French, though last to arrive, were second only to the Portuguese, their first voyage being to Sumatra in 1529.

What was the origin of this eagerness to reach the Indies? Why did the Portuguese, Spaniards, English, French and Dutch vie with one another in centuries of strenuous effort to find a sea route to India? The object was to obtain luxuries and particularly spices— chillies, cloves, nutings etc., which could be had only from India and the East. This seems rather strange— that all this run should be for spices. But the fact is that spices did play a very important part in this expansion of Europe.

How much spices were used and appreciated by the European peoples in the fifteenth and sixteenth centuries can be, seen, from the following data collected by Prof. Cheyney: "One of the chief luxuries of the Middle Ages was the edible spices. Wines and ale were constantly used spiced with various condiments. In Sir Thopa's forest grew *"notemuge to putte in ale"*. "Froissart has the king's guests led to the" palace, where wine and spices were set before them ". The dowry of a Marseilles girl, in 1224, makes mention of" mace, ginger, cardamom and galingale." "When John Ball wished to draw a contrast between the lot of the lords and the peasants, he said, "They have wines, spices and fine bread, when we have only rye and the refuse of the straw,". When old Latiner was being bound to the stake he handed nutmegs to his friends as keepsakes.

"Pepper, the most common and at the same time the most valued of these spices, was frequently treated as a gift of payment instead of money. "Matilda de Chaucer is in the gift of the king, and her land is worth'8s. 2*d.*, and I pound of pepper and I pound of cinnamon and I ounce of silk ", reads a chance record in an old English survey. The amount of these spices demanded and consumed was astonishing. Venetian galleys Genoese varracks, and other vessels of the Mediterranean brought many a cargo of them westward, and they were sold in fairs and markets every where. "Pepper-sack" was a derisive and yet not unappreciative epithet applied by German robber-barons to the merchants, who they plundered as they passed down the Rhine. For years the Venetians had a contract to buy from the Sultan of Egypt annually 420,000 pounds of pepper. One of the first vessels to make its way to India brought home 210,000 pounds. A fine of 200,000 pounds of pepper was imposed upon one petty prince of India by the Portuguese in 1520. In romances and chronicles, in cookbooks, trades-lists, and customs-tariffs spices are mentioned with a frequency and consideration known in modem times."

Why were spices so necessary to the European peoples of those days? One answer is taste. "The monotonous diet, the coarse food, the unskilful cookery of mediaeval Europe had all their deficiencies covered by a charitable mantle of Oriental seasoning." While it was a matter of taste for all it was a matter of necessity for the poor. The poor needed spices. In ancient I times when food was scarce and the productivity of man in the absence of machinery was very low; man could not afford to waste or throw away food as being stale. Whatever was left over or was not necessary for immediate consumption had to be preserved. Spices are the best preservatives. It was because of this as also for reasons of taste that spices were in mediaeval Europe in such universal demand.

Another question is why was a direct sea route necessary for these European nations to reach India and to obtain spices. Before the European nations discovered the sea route to India via the Cape of Good Hope there were in existence three well established land routes by which these luxuries and spices used to reach Europe and known as the Northern, the Middle and the Southern routes.

The Northern route lay between the Far East and the West, extending from the inland provinces of China westward across the great desert of Gobi, south of the Celestial mountains to Lake Lop then passing through a series of ancient cities, Khotan, Yarkand, Kashgar, Samaro and Bokhara, till it finally reached the region of the Caspian Sea. This main northern route was joined by others which crossed the passes of the Himalayas and the Hindookush, and brought into a United Stream, the products of India and China. A journey of eighty to a hundred days over desert, mountain, and steppes lay by this route between the Chinese wall and the Caspian. From still farther north in China a parallel road to this passed to the north of the desert and the mountains and by way of Lake

Balkash, to the same ancient and populous land lying to the east of the Caspian Sea.

Here the caravan routes again divided. Some led to the south-westward, where they united with the more central routes described above and eventually reached the Black Sea and the Mediterranean through Asia Minor and Syria. Others passed by land around the northern coast of the Caspian, or crossed it, reaching a further stage at Astrakhan. From Astrakhan the way led on by the Volga and on rivers, till its terminus was at last reached on the Black Sea at Tana near the mouth of the Don, or at Kaffa in the Crimea.

The Middle route lay through Mesopotamia and Syria to the Levant. Ships from India crept along the Asiatic shore to the Persian Gulf, and sold their costly freights in the marts of Chaldea or the lower Euphrates. A line of trading cities extending along its shores from Ormuz near the mouth of the gulf to Bassorah at its head served as ports of call for the vessels which carried this merchandise. Several of these coast cities were also termini of caravan routes entering them from eastward, forming a network which united the various provinces of Persia and reached through the passes of Afghanistan into northern India.

From the head of the Persian Gulf one branch of this route went up the line of the Tigris to Baghdad. From this point goods were taken by caravan through Kurdistan to Tabriz, the great northern capital of Persia, and thence westward either to the Black Sea or to Layas on the Mediterranean. Another branch was followed by the trains of camels which made their way from Bassorah along the tracks through the desert which spread like fan to the westward, till they reached the Syrian cities of Aleppo, Antioch, and Damascus. They finally reached the Mediterranean coast at Laodicea, Tripoli, Beirut, or Jaffa, while some goods were carried even as far south as Alexandria. The southern route was a sea route in all except its very latest stages. It lay through the Red Sea and brought the products of India and the Far East by sea to Egypt, whence they passed to Europe from the mouths of the Nile.

The land routes were devious and dangerous. They were insecure and transportation over them was difficult and expensive. Robbers plundered the merchants and Governments taxed them beyond measure. Of the two land routes the Northern was not a highway to the same extent as the middle one was. With its deadly camel journey of alternate shows and torrid wastes, rendered it available only for articles of small bulk. It never attained the importance of the Middle route. Even this Middle or Indo-Syrian route was not always open. It was blocked twice. Once between 632—651 A. D. when the Saracen Arabs under the conquering impulse of Islam seized the countries of this Indo-Syrian route. For a second time it was blocked during the crusades in the 11th Century. The southern route which was for most part a sea route was equally unsafe. "The storms of the Indian Ocean and its adjacent waters were destructive to vast numbers of the frail vessels of the East; piracy vied with storms in its destructiveness; and port dues were still higher than those of inland marts." But as Prof. Cheyney observed, "With all these impediments. Eastern products, nevertheless, arrived at the Mediterranean in considerable quantities" and were available to the European merchants.

When these land routes existed why did there arise the necessity for a sea route? The answer is the Turkish and Mongol upheaval in further Asia which overtherw the Saracenic culture and ruined the trade with Europe. This upheaval was a new force. It first came into operation when about 1038 the selfwill Turks burst upon Persia. Two centuries later the Mongols poured over Asia under Chengizkhan. In 1258, the Mongols captured Baghdad. In 1403 Timur captured Syria. In 1453 Constantinople fell to the Turks. This upheaval of the Turks and the Mongols completely blocked the two land routes. The Southern route was the only route that was open for some time. But even that was blocked when Egypt was conquered by the Turks in 1516.

Two factors are responsible for bringing the European Nations to India. First spices. Second the blockade of the old overland Trade routes by the Turks and the Mongols. It is these factors which drove the European nations to search for a sea route to India and which they ultimately found. Having come to trade with the East Indies, these Europeans remained there to conquer it. That evidently resulted in a struggle for supremacy. The struggle between the English and the Portuguese and the Dutch on the other band was for commercial supremacy. The theatre of the struggle between the English and the Portuguese was India and the Persian Gulf and ended in favour of the British in 1612, so far as India was concerned and in 1622 so far as the Persian Gulf was concerned. From 1622 India and the Persian Gulf lay open to England and the Portuguese ceased to be any menace to development of English trade and commerce. The theatre of the struggle between the English and the Dutch lay in Malaya Archipelego. It was decided against the English in 1823 by what is called the Mascaere of Amboyana whereby the English receded to India and left the Dutch to enjoy exclusively the trade with the Malaya Archipelego.

The struggle between the English and the French was a mighty I struggle. The theatre of this struggle was India proper. The object of this struggle was political sovereignty and not commerce. The French had established themselves in the South and the East. So far as Southern India is concerned the conflict began in 1744 and ended in 1760 at the battle of Wandiwash where the French were completely vanquished. So far as Eastern India is concerned the struggle was a single battle in 1757 — the battle of Plassey in which French lost along with the Nawab whom they supported as against the English. With the elimination of the French, the English alone were left to be the rulers of India.

*But how was the conquest of India received by the people of India?*

From a certain point of view the conquest of India by the British was an accident. As an accident it has come to be regarded as a part of destiny. In this sense Lord Curzon was justified when he said:

What have they done for the people of India? This is too large a question. Many volumes having been written on it, is unnecessary for me to add to what has already been said. I am reducing the question to a narrow compass and ask what have the British done for the Untouchables? What did the British do when they became rulers to emancipate and elevate the Untouchables? There are many heads in relation to which this question may be raised. But I propose to it Public Service, Education and Social Reform.

What did the British Government do to secure to the Untouchables adequate representation in the Public Services of the Country? I will take the Army first To understand and appreciate the fate that has befallen the Untouchables it is necessary to ask what is it that enabled the British to conquer India? The conquest of India is an extraordinary event. And this is for two reasons.

The countries which were suddenly thrown open to the European nations at the end of the fifteenth century fall into three classes. Vasco Da Gama threw open countries in which for the most part thickly populated and which were governed by ancient, extensive and well organised states existed. In the second category fell countries discovered by Columbus in which the population was small and the state was of a very rudimentary character. The third category consisted of countries discovered by. They were just empty areas with no population at all. India fell in the first of these three categories. This is one reason why the conquest of India must be said to be an extraordinary event.

The second reason why the conquest of India is an extraordinary event is the period during which this conquest has taken place. When was India conquered? India was conquered between 1757 and 1818.

In the year 1757 there was fought a battle between the forces of the East India Company and the Army of Siraj-ud-Daulah, the Nawab of Bengal. The British forces were victorious. It is known in history as the battle of Plassey and it is as a result of this battle that the British for the first time made territorial conquest in India. The last battle which completed the territorial conquest was fought in 1818. It is known as the battle of Koregaon. This was the battle which destroyed the Maratha Empire and established in its place the British Empire in India.

Thus the Conquest of India by the British took place during 1757 and 1818. What was the state of affairs in Europe during this very period and what was the position of the English people? This period was one of great turmoil in Europe. It was a period of Napoleonicwars the last of which was fought in 1815 at Waterloo. In these wars England was no idle spectator. It was deeply involved in these wars. It was at the head of all the European States which had formed an alliance to crush Napoleon and the French Revolution. In this grim struggle the English nation wanted every penny, every man, every ship and every gun for its own safety. If could spare nothing for the East India Company which was operating in a theatre far removed from the home base. Not only could they spare nothing to help the East India Company but they actually borrowed men, money and ships from the East India Company to fight Napolean in the European War thereat. The following date from Macpherson gives an idea as to how much the East India Company had to contribute to the English nation for the support of the wars in Europe.

It is during this period when the English people were wholly occupied in Europe in a deadly struggle with Napoleon and when they could not assist the East India Company in any way that India was conquered. It is this which makes the conquest such an extraordinary event. How did this extraordinary event become possible? What is the explanation?

Macaulay has given his explanation. He says:

*Macaulay's explanation is the explanation which all Englishmen believe, like to believe. Being current for a long time it has got a hold upon the minds of the English people and all European and American people. Indeed an endeavour is made to inculcate this view upon the minds of the younger generation of English people. It is quite understandable. An important element in the make up of an imperial race is the superiority complex and Macaulay's view goes to foster it as nothing else can.*

But is Macaulay's view right? Do the facts of history support that view? Professor Seely who has studied this subject in a more realistic way than Macaulay did say:

"In the early battles of the Company by which its power was decisively established, at the siege of Arcot, at Plassey, at Buxer, there seem almost always to have been more sepoys than Europeans on the side of the Company. And let us observe further that we do not hear of the sepoys as fighting ill, or of the English as bearing the whole brunt of the conflict. No one who has remarked the childish eagerness with which historians indulge their national vanity, will be surprised to find that our English writers in describing these battles seem unable to discern the sepoys. Read Macaulay's Essay on Clive; everywhere it is ' the imperial people,' ' the mighty children of the sea,' ' none could resist Clive and his Englishmen.' But if once it is admitted that the sepoys always outnumbered the English, and that they kept pace with the English in efficiency as soldiers, the whole theory which attributes our successes to an immeasurable natural superiority in valour falls to the ground. In those battles in which our troops were to the enemy as one to ten, it will appear that if we may say that one Englishman showed himself equal to ten natives, we may also say that one sepoy did the same. It follows that, though no doubt there was a difference it was not so much a difference of race as a difference of discipline, of military science, and also no doubt in many cases on difference of leadership.

Observe that Mill's summary explanation of the conquest of India says nothing of any natural superiority on the part of the English.' The two important discoveries for conquering India were; 1st the weakness of the native armies against European discipline, secondly the facility of imparting that discipline to natives in the European service '. He adds; ' Both discoveries were made by the French.' And even if we should admit that the English fought better than the sepoys, and took more than their share in those achievements which both performed in common, it remains entirely incorrect to speak of the English nation as having conquered the nations of India. The nations of India have been conquered by an army of which on the average about a fifth part was English. But we do not only exaggerate our own share in the achievement; we at the same time entirely misconceive and misdescribe the achievement itself. From what race were the other four-fifths of the I Army drawn? From the Natives of India themselves! India can I hardly be said to have been conquered at all by foreigners; She has rather I conquered herself."

This explanation of Prof. Seely is correct as far as it goes. But it is not going far enough. India was conquered by the British with the help of an Army composed of Indians. It is well for Indians as well as for the British not to overlook this fact.

But who were these Indians who joined the army of their foreigners? That question Prof. Seely did not raise. But it is a very pertinent question. Who were these people who joined the army of the East India Company and helped the British to conquer India? The answer that I can give—and it is based on a good deal of study— is that the people who joined the Army of the East India Company were the Untouchables of India.

The men who fought with Clive in the battle of Plassey were the Dusads, and the Dusads are Untouchables. The men who fought in the battle of Koregaon were the Mahars, and the Mahars are Untouchables. Thus in the first battle and the last battle it was the Untouchables who fought on the side of the British and helped them to conquer India. The truth of this was admitted by the Marquess of Tweedledale in his note to the Peel Commission which was appointed in 1859 to report on the reorganisation of the Indian Army.

There are many who look upon this conduct of the Untouchables in joining the British as an act of gross treason. Treason or no treason, this act of the Untouchables was quite natural. History abounds with illustrations showing how one section of people in a Country have shown sympathy with an invader, in the hope that the new comer will release them from the oppressions of their countrymen. Let those who blame the Untouchables read the following manifesto issued by the English Labouring Classes in 17 (Left incomplete).

Was the attitude of the Untouchables in any way singular? After all, the tyranny under which the English Labourer lived was nothing as compared with the tyranny under which the Untouchables lived and if the English workmen had one ground to welcome a foreign invader the Untouchable had one hundred.

Not only did the Untouchables enabled the British to conquer India, they enabled the British to retain. The Mutiny of 1857 was an attempt to destroy British Rule in India. It was an attempt to drive out the English and reconquer India. So far as the Army was concerned the Mutiny was headed by the Bengal Army. The Bombay Army and the Madras Army remained loyal and it was with their help that the Mutiny was suppressed. What was the composition of the Bombay Army and the Madras Army? They were mostly drawn from the Untouchables, the Mahars in Bombay and the Pariahs in Madras. It is therefore true to say that the Untouchables not only helped the British to conquer India they helped them to retain India.

How have the British treated the Untouchables so far as service in the Army is concerned? Strange as it may appear, the answer is that the British Government has since about 1890 placed a ban on the recruitment of the Untouchables in the Indian Army. The result was that, those who had already been recruited remained. It is a great mercy that they were not disbanded. But in course of time they died or went on pension and ultimately by about 1910 completely disappeared from the Army. Nothing can be more ungrateful than this exclusion of the Untouchables from the Army.

Why did the British commit an act which appears to be an act of treachery and bad faith? No reason has ever been given by the British Government for this ban on the recruitment of the Untouchables into the Army. It is often heard that this exclusion is not intentional but is the consequence of a policy initiated in the interest of the efficiency of the Army in about the year 1890. But is this so?

This policy is based on two principles, one relating to Organisation and the other relating to recruiting.

The principle of Organisation that was introduced in 1890 is known as the principle of class composition as against the old principle of a mixed regiment. Under the new principle, the Indian Army was organized on the principle of class regiment or the class squadron or company system. This means, in the first case, that the whole regiment is composed of one class (or caste) and in the second case, that every squadron or company is formed entirely of one class. The old principle of recruiting was to take the best men available, no matter what his race or religion was. Under the new principle, race of the man became a more important factor than his physique or his intellect. For the purposes of recruitment, the different castes and communities of India are divided into categories, those belonging to the martial races and those belonging to the non-material races. The non-martial races are excluded from military service. Only the castes and communities which are included in the category of martial races are drawn upon for feeding the Army.

It is difficult to approve of these two principles. The reasons which underlie the principle of class composition it is said, "are to a certain extent political, as tending to prevent any such formidable coalition" against the British, as occurred in the Mutiny. I should have thought that the old system of a mixed regiment was safer. But assuming that the principle is sound, why should it come in the way of the recruitment of the untouchables? If, under the system of class composition, there can be regiments of Sikhs, Dogras, Gurkhas, Rajputs etc., why can there not be regiment of Untouchables? Again, assuming that recruitment from martial races only is in sound principle, why should it affect adversely (to) the untouchables unless they are to be treated as belonging to the non-martial races? And what justification is there for classing the untouchables who formed the backbone of the Indian Army and who were the mainstay of the Indian fighting forces for over 150 years as non-martial? That the British Government does not deem the Untouchables as belonging to non-martial classes is proved by the fact, that in the Great War, when more men were necessary for the Army, this ban on the recruitment of the Untouchables in the Army was lifted and one full battalion was raised and was known as the 111 Mahars.

With this testimony who can say that the Untouchables are anon-martial race?

It is thus obvious that none of the two reasons supposed to be responsible for the exclusion of the Untouchables from the Army. What is then the real reason? In my opinion, the real reason for the exclusion of Untouchables from the Army is their Untouchability. Untouchables were welcome in the Army so long as their entry did not create a problem. It was no problem in the early part of the British history, because the touchable were out of British Army. They continued to be outside the British Army so long as there were Indian Rulers. When, after the Indian Mutiny, the Race of Indian rulers shrivelled, the Hindus began to enter the British Army which was already filled with the Untouchables; then arose a problem—a problem of adjusting the relative position of the two groups—

touchables and untouchables—and the "British, who always, in cases of conflict between justice and convenience, prefer convenience, solved the problem by just turning out the Untouchables and without allowing any sense of gratitude to come in their way.

Whatever the reasons of this' exclusion, whatever the justice of this exclusion, the fact remains that the effect of this exclusion has proved most disastrous in its social consequences to the life of the Untouchables. The Military Service was the only service in which it was possible for the Untouchables to earn a living and also to have a career. It is a part of history that many untouchables had done meritorious service in the field and hundreds had risen to the status of Jamadar, Subhedar and Subhedar Majors. The Military occupation had given them respectability in the eyes of the Hindus and had given them a sense of importance, by opening to them places of power, prestige and authority. Having been used to service in the Army for over 150 years, the Untouchables had come to regard it as a hereditary occupation and had not cared to qualify themselves for any other. Here in 1890 — they were told that they were not wanted in the Army, without giving them any time to adjust themselves to the new circumstances — as was done in the case of the Anglo-Indians in 1935. When this service was closed, the Untouchables received a stunning blow and setback from which they have not recovered. They were thrown from a precipice and without exaggeration, fell far below the level at which they had stood under the native Governments.

So much for the entry of the Untouchables in the Military service. What is the position with regard to their entry in the civil service?

The Civil Service requires a high degree of education from the entrant. Only those with University degrees can hope to secure admission. The Untouchables have been the most uneducated part of India's population. The Civil Service has been virtually closed to them. It is only recently, that there have been among them men, who have taken University degrees. What has been their fate? It is no exaggeration to say that they are begging from door to door. Two things have come in the way of their securing an entry in the Civil Services. Firstly, the British Government refused to give them any preference. Not that the British Government did not recognize the principle of giving preference to communities, which were not sufficiently represented in the Civil Services. For instance, the British Government has definitely recognized that the Mohammedans should get preference provided he has minimum qualification. That, this principle has been acted upon in their case, is evident from the nominations, which the Government of India has made to the I.C.S. since the year when the Government took over power to fill certain places in the I.C.S. by nomination.

Not a single candidate from the untouchables has been nominated by the British Government, although there were many, who called, have satisfied the test of minimum qualification.

The second reason, why the untouchables, though qualified by education, have not been able to find a place in the Civil Service is, because of the system of recruitment for these services, Under the British Government, the authority to fill vacancies is left with the head of the department. Heads of Department have been and will long continue to be high Caste Hindus. A caste Hindu by his very make up is incapable of showing any consideration to an untouchable candidate. He is a man (with) strong sympathies and strong antipathies. His sympathies make him look first to his family, then to his relations, then to his friends and then to members of his caste. Within this wide circle, he is sure to find a candidate for the vacancy. It is very seldom that he is required to travel beyond the limits of his caste. If he has to, then the Untouchable will have, only if there is no other touchable Hindu to compete with them. If there is a competitor from any of the touchable caste, the Untouchable will have no chance. Thus the Untouchable is always the last to be considered in the matter of appointments to the Civil Service. Being the last to be considered, his chances of securing a post are the least.

There are two services for which the Untouchable is particularly suited. One is the Police Service and the other is menial service in Government Offices. What is the position of the Untouchables so far as police service is concerned?

The answer is that the Police Service is closed to them.

On the 17th December 1925, a resolution was moved in the Legislative Council of the United Provinces, asking Government to remove all restrictions on the entry of the Untouchables in Government service and especially the Police Service, the Member of Government in charge of the Department, speaking on behalf of Government said: "No, if the Honourable members wish to leave it open to all, I have no objection. But I will certainly object to any member of a criminal tribe or a low caste man like a chamar in this force at present."

On 22nd July 1927, Lala Mohan Lal asked the following question in the Punjab Legislative Council:

***Lala Mohan Lal:*** Will the Hon'ble Member for Finance be pleased to state if members of the depressed classes are taken in the police? If not, does the Government intend to direct that, in the matter of recruitment of police constables, the members of the depressed classes should also be taken?

***The Hon'ble Sir Geoffrey de Montmorency:*** Members of the depressed classes are not enrolled in the police. When there is evidence that the depressed classes are treated on an equal footing by all sections of the community, (which may not happen till dooms day) or when Government is satisfied that enrolment of members of these classes will satisfy the requirements of efficiency and be in the best interests of the composition of the service. Government will be quite prepared to throw open recruitment to them, provided they come up to the physical and other standards required of all recruits.

As to menial service, that also has been closed to them. Few will believe it, nonetheless it is a fact and few will be able to guess the reason, though it is quite plain. The reason why the untouchable is excluded from menial service is the same for which he is excluded from the Police Service. It is Untouchability. As part of his duty, a constable has to arrest a person. As a part of his duty, a constable has to enter the house of a person, for instance, to execute a search warrant. What would happen if the person arrested is a Hindu and the constable is an Untouchable? Police constables have to live in lines as neighbours, use the water taps. What would be the reactions of a Hindu constable if his neighbour is an Untouchable constable? These are the considerations which have barred the entry of the Untouchable in the Police Service. Exactly the same consideration have been operative in the case of menial service. A menial in Government office is, in law, required to serve in the office. But his service brings him in contact with others who are Hindus.

His contact causes pollution. How could he be welcome. Besides, according to convention, a peon in office is supposed to serve the head of the Department and also his household. He has to bring tea for the boss, he has to do shopping for the wife of the boss, and he has to look after the children. The Head of the Department has to forego these services if the menial appointments went to the Untouchables. Rather than forego these services, the Untouchable was deprived of his right to serve. So complete was this exclusion that the Bombay Committee had to make a special recommendation in this behalf.

What did the British Government do about the education of the Untouchables? I will take the Presidency of Bombay by way of an illustration. The period of British administration, so far as Education is concerned, can be divided into three convenient periods.

### *From 1813 to 1854*

1. Education under the British Rule in the Bombay Presidency must be said to have begun with the foundation of the Bombay Education Society in 1815. That Society did not confine its efforts to the education of European children. Native boys were encouraged to attend its schools at Surat and Thana and at the beginning of 1820, four separate schools for natives had been opened in Bombay and were attended by nearly 250 pupils. In August of the same year, further measures were taken to extend native education. A special committee was appointed by the Society to prepare school books in the Vernacular languages, and to aid or establish Vernacular schools. But the wide scope of the undertaking was soon seen to be beyond the aims of a society established mainly for the education of the poor; and in 1822, the committee became a separate corporation, thenceforth known as the Bombay Native

School Book and School Society, which name was in 1827 changed into the Bombay Native Education Society. The Honourable Mountstuart Elphinstone was the new Society's first President.

The Vice-Presidents were the Chief Justice and the three members of the Executive Council of the Bombay Government; and the managing committee consisted of twelve European and twelve native gentlemen, with Captain George Jervis R. E., and Mr. Sadashiv Kashinath Chhatre as Secretaries. The Society started its work with a grant of Rs. 600 per mensern from the Government. As early as 1825, the Government of Bombay had along side, began to establish primary schools at its own expense in district towns and had placed them under the control of the Collectors. To coordinate the activities of these two independent bodies, there was established in 1840 a Board of Education composed of six members, 3 appointed by Government and 3 appointed by the Native Education Society. This Board was in charge of the Education Department till the appointment of the Director of Public Instruction in 1855.

2. On the 1st March 1855, when the Board was dissolved, there was in the Presidency of Bombay under the charge of the Board, 15 English Colleges and Schools having 2850 students on the Register and 256 vernacular schools having 18,883 students on the Register. In the same report it is stated by the Board: "In August (1855) we received a petition from certain inhabitants of Ahmednagar, praying for the establishment of a school for the education of low castes and engaging to defray one-half of the teacher's salary, in accordance with the terms of the late rules. A school room had been built by the petitioners and the attendance of boys was calculated at thirty. The establishment of such a school was opposed to the prejudice of the richer and higher castes, and there was some difficulty in procuring a teacher on a moderate salary, but as the application was made in strict accordance with the conditions stated in the late notification on the subject, we readily

complied with the request, and the school was opened in November. We merely mention the subject, as it is the first occasion on which we have established a school for these castes".

3. The statement by the Board, that this was the first occasion when a school for the low castes was established in this Presidency, naturally raises the question what was the policy of the British Government in the matter of the education of the Depressed Classes before 1855? To answer this question, it is necessary to have a peep into the history of the educational policy of the British Government in this Presidency from 1813 to 1854. It must be admitted that under the Peshwa's Government the Depressed classes were entirely out of the pale of education. They did not find a place in any idea of state education, for the simple reason that the Peshwa's Government was a theocracy based upon the cannons of Manu, according to which the Sudras and Atisudras (classes corresponding to the Backward classes of the Education department), if they had any right of life, liberty and property, had certainly no right to education. The Depressed classes who were labouring under such disabilities, naturally breathed a sigh of relief at the downfall of this hated theocracy. Great hopes were raised among the Depressed classes by the advent of the British Rule. Firstly, because, it was a democracy which, they thought, believed in the principle of one man (one) value, be that man high or low. If it remained true to its tenets, such a democracy was a complete contrast to the theocracy of the Peshwa. Secondly, the Depressed classes had helped the British to conquer the country and naturally believed that the British would in their turn help them, if not in a special degree, at least equally with the rest.

4. The British were for a long time silent on the question of promoting education among the native population. Although individuals of high official rank in the administration of India were not altogether oblivious of the moral duty and administrative necessity of spreading knowledge among the people of India, no

public declaration of the responsibility of the State in that behalf was made till the year 1813, when by section 43 of the Statute 53 George IV chap. 155 Parliament laid down that" out of the surplus revenues of India, a sum of not less than one lakh of rupees in each year shall be set apart and applied to the revival and improvement of literature and the encouragement of the learned natives of India, and for the introduction and promotion of a knowledge of sciences among the inhabitants of British territories in India etc. "This statutory provision, however, did not result in any systematic effort, to place the education of the natives upon a firm and organised footing till 1823. For, the Court of Directors in their despatch dated 3rd June 1814 to the Governor General in Council, in prescribing the mode of giving effect to section 43 of the statute of 1813, directed that the promotion of Sanskrit learning among the Hindus would fulfil the purposes which Parliament had in mind. But what a disappointment to the Depressed classes, there was, when systematic efforts to place the education of the natives upon a firm and organized footing came to be made! For, the British Government deliberately ruled that education was to be a preserve for the higher classes. Lest this fact should be regarded as a fiction, attention is invited to the following extracts from the Report of the Board of Education of the Bombay Presidency for the year 1850-51.

***Paragraph 5th.— System Adopted by the Board based on the Views of Court of Directors:*** Thus the Board of Education at this Presidency having laid down a scheme of education, in accordance with the leading injunctions of Despatches from the Honourable Court, and founded not more on the opinions of men who had been attentively considering the progress of education in India such as the Earl of Auckland, Major Candy and others, than on the openly declared wants of the most intelligent of the natives themselves, the Board, we repeat, were informed by your Lordships predecessor in Council that the process must be reversed."

***Paragraph 8th.— Views of Court on the Expediency of Educating the Upper Classes*:** Equally wise, if we may be permitted, to use the expression, do the indications of the Hon. Court appear to us to be as to the quarters to which Government education should be directed, and specially with the very limited funds which are available for this branch of expenditure. The Hon. Court write to Madras in 1830 as follows: "The improvements in education, however, which most effectively contribute to elevate the moral and intellectual condition of a people, are those which concern the education of the higher classes—of the persons possessing leisure and natural influence over the minds of their countrymen. By raising the standard of instruction amongst these classes, you would eventually produce a much greater and more beneficial change in the ideas and the feelings of the community than you can hope to produce by acting directly on the more numerous class.

You are, moreover, acquainted with our anxious desire to have at our disposal a body of natives qualified by their habits and acquirements to take a larger share and occupy higher situations, in the civil administration of their country than has been hitherto the practice under our Indian Government; ' Nevertheless, we hear on so many sides, even from those who ought to know better of the necessity and facility for educating the masses for diffusing the arts and sciences of Europe amongst the hundred or the hundred and forty millions (for numbers count for next to nothing) in India, and other like generalities indicating cloudy notions on the subject, that a bystander might almost be tempted to suppose the whole resources of the State were at the command of Educational Boards, instead of a modest pittance inferior in amount to sums devoted to a single establishment in England.

***Paragraph 9th.— Retrospect of Principal Educational Facts during the Last Ten Years Necessary*:** The arguments adduced in the few last paragraphs appear to show that a careful examination of the real facts, and an analysis of the principal phenomena which have displayed themselves in the course of educational proceedings in the Presidency, would not be without their uses, if made with sufficient industry and impartiality to ensure confidence, and with a firm determination to steer clear of bootless controversy and all speculative inquiries.

The present epoch, also, appears especially to commend itself for such a retrospect, as in 1850 the second decennial period commenced, during which the Schools of the Presidency have come under exclusive control of a Government Board; and it is obvious that as a considerable body of information ought now to have been accumulated, and as the majority of the present members have had seats at the Board during the greater portion of that time, they would fain hope that by recording their experience, they may shed some light on certain obscure but highly interesting questions, which are certain to arise from time to time before their successors at this Board.

***Paragraph 10th.— A Uniform System Developing itself Spontaneously Both in Bengal and Bombay:*** We now proceed to give as minute a detail as comports with our limits, of the principal educational facts which have forced themselves upon our notice, and we think it will clearly appear, when those facts are duly appreciated, that many of the disputed questions, which arise in the Indian field of education, will be seen to solve themselves and that a system is generally evolving itself in other Presidencies as well as in Bombay, which is well suited to the circumstances of the country, and which, as the growth of spontaneous development, denotes that general causes are at work to call it forth.

***Paragraph IIth.— Statistics of Education in Bombay:*** In the return on the following page, a comparative view is given of the number of schools and of pupils receiving education under Government at the period when the Establishments first came under the control of the Board, in 1840 and in April 1850. It shows, in the latter period, an addition of four English and 83 vernacular schools and a general increase in pupils of above a hundred per cent. The total number receiving Government education at present is 12,712 in the following proportion:—

English Education...... 1,699

Vernacular Education...... 10,730

Sanskrit Education...... 283

(comparison from tables: in 1840 there were 97 schools, number of pupils 5,491; number of schools 185 and number of pupils 12,712).

***Paragraph 12th.— Same Subject:*** But the population of the Bombay Presidency is now calculated by the most competent authorizes to amount to ten millions. Now on applying the rule of statistics deduced from the Prussian census as noticed in a former Report (1842-43 page 26) a population of this amount will be found to contain no fewer than 900,000 male children between the ages of seven and fourteen years and of course, fit subjects for school. It follows, therefore, that Government at this Presidency has not been able to afford an opportunity for obtaining education to more than one out of every sixty-nine boys of the proper school going age.

***Paragraph 13th.— Same Subject:*** Further, it is admitted that education afforded in the Vernacular School is far from efficient. A great portion of the strictures of Mr. Willoughby's Minute is directed against the defective character and insignificant results of these schools. The Board, not only acknowledge this fact, but they have been studious to point it out prominently for many years past, and indeed, in the opinion of some competent observers, have drawn too unfavourable a picture of the vernacular schools. But what are the obvious remedies for the defects indicated? Mr. Willoughby describes them very correctly: —" a superior class of school masters, normal schools, more efficient supervision, additions to the vernacular literature. "These are all subjects however, which have occupied the attention of the Board for many years past, and as to which not a step can be made in advance without additional expenditure. But we are given to understand from the letter of your Lordship in council that "it is not probable that the Government will have the power, for a considerable time to come, to afford the Board additional pecuniary assistance."

***Paragraph 14th.—Conclusion that no Means exist- for Educating the Masses:*** It results most clearly from these facts that if sufficient funds are not available to put 175 Vernacular schools into a due state of organisation, and to give a sound elementary education to 10,730 boys, all question as to educating "the masses "the" hundred and forty millions "the 900,000 boys in the Bombay Presidency disappears. The object is not one that can be attained or approximated to by Government; and Educational Boards ought not to allow themselves to be distracted from a more limited practical field of benevolence.

***Paragraph 15th.— Views of Court of Directors as to the Best Method of Operation with Limited Means:*** The Hon'ble Court appear to have always kept the conclusion which has been arrived at in the last paragraph very distinctly in view. Perceiving that their educational efforts to improve the people could only be attempted on a very small scale, they have deemed it necessary to point out to their different Governments the true method of producing the greatest results with limited means. We have already cited their injunctions to the Madras Government on this head, (Para 7) and their despatch to the Government on the same date enforce sentiment of exactly the same import:— "It is our anxious desire to afford to the higher classes of the Natives of India the means of instruction in European sciences and of access to the literature of civilised Europe. The character which may be given to the classes possessed of leisure and natural influence ultimately determines that of the whole people."

***Paragraph 16th.—Inquiry as to Upper Classes of India.:*** It being then demonstrated that only a small section of the population can be brought under the influence of Government education in India, and the Hon'ble Court having in effect decided that this section should consist of the "upper classes" it is essential to ascertain who these latter consist *of*.— Here it is absolutely necessary for the European inquirer to divest his mind of European analogies which so often insinuate themselves almost involuntarily into Anglo-Indian speculations. Circumstances in Europe, especially in England have drawn a marked line, perceptible in manners, wealth, political and social influence, between the upper and lower classes. No such line is to be found in India, where, as under all despotisms the will of the Price was all that was requisite to raise men from the humblest condition in life to the highest station, and where consequently great uniformity in manners has always prevailed. A beggar, according to English notions, is fit only for the stocks or compulsory labour in the workhouse; in India he is a respectable character and worthy indeed of veneration according to the Brahminical theory, which considers him as one who has renounced all the pleasures and temptations of life for the cultivation of learning and undisturbed meditation of the Deity.

***Paragraph 17th.—Upper Classes in India:*** The classes who may be deemed to be influential and in so far the upper classes in India may be ranked as follows:

*1st.*— The landowners and Jagirdars, representatives of the former feudatories and persons in authorities under Native powers and who may be termed the Soldier class.

*2nd.*— Those who have acquired wealth in trade or commerce or the commercial class.

*3rd.*— The higher employees of Government.

*4th—Brah*mins, with whom may be associated, though at long interval, those of higher castes of writers who live by the pen such as Parbhus and Shenvis in Bombay, Kayasthas in Bengal provided they acquire a position either in learning or station.

***Paragraph 18th.— Brahmins, the Most Influential:*** Of these four classes, incomparably the most influential, the most numerous, and on the whole easiest to be worked on by the Government, are the latter. It is a well-recognized fact throughout India that the ancient Jagirdars or Soldier class are daily deteriorating under our rule. Their old occupation is gone, and they have shown no disposition or capacity to adopt new one, or to cultivate the art of peace. In the Presidency, the attempts of Mr. Elphinstone and his successors to bolster up a landed aristocracy have lamentably failed; and complete discomfiture has hitherto attended all endeavours to open up a path to distinction through civil honours and education, to a race to whom nothing appears to excite but vain pomp and extravagance, of the reminiscences of their ancestors' successful raids in the plains of Hindustan'. Nor among commercial classes, with a few exceptions, is there much greater opening for the influences of superior education.

As in all countries, but more in India than in the higher civilized ones of Europe, the young merchant or trader must quit his school at an early period in order to obtain the special education needful for his vocation in the market or the counting house. Lastly, the employees of the State, though they possess a great influence over the large numbers, who come in contact with Government, have no influence, whatever, with the still larger numbers who are independent of Government; and, indeed, they appear to inspire the same sort of distrust with the public as Government functionaries in England, who are often considered by the vulgar as mere hacks of the State.

***Pharagraph 19th.— Poverty of Brahmins:*** The above analysis, though it may appear lengthy, is nevertheless, indispensable, for certain important conclusions deducible from it. First, it demonstrates that the influential class, whom the Government are able to avail themselves of in diffusing the seeds of education, are the Brahmins and other high castes Brahmins proxmi. But the Brahimins and these high castes arc, for the most part, wretchedly poor; and in many parts of India, the term Brahmin is synonymous with "beggar."

***Paragraph 20th.— Wealthy Classes will not at Present Support Superior Education:*** We may see, then, how hopeless it is to enforce what your Lordship in council so strongly enjoined upon us in your letter of the 24th April 1850— what appears, *prima fade,* so plausible and proper in itself — what in fact, the Board themselves have very often attempted, *viz,* the strict limitation of superior education "to the wealthy, who can afford to pay for it, and to youths of unusual intelligence. "The invariable answer the Board has received, when attempting to enforce a view like this, has been, that the wealthy are wholly indifferent to superior education and that no means for ascertaining unusual intelligence amongst the poor exist, until their faculties have been tested and developed by school training.

A small section, from among the wealthier classes, is no doubt displaying itself, by whom the advantages of superior education are recognized, it appears larger in Bengal, where education has been longer fostered by Government, than in Bombay, and we think it inevitable that such class must increase, with the experience that superior attainments lead to distinction, and to close intercourse with Europeans on the footing of social equality; but as a general proposition at the present moment, we are satisfied that the academic instruction in the arts and sciences of Europe cannot be based on the contributions, either of students or of funds, from the opulent classes of India.

***Paragraph 21st.— Question as to Educating low Castes:*** The practical conclusion to be drawn from these facts which years of experience have forced upon our notice, is that a very wide door should be opened to the children of the poor higher castes, who are willing to receive education at our hands. But here, again, another embarrassing question arises, which it is right to notice: If the children of the poor are admitted I freely to Government Institutions, what is there to prevent all the despised castes—the Dheds, Mahars etc., from flocking in numbers to their walls?

***Paragraph 22nd.— Social Prejudice of the Hindus:*** There is a little doubt, that if a class of these latter were to be formed in Bombay, they might be trained, under the guiding influence of such Professors and masters as are in the service of the Board, into men of superior intelligence to any in the community; and with such qualifications, as they would then possess, there would be nothing to prevent their aspiring to the highest offices open to Native talent—to Judgeship the Grand Jury, Her Majesty's Commission of the Peace. Many benevolent men think, it is the height of illiberality and weakness in the British Government, to succumb to the prejudices, which such appointments would excite into disgust amongst the Hindu community, and that an open attack should be made upon the barriers of caste.

***Paragraph 23rd.—Wise Observations of the Hon. Mount Stuart Elphinstone Cited:*** But here the wise reflections of Mr. Elphinstone, the most liberal and large minded administrator, who has appeared on this side of India, point out the true rule of action. "It is observed" he says, "that the missionaries find the lowest castes the best pupils; but we must be careful how we offer any special encouragement to men of that description; they are not only the most despised, but among the least numerous of the great divisions of society, and it is to be feared that if our system of education first took root among them it would never spread further, and we might find ourselves at the head of a new class, superior to the rest in useful knowledge, but hated and despised by the castes to whom these new attainment would be desirable, if we were contented to rest our power on our army or on the attachment of a part of the population but is inconsistent with every attempt to found it on a more extended basis."

5. It is, therefore obvious, that if no schools were opened for Depressed classes before 1855 in the Bombay Presidency, it was because the deliberate policy of the British Government was to restrict the benefits of education to the poor higher castes, chiefly the Brahmins. Whether this policy was right or wrong is another matter. The fact, however, is that during this period the Depressed classes were not allowed by Government to share in the blessings of education.

### *From 1854 to 1882*

6. In their Despatch No. 49 of 19th July 1854, the Court of Directors observed: "Our attention should now be directed to a consideration, if possible, still more important, and one which has hitherto, we are bound to admit, too much neglected, namely, how useful and practical, knowledge suited to every station in life, may be best conveyed to the great mass of the people who are utterly incapable of obtaining any education worthy of the name by their own efforts; and we desire to see the active measures of Government more especially directed, for the future, to this object, for the attainment of which, we are ready to sanction a considerable increase of expenditure."

This despatch is very rightly regarded as having laid the foundation of mass education in this country. The results of this policy were first examined by the Hunter Commission on Indian Education in 1882. The following figures show what was achieved during the period of 28 years.

***Primary Education 1881-82***

| | No. of Scholars at School | Per cent on Total |
|---|---|---|
| Christians | 1,521 | .49 |
| Brahmins | 63,071 | 20.17 |
| Other Hindus | 202,345 | 64.69 |
| Mohammedans | 39,231 | 12.54 |
| Parsis | 3,517 | 1.12 |
| Aboriginal and Hill Tribes | 2,713 | .87 |
| Low Caste Hindus | 2,862 | .87 |
| Jews and Others | 373 | .12 |

## *Secondary Education 1881-82*

| | | Middle Schools | | High Schools | |
|---|---|---|---|---|---|
| | | No. of scholars at School | Per cent on total | No. of scholars at School | Per cent on total |
| Christians | | 1,429 | 12.06 | 111 | 2.26 |
| Brahmins | | 3,639 | 30.70 | 1,978 | 40.29 |
| Other Hindus | Cultivators | 624 | 5.26 | 140 | 2.85 |
| | Low Castes | 17 | .14 | --- | --- |
| | Other Castes | 3,823 | 32.25 | 1,573 | 32.04 |
| Mohammedans | | 687 | 5.80 | 100 | 2.04 |
| Parsis | | 1,526 | 12.87 | 965 | 19.66 |
| Aboriginal and Hill Tribes | | 6 | .05 | --- | --- |
| Others ( including Jews etc. | | 103 | .87 | 92 | .86 |

## *Collegiate Education 1881-82*

| | | No. of scholars at School | Per cent on total No. of Scholars |
|---|---|---|---|
| Christians | | 14 | 3 |
| Brahmins | | 241 | 50 |
| Other Hindus | Cultivators | 5 | 1 |
| | Low Castes | 0 | 0 |
| | Other Castes | 103 | 21.3 |
| Mohammedans | | 7 | 1.5 |
| Parsis | | 108 | 21.5 |
| Aboriginal and Hill Tribes | | 0 | 0 |
| Others ( including Jews) etc. | | 2 | 0.4 |

7. What do these figures show? They show that although mass education was the policy of the Government, the masses were as outside the pale of education as they were before the year 1854 and that the lowest and aboriginal classes of the Hindus still remained lowest in order of education; so much so, that in 1881-82, there was no student from that community either in the High Schools or in the Colleges of this Presidency. What can this failure to bring the Depressed Classes to the level of the rest in the matter of education be due to? To

answer this question, it is necessary again to go into the history of the educational policy of the Government of this Presidency.

8. The Despatch of the Court of Directors of the year 1954, for the first time recognised after a lapse of full 40 years that the duty of the State was to undertake the education of the great mass of the people. But there were still die-hards, who had great misgivings as to the wisdom of the principle laid down in that Despatch and who were agitating for a reversal of that policy. The fears of dire consequences to the British Rule arising from elevating the Backward Classes above their station in life, still haunted men like Lord Ellenborough, President of the Board of Control, who in a letter to the Chairman of the Court of Directors dated 28th of April 1858, did not hesitate to strike the following note of caution: "Gentlemen:— Many letters have been lately before me, reviewing the state of education in different parts of India, under the instructions sent by the Court of Directors in 1854, and I confess, that they have not given me the impression that the expected good has been derived from the system which was then established, while all the increase of charge which might have been expected, appears to be in progress of realization.

***"Paragraph 11:*** I believe, we rarely, if even induce parents above the lower class to send their children to our schools, and we should practically, if we succeeded in intending education as we desire, give a high degree of mental cultivation to the labouring class, while we left the more wealthy in ignorance.

***"Paragraph 12:*** This result would not tend to create a healthy state of society. Our Government could not offer to the most educated of the lower class the means of gratifying the ambition we should excite.

***"Paragraph 13:*** We should create a very discontented body of poor persons, having, through the superior education we had given to them, a great power over the mass of the people.

***"Paragraph 14:*** Education and civilization may descend

from the higher to the inferior classes, and so communicated may impart new vigour to the community, but they will never ascend from the lower classes to those above them; they can only, if imparted solely to the lower classes, lead to general convulsion, of which foreigners would be the first victims.

***"Paragraph 15:*** If we desire to diffuse education, let us endeavour to give it to the higher classes first.

***"Paragraph 16:*** These are but two ways of doing this—by founding colleges to which the higher classes alone should be admitted, and by giving in the reorganisation of the army, commissions at once, to such sons of native gentlemen as may be competent to receive them."

9. This antipathy of the European officers towards the untouchable classes was finally corrected by the Secretary of State for India in his despatch of 1859, which again reiterated the responsibility of Government for mass education.
10. Singular as it may appear, the recognition by the Government of its responsibility for mass education conferred upon the Depressed classes a benefit only in name. For, although, schools were opened for the masses in the various districts, the question of the admission of the Depressed classes to these schools had yet to be solved. Such a question did practically arise in the year 1856. But the decision of the Government was not favourable to the Depressed classes as will be seen from the following extracts from the Report of the Director of Public Instruction for the Bombay Presidency for the year 1856-57:—

***"Paragraph 177:*** Schools of Low castes and wild tribes.—There are no low class schools established directly by Government and the Supreme Government has expressed disapproval of such schools. The ordinary schools entirely supported by the state are in theory open indifferently to all castes. In the course of observation of my Report 1855-56 the Government issued the following order:— "The only case as yet brought before Government in which the question as to the admissions of the pupils of the lowest class to Government schools has been raised was that of a Mahar boy on whose behalf a petition was submitted in June 1856, complaining that though willing to pay the usual schooling fee, he had been denied admission to the Dharwar Government School.

> *"On this occasion. Government felt a great practical difficulty which attended the adjudication of a question in which their convictions of abstract right would be in antagonism to the general feelings of the mass of the natives, for whose enlightenment, to the greatest possible extent, the Government Educational Department has been established; and it was decided, as will appear from the Resolution passed at the time with some hesitation, that it would not be right, for the sake of single individual, the only Mahar who had ever come forward to beg for admission into a school attended only by the pupils of castes and to force him into association with them, at the probable risk of making the institution practically useless for the great mass of natives".*

The proceedings of the Government of Bombay in this matter were noticed in the following terms by the Government of India, in a letter No. 111 dated 23rd January 1857: "Governor General in Council thinks it very probable that the Bombay Government has acted wisely in the matter; but it desires me (*i.e.* Secretary to the Government of India) to say that the boy would not have been refused admission to any Government school in the Presidency of Bengal".

On receipt of this letter, it was resolved that Government of India should be assured that this Government would be most unwilling to neglect any means of rendering the schools throughout the country less exclusive than they practically are in the matter of caste; provided this could be effected without bringing the Government school into general disrepute, and thus destroying their efficiency and defeating the object for which they were intended. It was also determined that an enquiry should be made as to the practical working of the principle which was said to prevail in Bengal as affecting the general usefulness of the Government schools.

11. Inquiries as to the practice prevalent in Bengal revealed that the Bengal authorities, contrary to the supposition of the "Government of India" had left it to the District

Committees of Instructions to grant or refuse admittance to candidates of inferior castes, with reference to the state of local native feeling in each case. The result of this was that the Depressed classes were left in the cold, because the touchable classes would not let them sit at the fire of knowledge which the Government had lit up in the interest of all its subjects.

12. Under these circumstances, mass education as contemplated by the Despatch of 1854 was in practice available to all except the Depressed classes. The lifting of the ban on the education of the Depressed classes in 1854 was a nominal affair only. For, although the principle of non-exclusion was affirmed by the Government, its practical operation was very carefully avoided; so that, we can say, that the ban was continued in practice as before.

    The only agency which could take charge of the education of the Depressed classes was that of Christian Missionaries. In the words of Mount Stuart Elphinstone they "found the lowest classes the best pupils". But the Government was pledged to religious neutrality and could not see its way to support missionary schools, so much so that no pecuniary grant was made in this Presidency to any missionary school in the early part of this period although the Educational Despatch of 1854 had not prohibited the giving of grants to missionary schools.

13. To find a way out of this *impasse* the Government adopted two measures: (1) the institution of separate Government schools for low caste boys, and (2) the extension of special encouragement to missionary bodies to undertake their education by relaxing the rules of grants-in-aid. Had these two measures not been adopted, the education of the Depressed classes would not have yielded the results, most meager as they were, at the stocktaking by the Hunter Commission in 1882.

### *From 1882 to 1923*

14. After the year 1882, the year 1923 forms the next landmark in the educational history of the Bombay

Presidency. That year marks the transfer of primary education from the control of Provincial Governments to the control of local bodies. It will therefore be appropriate to take stock of the position as it stood in 1923. The position of the different communities in the Bombay Presidency in 1923 in the matter of educational advancement may be summed up in a tabular form as follows:

| *Classes of population in the Presidency* | *Order in respect of education* | *Order in respect of education* | | |
|---|---|---|---|---|
| | | *Primary* | *Secondary* | *Collegiate* |
| **Advanced Hindus** | 4th | 1st | 1st | 1st |
| **Intermediate Hindus** | 1st | 3rd | 3rd | 3rd |
| **Backward Hindus** | 2nd | 4th | 4th | 4th |
| **Mahomedans** | 3rd | 2nd | 2nd | 2nd |

15. From this table, one notices a great disparity in the comparative advancement of these different communities in the matter of education. Comparing these classes of people according to the order in which they stand in respect of their population and according to the order in which they stand in respect of their educational progress, we find that the Intermediate class, which is first in order of population is third in order of college education, third in order of secondary education and third in order of primary education. The Depressed classes who are second in order of population, stand fourth *i.e.* last in order of college education, last in order of secondary education and last in order of primary education. The Mohammedans who are third in order of population are second in order of college education, second in order of secondary education and second in order of primary education; while the "Advanced Hindoos" who occupy the fourth place in order of population stand first in order of college education, first in order of secondary education and first in order of primary education. From this we can safely say that in this respect there has been no improvement over the situation as it stood in 1882 relatively speaking.

16. The above statement which is based upon the Report of the Director of Public Instruction, Bombay Presidency for the year 1923-24 merely reveals the disparity that exists in the educational advancement of the different communities. But the disparity in the level of education among the different communities would be a very small matter if it be not very great. We can form no important conclusion unless we know the degree of disparity. To make this position clear from this point of view, the following table is presented:—

| *Classes of Population* | *Primary Education, Students per 1000 of the population of the class* | *Secondary Education, Students per 1000 of the population of the class* | *College Education, Students per 1000 of the population of the class* |
|---|---|---|---|
| Advance Hindus | 119 | 3,000 | 1,000 |
| Mahomedans | 92 | 500 | 52 |
| Intermediate class.. | 38 | 140 | 24 |
| Backward class .. | 18 | 14 | Nil (or nearly one if at all). |

17. The above figures give the lengths, as it were, by which each community is ahead of the rest in the matter of primary, secondary and collegiate education. They reveal a range of disparity between the different communities in this Presidency which shows that the position of some of the communities in the matter of education is most shocking. From the statistics as given above, two facts stand out to be indisputable. (1) That the state of education of the Backward classes in this Presidency is deplorable. In the matter of population they occupy a place as high as second. But in the matter of Education, they occupy a place which is not only last but which also is the least; (2) That the Muhammedans of the Presidency have made enormous strides in education; so much so that within the short span of 30 years, they have not only stolen a march over other communities such as the Intermediate and the

Backward class, but have also come close to the Brahmins and allied castes.

18. What can this be due to? To the policy of unequal treatment adopted by the Government must again be our reply to this ever present question. How unequal was the treatment of the two classes will be evident from the following extracts from the Quinquennial Reports on Education. With regard to the treatment of the Mohammedans in the matter of education, the following observations in the third Quinquennial Report (1892-96) are noteworthy:

    "Concerning the figures for Mohammedan Education in Bombay the Director remarks that the increase would have been larger "but for adverse circumstances". It has long been recognized in Bombay that Mohammedans make a larger use of Public Institutions than the rest of the population. On the general question of what has been done to encourage Mohammedan education, the Director writes:

    "In the first place, a Mohammedan officer is appointed to every District, either as Deputy or Assistant Deputy Inspector; and we have three Mohammedan graduates as Deputies, at Kaira, Sholapur, and Hyderabad, while a fourth has been drafted into the higher grades of the Revenue Department. There is thus, not a District where the staff is out of touch with the Mohammedan population. Again at Bombay, Karachi and Junagadh (a Muhammadan State in Kathiawar), special efforts have been made to provide High Schools for Muhammadans with low fee rates, and smaller schools have been opened by other Anjumans (Muhammadan associations) elsewhere. The Department also provides for their benefit, special standards and maintains special schools in certain localities, and reserves for them one-third of the Provincial and Local Boards scholarships. Then, there are the special scholarships founded by Khan Bahadur Kazi Shahbuddin (at one time Diwan of Baroda); and in Sindh, a certain number of food scholarships have been given by the heir of the Native State of Khairpur for students attending in Arts College.

(I had great difficulty in filling these up last year, though they are of the value of Rs. 25 a month). In Primary schools, Muhammadans are very leniently treated in the matter of fees. They are encouraged to come to the Training Colleges by special rules which (regime) from them an easier test than from Hindus; The Joint Schools Committee at Bombay has lately made special efforts to encourage Muhammadan education by the appointment of a Mahommadan Deputy Inspector"

19. Compare with this the observations regarding the education of the Depressed classes in the fifth Quinquennial Report (1902-1907): "959. Bombay— In the Central Division of Bombay, the low caste children are admitted free into schools and receive presents in the form of books, slates etc. In Kathiawar only three children of the Depressed castes are receiving education. In the Southern division there are 72 special schools or classes of them, most of which are under unqualified teachers."

20. This unequal treatment has its origin in the recommendations of the Hunter Commission. How partial was the Hunter Commission to the Mohammedans will be evident, if we compare the recommendations it made in their behalf to those it made in the interests of the Depressed classes. With respect to the Mohammedans the Commission made seventeen recommendations of which the following are worthy of note:

(1) that the special encouragement of Mohammedan education be regarded as a legitimate charge on local, on Municipal, and on Provincial funds.

(7) that higher English education for Mohammedans, being the king of education in which that community needs special help, be liberally encouraged.

(8) that, where necessary, graduated system of special scholarships for Mohammedans be established to be awarded (a) in primary schools, and tenable in middle schools; (b) in middle schools, and tenable in high schools; (c) on the results of Matriculation

and First Arts examinations, and tenable in colleges also.

(9) that in all classes of schools maintained from public funds, a certain proportion of free studentship be expressly reserved for Mohammedan students.

(10) that in places where educational endowments for the benefit of Mohammedans exist and are under the management of Government, the funds arising from each endowments be devoted to the advancement of education among the Mohammedans exclusively.

(11) that where Mohammedans exist, and are under the management of private individuals or bodies, inducements by liberal grants-in-aid be offered to them to establish English teaching schools or colleges on the grants-in-aid system.

(12) that, where necessary, the Normal Schools or classes for the training of Mohammedan teachers be established.

(16) that Mohammedan Inspecting Officers be employed more largely than hitherto for the inspection of primary schools for Mohammedans.

(17) that the attention of Local Governments be invited to the question of the proportion in which patronage is distributed among educated Mohammedans and others.

21. Every one of these recommendations made by the Hunter Commission was necessary in the interests of the Depressed classes also. But when we come to analyse the recommendations made by the Commission in the interest of the Backward classes, we do not find them directing that education of the Backward Classes be regarded a legitimate change on Government funds, that scholarships and proceedings be reserved for them, that special inspecting staff be kept to look after their educational needs or that public patronage be given to them by way of encouraging the growth of education amongst them. All we find the Commission saying is that (1) the principle that "no boy be refused admission

to a Government College or school merely on the ground of caste", be now reaffirmed as a principle and be applied with due caution to every institution, not reserved for special races, which is wholly maintained at the cost of public funds, whether provincial, municipal or local. (2) that the establishment of special schools or classes for children of low castes be liberally encouraged in places where there are a sufficient number of such children to form separate schools or classes and where the schools already maintained from public funds do not sufficiently provide for their education. "As a matter of fact the recommendations made by the Commission for the Mohammedans were far more necessary in the interests of the Backward classes than in the interests of the Mohammedans." For even the Hunter Commission, presided as it was by a chairman of pronounced sympathies for the Mohammedans, had to admit that "the inquiries made in 1871-73 went to prove that except in the matter of the higher education, there had been a tendency to exaggerate the backwardness of the Muhamadans. "Notwithstanding this the only recommendations made by the Hunter Commission were the two mentioned above. Even these two recommendations, made by the Commission regarding the Depressed classes were not calculated to do much good. They were bound to be futile. The reaffirmation of the principle even if it be for the fifth time was useless. For under the proviso inserted by the Commission, the enforcement was to be avoided in practice. Similarly, the opening of the separate schools for the Depressed classes was hardly possible, which again was bound to be sterile. Separate schools involving additional expense could hardly be acceptable to a Government to which primary education was a task. Besides, the proviso, that such schools should be opened where Backward classes were in large numbers, was sufficient to negative the recommendations simply because in rural parts the Backward classes can seldom be found to be living in one locality in large numbers.

22. It is difficult to understand why the Hunter Commission paid such a scant attention to the educational needs of the Backward classes. If it felt necessary to be generous towards the Mohammedans, it should have at least seen that it was just to the Backward classes who were far behind the Mohammedans in education, wealth and social status. Once the Hunter Commission had thrown the Depressed classes into the background, they remained there and the Government never paid any attention to them. As an example of this neglect, attention may be drawn to the Resolution of the Government of India in the Department of Education dated Delhi the 21st February 1923. It was one of the most important resolutions ever issued by the Government of India in which they decided to assist local Government by means of large grants from imperial revenues as funds became available, to extend comprehensive systems of education in the several provinces. In that resolution, they were particular to point out to the provincial Governments, the educational needs of "Domiciled community" and the Mohammedan community. But they had not a word to say in the whole Resolution about the Backward classes. The Bombay Government readily accepted the suggestion and appointed in 1913 a Mohammedan on Education Committee to make recommendations for the promotion of education among the Mohammedans. One feels righteous indignation against such criminal neglect on the part of the Government, particularly when, it is realized that the large grants given by the Government of India after 1913, were given by way of fulfilment of the declaration made by His Most Gracious Imperial Majesty, the King Emperor, in replying to the address of the Calcutta University on the 6th January, in which he said: "It is my wish that there may be spread *over* the land a network of Schools and Colleges, from which will go forth loyal and manly and useful citizens, able to hold their own industries and agriculture and all the vocations in life. And it is my wish too, that the homes of my Indian subjects may be brightened and their

labour sweetened by the spread of knowledge with all that follows in its train, a higher level of thought, of comfort and health. It is through education that my wish will be fulfilled, and the cause of education in India will ever be very close to my heart."

What about social Reform under the British Government?

It was Raja Sir T. Madhavrao, a very prominent and progressive Hindu of the last generation, who said: "The longer one lives, observes, and thinks, the more deeply does he feel that there is no community on the face of the earth which suffers less from political evils and more from self-inflicted or self-accepted or self-created, and therefore avoidable evils, than the Hindu Community."

Leaving aside the question of the comparative cost of the observation, there can be no doubt that Hindu Society suffers from social evils as no other community does.

Mahadeo Govind Ranade, another venerable name among earnest social reformers has made another and equally important observation, emphasizing another aspect of the Hindu Community: "Mere considerations of expediency or economical calculations of gains or tosses can never move a community to undertake and carry through social reforms, especially with a community like ours, so spellbound by custom and authority.

Our people feel, and feel earnestly, that some of our social customs are fraught with evil; but as this evil is of a temporal character, they think that it does not justify a breach of commands divine, for" such breach involves a higher penalty.— The truth is, the 'orthodox society has lost its power of life, it can initiate no reform nor sympathise with it."

In other words all the social evils are based on religion. A Hindu man or woman, whatever he does, he does as a religious observance. A Hindu eats religiously, drinks religiously, bathes religiously, dresses religiously, is born religiously, is married religiously and is burned religiously. His acts are all pious acts. However evil they may be from a secular point of view, to him, they are not sinful because they are sanctioned and enjoined by his religion. If any one accuses a Hindu of Sin, his reply is, ' If I sin, I am sinning religiously.

Society is always conservative. It does not change unless it is compelled to and that too very slowly. When change begins, there is always a struggle between the old and the new, and the new is always in danger of being eliminated in the struggle for survival unless it is supported. The one sure way of carrying through a reform is to back it up by law. Without the help of legislation, there can never be any reform in any evil. The necessity of legislation is very great when the evil to be reformed based on religion.

What is the sum total of legislation in favour of social reform under the British Government? The record of the British Government, in the matter of social reform, is to say the least, very halting and very disappointing. In the course of 150 years, there are just six social evils which have been subjected to Legislation.

The first piece of Social Legislation which the British undertook, is contained in Bengal Regulation XXI of 1795. It is a regulation for Preventing the Brahmins in the Province of Benares establishing Koorhas, wounding or killing their female relations or children or sitting Dhurna and for preventing the Tribe of Raj Koomars in that Province killing their female children.

3

# Ambedkar Notes on Caste Systems

## Manu and the Sudras

The reader is now aware that in the Scheme of Manu there were two principal social divisions: those outside the Chaturvarna and those inside the Chaturvarna. The reader also knows that the present day Untouchables are the counterpart of those outside the Chaturvarna and that those inside the Chaturvarna were contrasted with those outside. They were a composite body made up of four different classes, the Brahmins, the Kshatriyas, the Vaishyas and the Sudras. The Hindu social system is not only a system in which the idea of classes is more dominant than the idea of community but it is a system which is based on inequality between classes and therefore between individuals.

To put it concretely, the classes *i.e.* the Brahmins, Kshatriyas, Vaishyas, Sudras and Antyajas (Untouchables) are not horizontal, all on the same level. They are vertical *i.e.* one above the other. No Hindu will controvert this statement. Every Indian knows it. If there is any person who would have any doubt about it he can only be a foreigner. But any doubt which a foreigner might have will be dissolved if he is referred to the law of Manu who is the chief architect of the Hindu society and whose law has formed the foundations on which it is built. For his benefit I reproduce such texts from the Manusmriti as go to prove that Hindu society is based on the principle of inequality.

It might be argued that the inequality prescribed by Manu in his Smriti is after all of historical importance. It is past history and cannot be supposed to have any bearing on the present conduct of the Hindu. I am sure nothing can be greater error than this. Manu is not a matter of the past. It is even more than a past of the present. It is a 'living past' and therefore as really present as any present can be.

That the inequality laid down by Manu was the law of the land under the pre-British days may not be known to many foreigners. Only a few instances will show that such was the case. Under the rule of the Marathas and the Peshwas the Untouchables were not allowed within the gates of Poona city, the capital of the Peshwas between 3 p.m. and 9 a.m. because, before nine and after three, their bodies cast too long a shadow; and whenever their shadow fell upon a Brahmin it polluted him, so that he dare not taste food or water until he had bathed and washed the impurity away. So also no Untouchable was allowed to live in a walled town; cattle and dogs could freely enter but not the Untouchables

Under the rule of the Marathas and the Peshwas the Untouchables might not spit on the ground lest a Hindu should be polluted by touching it with his foot, but had to hang an earthen pot round his neck to hold his spittle. He was made to drag a thorny branch of a tree with him to brush out his footsteps and when a Brahman came by, had to lie at a distance on his face lest his shadow might fall on the Brahman

In Maharashtra an Untouchable was required to wear a black thread either in his neck or on his wrist for the purpose of ready identification.

In Gujarat the Untouchables were compelled to wear a horn as their distinguishing mark.

In the Punjab a sweeper was required while walking through streets in towns to carry a broom in his hand or under his armpit as a mark of his being a scavenger.

In Bombay the Untouchables were not permitted to wear clean or untorn clothes. In fact the shopkeepers took the precaution to see that before cloth was sold to the Untouchable it was torn & soiled.

In Malabar the Untouchables were not allowed to build

houses above one storey in height and not allowed to cremate their dead.

In Malabar the Untouchables were not permitted to carry umbrellas, to wear shoes or golden ornaments, to milk cows or even to use the ordinary language of the country.

In South India Untouchables were expressly forbidden to cover the upper part of their body above the waist and in the case of women of the Untouchables they were compelled to go with the upper part of their bodies quite bare.

In the Bombay Presidency so high a caste as that of Sonars (goldsmiths) was forbidden to wear their Dhoties with folds and prohibited to use *Namaskar* as the word of salutation#.

The following letter will be interesting to the reader as it throws a flood of light as to whether the Dhamia prescribed by Manu was or was not the law of the land-

"To

Damulsett Trimbucksett

Head of the Caste of Goldsmiths.

"The Hon'ble the President in Council having thought proper to prohibit the Caste of Goldsmiths from making use of the form of salutation termed Namaskar, you are hereby pre-emptorily enjoined to make known this order and resolution to the whole caste and to take care that the same be strictly observed.

By order

Secretary to Government

sig. W. Page

Bombay

9th August 1779

***Resolution of Government***

Dated 28th July 1779.

"Frequent disputes having arisen for some time between the Brahmins and Goldsmiths respecting a mode of salutation termed "Namaskar" made use of by the latter, and which the Brahmins allege they have no right to perform, and that the exercise of such ceremony by the Goldsmiths is a great breach and profanation of the rights of the Gentoo (Hindu] Religion, and repeated complaints having been made to us by the Brahmins, and the Peishwa also having several times written to the President, requesting the use of the Namaskar might be prohibited to the Goldsmiths-Resolved as it i« necessary. This matter should be decided by us in order that the dispute between the two castes may be put an end to, and the Brahmins appear to have reason for their complaint, that the Goldsmiths be forbidden the use of the Namaskar, and this being a matter wherein the Company's interest is not concerned, our Resolution may be put on the footing of a compliment to the Peshwa whom the President is desired to make acquainted with our determination."

Under the Maratha rule any one other than a Brahmin uttering a Veda Mantra was liable to have his tongue cut off and as a matter of fact the tongues of several Sonars (goldsmiths) were actually cut off by the order of the Peshwa for their daring to utter the Vedas contrary to law.

All over India Brahmin was exempt from capital punishment. He could not be hanged even if he committed murder.

Under the Peshwas distinction was observed in the punishment of the criminals according to the caste. Hard labour and death were punishments mostly visited on the Untouchables.

Under the Peshwas Brahmin clerks had the privilege of their goods being exempted from certain duties and their imported corn being carried to them without any ferry charges; and Brahmin landlords had their lands assessed at distinctly lower rates than those levied from other classes. In Bengal the amount of rent for land varied with the caste of the occupant and if the tenant was an Untouchable he had to pay the highest rent.

These facts will show that Manu though born some time before B. C. or sometime after A. D. is not dead and while the Hindu Kings reigned, justice between Hindu and Hindu, touchable and untouchable was rendered according to the Law of Manu and that law was avowedly based on inequality.

This is the Dharma laid down by Manu. It is called Manav Dharma *i.e.* Dharma which by its inherent goodness can be applied to all men in all times and in all places. Whether the fact that it has not had any force outside India is a blessing or a curse I do not stop to inquire. It is important to note that this Manav Dharma is based upon the theory that the Brahman is to have all the privileges and the Sudra is not to have even the rights of a human being, that the Brahman is to be above everybody in all things merely by reason of his high birth and the Sudra is to be below everybody and is to have none of the things no matter how great may be his worth.

Nothing can show the shamelessness and absurdity of this Manava Dharma better than turning it upside down. I know of no better attempt in this behalf than that of Dr. R. P. Pranjape a great Educationist, Politician and Social reformer and I make no apology for reproducing it in full.

## *Peep Into the Future*

This piece Was written against the Non-Brahmin Parties which were then in power in the Bombay and Madras Presidency and in the Central Provinces. The Non-Brahmin parties were founded with the express object of not allowing a single community to have a monopoly in State Service. The Brahmins have a more or less complete monopoly in the State services in all provinces in India and in all departments of State. The Non-Brahmin parties had therefore laid down the principle, known as the principle of communal ratio, that given minimum qualifications candidates belonging to non-Brahmin communities should be given preference over Brahmin candidates when making appointments in the public services. In my view there was nothing wrong in this principle. It was undoubtedly wrong that the administration of the country should be in the hands of a single community however clever such a community might be.

The Non-Brahmin Party held the view that good Government was better than efficient Government was not a principle to be confined only to the composition of the Legislature & the Executive. But that it must also be made applicable to the field of administration. It was through administration that the State came directly in contact with the masses. No administration could do any good unless it was sympathetic. No administration could be sympathetic if it was manned by the Brahmins alone. How can the Brahmin who holds himself superior to the masses, despises the rest as low caste and Sudras, is opposed to their aspiration, is instinctively led to be partial to his community and being uninterested in the masses is open to corruption be a good administrator? He is as much an alien to the Indian masses as any foreigner can be. As against this the Brahmins have been taking their stand on efficiency pure & simple. They know that this is the only card they can play successfully by reason of their advanced position in education. But they forget that if efficiency was the only criterion then in all probability there would be very little chance for them to monopolise State service in the way and to the extent they have done. For if efficiency was made the only criterion there would be nothing wrong in employing Englishmen, Frenchmen, Germans & Turks instead of the Brahmins of India. Be that as it may, the Non-Brahmin Parties refused to make a fetish to efficiency and insisted that there must be introduced the principle of communal ratio in the public services in order to introduce into the administration an admixture of all castes & creeds and thereby make it a good administration.

In carrying out this principle the Non-Brahmin Parties in their eagerness to cleanse the administration of Brahmindom while they were in power, did often forget the principle that in redressing the balance between the Brahmins and non-Brahmins in the public services they were limited by the rule of minimum efficiency. But that does not mean that the principle they adopted for their guidance was not commendable in the interests of the masses.

This policy no doubt set the teeth of many Brahmins on edge. They were vehement in their anger. This piece by Dr. Paranjpe is the finest satire on the policy of the non-Brahmin Party. It caricatures the principle of the non-Brahman party in a manner which is inimitable and at the time when it came out, I know many non-Brahmin leaders were not only furious but also speechless. My complaint against Dr. Paranjpe is that he did not see the humour of it. The non-Brahmin Party was doing nothing new. It was merely turning Manusmriti upside down. It was turning the tables. It was putting the Brahmin in the position in which Manu had placed the Sudra. Did not

Manu give privileges to Brahmin merely because he was a Brahmin? Did not Manu deny any right to the Sudra even though he deserved it? Can there be much complaint if now the Sudra is given some privileges because he is a Sudra? It may sound absurd but the rule is not without precedent and that precedent iș the Manusmriti itself. And who can throw stones at the non-Brahmin Party? The Brahmins may if they are without sin. But can the authors and worshippers, upholders of Manusmriti claim that they are without sin? Dr. Paranjpe's piece is the finest condemnation of the inquiry that underlies this Manav Dharma. It shows as nothing else does what a Brahmin feels when he is placed in the position of a Sudra.

Inequality is not confined to Hindus. It prevailed elsewhere also and was responsible for dividing society into higher and lower free and servile classes. (Left incomplete in Ms.-ed.)

## Preservation of Social Order

The second technique devised for the maintenance and preservation of the Established Order is quite different from the first. Really speaking it is this, which constitutes a special feature of the Hindu Social Order.

In the matter of the preservation of the Social Order from violent attack it is necessary to bear in mind three considerations. The outbreak of a Revolution is conditioned by three factors.

(1) The existence of a sense of wrong,

(2) Capacity to know that one is suffering from a wrong and

(3) Availability of arms.

The second consideration is that there are two ways of dealing with a rebellion. One is to prevent a rebellion from occurring and the other is to suppress it after it has broken out. The third consideration is that whether the prevention of rebellion would be feasible or whether the suppression of rebellion would be the only method open, would depend upon the rules which govern the three prerequisites of rebellion.

Where the Social Order denies opportunity to rise, denies right to education, and denies right to use arms it is in a position to prevent rebellion against the Social Order. Where on the other hand a Social Order allows opportunity to rise, allows right to education, and permits the use of arms it cannot prevent rebellion by those who suffer wrongs. Its only remedy to preserve the Social Order by suppressing rebellion by the use of force and violence. The Hindu Social Order has adopted the first method. It has fixed the social status of the lower orders for all generations to come. Their economic status is also fixed. There being no disparity between the two there is no possibility of a grievance growing up. It has denied education to the lower orders.

The result is that no one is conscious that his low condition is a ground for grievance. If there is any consciousness it is that no one is responsible for the low condition. It is the result of fate. Assuming there is a grievance, assuming there is consciousness of grievance there cannot be a rebellion by the lower orders against the Hindu Social Order' because the Hindu Social order denies the masses the right to use arms.... Social Orders such as use of follow the opposite course. They allow equal opportunity to all. They allow freedom to acquire knowledge, they allow the right to bear arms and take upon themselves the odium of suppressing rebellious force & violence. To deny freedom of opportunity, to deny freedom to acquire knowledge, to deny the right to arms is a most cruel wrong. Its result to and man. The Hindu Social Order is not ashamed to this. It has however achieved two things. It has found the most effective even though it be the most shameless method of preserving the established Order. Secondly notwithstanding the use of most inhuman means of killing manliness, it has given to the Hindus the reputation of being a very humane people.

Another special feature of the Hindu Social Order relates to the technique devised for its preservation.

The technique is twofold.

The first technique is to place the responsibility of upholding and maintaining the social order upon the shoulders of the King. Manu does this in quite express terms.

VIII. 410. "The king should order each man of the mercantile class to practice trade, or money-lending, or agriculture and attendance on cattle; and each man of the servile class to act in the service of the twice-born."

VIII. 418. "With vigilant care should the King exert himself in compelling merchants and mechanics to perform their respective duties; for, when such men swerve from their duty, they throw this world into confusion."

Manu does not stop with the mere enunciation of the duty of the King in this behalf. He to ensure that the King shall at all times perform his duty to maintain and preserve the Established Order. Manu therefore makes two further provisions. One provision is to make the failure of the King to maintain the Established Order an offence for which the King become liable for prosecution and punishment like a common man. This would be clear from the following citations from Manu:

VIII. 335. "Neither a father, nor a preceptor, nor a friend, nor a mother, nor a wife, nor a son, nor a domestic priest must be left unpunished by the king, if they adhere not with firmness to their duty."

VIII. 336. "Where another man of lower birth would be fined one pana, the king shall be fined a thousand, and he shall give the fine to the priests, or cast it into the river, this is a sacred rule."

The other provision made by Manu against a King who is either negligent or opposed to the Established Order is to invest the three classes. Brahmins, Kshatriya and Vaishya with a right to rise in armed rebellion against the King.

VIII. 348. "The twice-born may take arms, when their duty is obstructed by force; and when, in some evil time, a disaster has befallen the twice-born classes."

## With the Hindus

It is impossible to believe that Hindus will ever be able to absorb the Untouchables in their society. Their Caste System and the Religion completely negative any hope being entertained in this behalf. Yet there are incorrigible optimists more among the Hindus than among the Untouchables, who believe in the possibility of the Hindus assimilating the Untouchables. Whether these incorrigible optimists are honest or dishonest in their opinion is a question which cannot be overlooked. Within what time this assimilation will take place, they are unable to define. Assuming that the optimists are honest, there can be no question that this process of assimilation is going to be a long drawn process extending over many centuries.

In the meantime the Untouchables will have to live under the Social and political sway of the Hindus, and continue to suffer all the tyrannies and oppressions to which they have been subjected in the past. Obviously no sane man will think of leaving them to the will and the pleasure of the Hindus in the hope that some day in the unpredictable future they will be assimilated by the Hindus. Long or short, there will be a period of transition and some provision must be made against the tyranny and oppression by the Hindus. What provisions should be made in this behalf? If the question is left to the Untouchables they will ask for two provisions being made: one for Constitutional Safeguards and two for Separate Settlements.

The nature of Constitutional Safeguards for the protection of the Untouchables have been defined by the All-India Scheduled Caste Federation, a political organisation of the Untouchables of India in the form of resolutions.

The Hindus are very reluctant to allow the Untouchables these safeguards. The objection is general. There is also objection to particular safeguards. The general objection that the Untouchables are not a minority and therefore they are not entitled to safeguards which may be allowed to other minorities. The argument proceeds that the basis of a community to be called a minority is Religion if one is entitled to be recognised as a minority. The Untouchables are not separate from the Hindus in the matter of the religion. Consequently they are not a minority. That this definition of a minority is childish will be obvious to all those who have studied the question.

## Frustration

The Untouchables are the weariest, most loathed and the most miserable people that history can witness. They area spent and sacrificed people. To use the language of Shelley they are—"pale for weariness of climbing heaven, and gazing on earth, wandering companionless Among the stars that have a different birth" To put it in simple language the Untouchables have been completely overtaken by a sense of utter frustration. As Mathew Arnold says "life consists in the effort to affirm one's own essence; meaning by this, to develop one's own existence fully and freely, to have ample light and air, to be neither (.......) nor overshadowed.. Failure to affirm ones own essence is simply another name for frustration. Its non fulfilment of one's efforts to do the best, the withering of one's faculties, the stunting of one's personality."

Many people suffer such frustrations in their history. But they soon recover from the blight and rise to glory again with new vibrations. The case of the Untouchables stands on a different footing. Their frustration is frustration for ever. It is unrelieved by space or time. In this respect the story of the Untouchables stands in strange contrast with that of the Jews.

Their captivity in Egypt was the first calamity that visited the Jewish people. As the Bible says.

Ultimately Pharaoh yielded. The Jewish people escaped captivity and went to Cannan and settled there in the land flowing with milk and honey.

The second calamity which overtook the Jews was the Babylonian Captivity.

We can now explain why the Untouchables have suffered frustration. They have no plus condition of body and mind. They have nothing in their dull drab deadening past for a hope of a rise in the future to feed upon. This is due to no fault of theirs. The frustration which is their fate is the result of the unpropitious social environment born out of the Hindu Social Order which is so deadly inimical to their progress.

The Covenant with God may be interpreted to mean in the language of Emerson a plus condition of mind and body. As Emerson has said "Success is constitutional-depends, on a plus condition of mind and body—on power of work—on courage. Success goes invariably with a certain plus or positive power: An ounce of Power must balance an ounce of weight."

If the Jews rose after their first captivity, it was primarily because of their plus condition of mind and body. This plus condition of mind and body can arise from two sources. It can arise from reliance on God. God, if nothing else is at least a source of power and in emergency man needs mental power, the plus condition of mind and body which is necessary for success. There is therefore nothing wrong in the suggestion that the Jews succeeded because of their Covenant of God if it is interpreted in the right way.

This plus condition of body and mind is also the result of Social Environment, if the Environment is propitious. In a society where there is exemption from restraint, a secured release from obstruction, in a society where every man is entitled not only to the means of being, but also of well-being, where no man is forced to labour so that another may abound in luxuries, where no man is deprived of his right to cultivate his faculties and powers so that there may be no competition with the favoured, where there is emphasis of reward by mento, where there is goodwill towards all.

## The Problem of Political Suppression

The introduction of the principle of political liberty in India has been very tardy & gradual. It began in the year 1892 when the principle of popular representation in the Constitution of the Legislatures was introduced. It was expanded in 1909. There were two defects in the popular representation as it stood in 1909. The first defect was the franchise was very high. It was so high that a large mass of people were excluded. Those to whom it reached were the aristocracy of the Hindus and the Muslims. The second defect was that the scheme of popular representation was confined to the Legislature. It did not extend to the Executive.

The Executive continued to be independent. The Legislature could neither make or unmake the Executive. The next was taken in 1919. Curiously enough, in the scheme of 1919 the principle of popular representation was applied to the Executive without applying it in commensurate degree to the Legislature. This happened because the political movement in India was led largely by the higher classes. They have always been more anxious for Executive power than for extension of franchise. It is natural. For they stood to gain by executive power. While those who would gain by franchise were the masses.

The higher classes having the ear of the British authorities pressed for executive power and succeeded getting it without the extension of franchise. The franchise was no doubt extended much beyond the bounds fixed in 1909. But it did not touch the Untouchables. Indeed they are so poor that nothing except adult franchise would bring the Untouchables on the electoral roll.

The Government of India was very much perturbed. They could do very little. But they did express their anxiety about placing the Untouchables under the political domination of the high caste Hindus without giving the Untouchables the right to vote in the election. In their despatch of 19th March 1919 the Government of India observed— [Quote] The situation was altered in 1935 under the scheme proposed by the British Government under what is called the Communal Award.

(i) The Untouchables were to have a differential franchise so as to enfranchise about ten per cent of their population.

(ii) The Untouchables were not only to have a differential franchise, they were to have certain number of seats reserved for them in the Provincial and Central Legislatures.

(iii) The seats reserved for them were to be filled by separate Electorates formed exclusively of voters belonging to the Untouchable Community.

(iv) In addition to having a vote in the Separate Electorates the Untouchables were to have a second or additional vote in the general election for seats open to Hindus other than the Untouchables.

Mr. Gandhi who had been objecting to separate representation of the Untouchables raised a protest against the proposal of the British Government and threatened to fast unto death if these concessions were not withdrawn. Mr. Gandhi's objection was mainly to Separate Electorates and as the British Government refused to withdraw their proposals unless there was an agreement between the Untouchables and the Hindus. There upon Mr. Gandhi started his fast. Eventually an agreement was arrived at between the Hindus and the Untouchables in September 1932. That agreement is known as the Poona Pact. Its terms are reproduced below:

## Poona Pact

(1) There shall be seats reserved for the Depressed Classes out of the general electorate seats in the Provincial Legislatures as follows:

| | |
|---|---|
| Madras | 30 |
| Bombay with Sindh | 15 |
| Punjab | 8 |
| Bihar and Orissa | 18 |
| Central Provinces | 20 |
| Assam | 7 |
| United Provinces | 20 |
| Total | 148 |

These figures are based on the total strength of the Provincial Councils, announced in the Prime Minister's decision.

(2) Election to these seats shall be by joint electorates subject, however, to the following procedure:

All the members of the Depressed Classes registered in the fengral electoral roll in a constituency will form an electoral college, which will elect a panel of four candidates belonging to the Depressed Classes for each of such reserved seats, by the method of the single vote; the four persons getting the highest number of votes in such primary election, shall be candidates for election by the general electorate.

(3) Representation of the Depressed Classes in the Central Legislature shall likewise be on the principal of joint electorates and reserved seats by the method of primary election in the manner provided for in Clause two above, for their representation in the Provincial Legislatures.

(4) In the Central Legislatures, eighteen per cent of the seats allotted to the general electorate for British India in the said legislature shall be reserved for the Depressed Classes.

(5) The system of primary election to a panel of candidates for election to the Central and Provincial Legislatures, as here in before mentioned, shall come to an end after the first ten years, unless terminated sooner by mutual agreement under the provision of Clause six below.

(6) The system of representation of the Depressed Classes by reserved seats in the Provincial and Central Legislature as provided *for* in Clauses I and 4 shall continue until determined by mutual agreement between the communities concerned in the settlement.

(7) Franchise for the Central and Provincial Legislatures for the Depressed Classes shall be as indicated in the Lothian Committee Report.

(8) There shall be no disabilities attaching to any one on the ground of his being a member of the Depressed Classes in regard to any elections to local bodies or appointment to the Public Services. Every endeavour shall be made to secure fair representation of the Depressed Classes in these respects, subject to such educational qualifications as may be laid down for appointment to the Public Services.

(9) In every province out of the educational grant, an adequate sum shall be earmarked for providing educational facilities to the members of the Depressed Classes.

This pact forms the charter of the political liberty of the Untouchables. The first election.......

## Which is Worse?—Slavery or Untouchability?

### *Slavery in India*

Among the claims made by the Hindus for asserting their superiority over other nations the following two are mentioned. One is that there was no slavery in India among the Hindus and the other is that Untouchability is infinitely less harmful than slavery.

The first statement is of course untrue. Slavery is a very ancient institution of the Hindus. It is recognised by Manu, the law giver and has been elaborated and systematised by the other Smriti writers who followed Manu. Slavery among the Hindus was never merely ancient institution, which functioned, only in some hoary past. It was an institution which continued throughout all Indian history down to the year 1843 and, if it had not been abolished by the British Government bylaw in that year, it might have continued even today. While slavery lasted it applied to both the touchables as well as the untouchables.

The untouchables by reason of their poverty became subject to slavery of tener than did the touchables. So that up to 1843 the untouchables in India had to undergo the misfortune of being held in double bondage-the bondage of slavery and the bondage of untouchability. The lighter of the bonds has been cut and the untouchable is made free from it. But because the untouchables of today are not seen wearing the chains of slavery on them, it is not to be supposed that they never did. To do so would be to tear off whole pages of history.

The first claim is not so widely made. But the second is. So great a social reformer and so great a friend of the untouchables as Lala Lajpat Rai in replying to the indictment of the Hindu Society by Miss Mayo insisted that untouchability as an evil was nothing as compared with slavery and he fortified his conclusion by a comparison of the Negro in America with the untouchables in India and showed that his conclusion was true. Coming as it does from Lala Lajpat Rai the matter needs to be more closely examined.

Is untouchability less harmful than slavery? Was slavery less human than untouchability? Did slavery hamper the growth more than untouchability does? Apart from the controversy raised by Lala Lajpat Rai, the questions are important and their discussions will be both interesting and instructive. To understand this difference it is necessary to begin by stating the precise meaning of the term slavery. This is imperative because the term slavery is also used in a metaphorical sense to cover social relationship which is kindered to slavery but which is not slavery.

Because the wife was entirely in the power of the husband, because he sometimes ill-used her and killed her, because the husband exchanged or lent his wife and because he made her work for him, the wife was sometimes spoken of as a slave. Another illustration of the metaphorical use of the term is its application to I serfs. Because a serf worked on fixed days, performed fixed I services, paid fixed sums to the lord and was fixed to the land, he was spoken of as a slave. These are instances of curtailment of I freedom, and inasmuch as they are akin to slavery because slavery also involves loss of freedom. But this is not the sense in which the word is used in law, and to avoid arguing at cross purpose, it would be better to base the comparison on the legal meaning of the word slavery.

In layman's language, a person is said to be slave when he is the property of another. This definition is perhaps too terse for the lay reader. He may not understand the full import of it without further explanation, property means something, a term which is used to denote a bundle of rights which a person has over something which is his property, such as the right to possess, to use, to claim the benefit of, to transfer by way of sale, mortgage or lease and destroy. Ownership therefore means complete dominion over property. To put it concretely, when it is said that the slave is the property of the master, what it means is that the master can make the slave work against his will, take the benefit of whatever the slave produces without the consent of the slave.

The master can lease out, sell or mortgage his slave without consulting the wishes of the slave and the master can even kill him in the strictest legal connotation of the term. In the eye of the law the slave is just a material object with which his master may deal in any way he likes.

In the light of this legal definition, slavery does appear to be worse than untouchability. A slave can be sold, mortgaged or leased; an untouchable cannot be sold, mortgaged or leased. A slave can be killed by the master without being held guilty for murder; an untouchable cannot be. Whoever causes his death will be liable for murder. In fact, the slave could not be killed with impunity, the law did recognise his death as being culpable homicide as it did in the case of the death of a freeman. But taking the position of the slave as prescribed by laws the difference between the condition of the slave and the untouchable is undoubtedly clear-that the slave was worse off than the untouchable.

There is however another way of defining a slave which is equally legal and precise although it is not the usual way. This other way of defining a slave is this; A slave is a human being who is not a person in the eye of the law. This way of defining a slave may perhaps puzzle some. It may therefore be necessary to state that in the eye of the law the term person is identical with the term human being. In law, there may be human beings whom the law does not regard as persons. Contrariwise there are in law persons who are not human brings.

This curious result arises of the meaning which the law attaches to the word person. For the purposes of law a person is defined as an entity, human or non-human, in whom the law recognised a capacity for acquiring rights and bearing duties, A slave is not a person in the eye of the law although he is a human being. An idol is a person in the eye of the law although an idol is an inanimate object. The reason for this difference will be obvious. A slave is not a person although he is a human being, because the law does not regard him as an entity endowed with the capacity for rights and duties. Concisely an idol is a person though not a human being because the law does-whether wisely or not is another question-recognise the capacity for rights and duties. To be recognised as a person is of course a very important fact fraught with tremendous consequences. Whether one is entitled to rights and liberties upon this issue, the rights which flow from this recognition as person are not only as life but are as vital as life.

They include right over material things, their acquisition, their enjoyment and their disposal—called right to property. There are others far more important than these rights over material things. Firstly, there is the right in respect of one's own person—a right not to be killed, maimed or injured without due process of law called a right to life, a right not to be imprisoned save in due process of law-called right to liberty. Secondly, there is a right to reputation-a right not to be ridiculed or lowered in the estimation of fellow men, the right to his good name *i.e.* the right to the respect so far as it is well founded which others feel for him shall not be diminished. Thirdly, there is the right to the free exercise of powers and liberties

Every person is entitled without molestation to perform all lawful acts and to enjoy all the privileges which attach to him as a person. The most specific right of this kind is to be the unmolested pursuit of the occupation by which a man chooses to gain his livelihood. Under the same head falls the right of every person to the free use of the public highways, of navigable rivers and all public utilities. It also includes the right of every person that the machinery of the law, which is established for the protection of all persons shall not be maliciously set in motion to his detriment. Thirdly, there is the right of immunity from damage by fraud or coercion-it is a right not to be induced by fraud to assent to a transaction which causes damage, and not to be coerced into acting contrary to one's desire by force.

Fourthly, the rights of a person are those which are collectively called Family Rights. These family rights may be distinguished as 'marital', 'parental', 'tutelary', and 'dominical'. The marital right, the right of a husband as against the world, is that no other man shall, by force or persuasion, deprive him of his wife's society, still less be criminally intimate with her. An analogous right might conceivably be recognised as being vested in the wife and is recognised in parts of America. The parental right extends to the custody and control of children, to the produce of their labour till they arrive at the age of discretion without interference. The tutelary right is the right of the parent to act as the guardian not for the benefit of the guardian but for that of the ward......... whose want of understanding he supplements and whose affairs he manages. The dominical right is the right to use labour of the ward. The right is infringed by killing, by injuring so as to make him less valuable or by enticing him away.

Not being a person, a slave had, so far as law is concerned, none of these rights. The untouchable is a person in the eye of the law. It cannot therefore be said that he has none of the rights which the law gives to a 'person'. He has the right to property, to life, liberty, reputation, family and to the free exercise of his liberties and his powers. Define the slave as one may, either as a piece of property or as one who is not a person, *it* appears that the slave was worse off than the untouchable.

This is so if we consider only the *de jure* position of the slave. Let us consider what was the *defacto* position of the slave in the Roman Empire and in the United States. I take the following extracts from Mr. Barrow:

> *"Hitherto, it is the repulsive side of household slavery that has been sketched. There is also another aspect. The literature reveals the vast household as normal. It is, of course, the exception. Large slave staffs undoubtedly existed, and they are generally to be found in Rome. In Italy and the Provinces there was less need of display; many of the staff of the Villa were engaged in productive work connected with land and its produce. The old-fashioned relationship between foreman and slave remained there; the slave was often a fellow worker. The kindliness of Pliny towards his staff is well-known. It is in no spirit of self-righteousness and in no wish to appear in a favourable light in the eyes of the future generations which he hoped would read his letters that he tells of his distress at the illness and death of his slaves. The household (of Pliny) is the salves' republic. Pliny's account of his treatment of his slaves is sometimes regarded as so much in advance of general or even occasional practice as to be valueless as evidence. There is no reason for this attitude."*

From reasons both of display and genuine literary interest, the rich families attached to their households, slaves trained in literature and art. Calvisices Sabinus is said by Seneca to have had eleven slaves taught to recite Homer, Hesioid, and nine lyric poets by heart. ' Book cases would be cheaper ', said a rude friend. ' No, what the household knows the master knows ' was the answer. But, apart from such abuses, educated slaves must have been a necessity in the absence of printing;..... The busy lawyer, the dilettante poet, the philosopher and educated gentlemen of literary tastes had need of copyists and readers and secretaries. Such men were naturally linguistic also; a librarius who dies at the age of twenty boasts that he was ' *literatus Graecis at Latinis*'. *Amanuensis* were common enough; librarians are to be found in public and private libraries.....Shorthand writing was in common use under the Empire, and slave Notary were regularly employed....

Many freemen, rhetoricians and grammarians are collected by Snetonius in a special treatise. Verrius Flaccus was tutor to Austus's grandsons, and at death was publicly honoured by a statue. Scribonius Aphrodisius was the slave and disciple of

Orbilius and was afterwards freed by Scribenia. Hyginus was librarian of the Palatine Library, in which office he was followed by Jullius Modestus, his own freedman. We hear of freedmen historians of a slave philosopher who was encouraged to argue with his master's, friends' slaves and freed architects. Freemen as doctors occur frequently in the inscriptions, some of them specialists; they had been trained in big households as slaves, as is shown by one or two examples; after Manumission they rose to eminence and became notorious for their high fees."

"The tastes of some section of society demanded that dancers, singers, musicians, montebanks, variety artists, athletic trainers and messeiurs should be forthcoming. All these are to be found in slavery, often trained by teachers who had acquired some reputation."

"The age of Augustus was the beginning of a period of commercial and industrial expansion..... slaves had indeed been employed (in arts and crafts) before, but the sudden growth of trade....their employment in numbers that would otherwise have been unnecessary. Romans engaged more freely and more openly in various forms of commercial and industrial venture. Yet, even so the agent became more important, for commercial activities became more widespread; and such agents were almost necessarily slaves..... (this is so) because the bonds of slavery (are elastic). They could be so relaxed as to offer an incentive (to the slave) to work by the prospect of wealth and freedom, and so tightened as to provide a guarantee to the master against loss from the misconduct of his slave. In business contracts between slave and master third person seem to have been common, and the work thus done, and no doubt, the profits were considerable........ Renting of land to the slave has already been noticed.... and in industry much the same system was used in various forms; the master might lease a bank, or a business of the use of a ship, the terms being a fixed return or the slave being paid on a commission basis".

"The earnings of the slave became in law his peculium. Once the peculium was saved it might be used to a variety of purposes. No doubt in many cases this fund was expended in providing food or pleasure...... But peculium must not be regarded merely as petty savings, casually earned and idly spent. The slave who made his master's business yield profits, to his own profit too, very often, had a keen sense of the best use to make up his own money. Often he reinvested it in his master's business or in enterprises entirely unrelated to it. He could enter into business relations with hi master, from whom he came to be regarded as entirely distinct, or he could make contracts with a third person. He could even have procurators to manage his own property and interests. And so with the peculium may be found not only land, houses, shops but rights and claims.

"The activities of slaves in commerce are innumerable; numbers of them are shopkeepers selling every variety of food, bread, meat, salt, fish, wine vegetables, beans, Aupine-seed, honey, curd, ham, ducks and fresh fish, others deal inclothing—sandals, shoes, gowns and mantles. In Rome, they plied their trade in the neighbourhood of the Circus Maximus, or the Portions Trigeminus; or the Esquiline Market, or the Great Mart (on the Caolian Hill) or the Suburra.

The extent to which slave secretaries and agents acted for their masters is shown very clearly in the receipts found in the house of Caecilius Jucundus at Pompei.

That the State should possess slaves is not surprising; war, after all, was the affair of the State and the captive might well be State-property. What is surprising is the remarkable use made of public slaves under the Empire and the extraordinary social position occupied by them.....

"Public slave came to mean before the Empire a slave of the state employed in its many offices, and the term implied a given occupation and often social position. The work of slaves of the State, slaves of the townships, and slaves of Caesar comprises much of what would now fall to parts of the higher and the whole of the lower branches of the civil services and of the servants of Municipal Corporations, working both with head and hands... In the subordinate levels (of the Treasury) there worked numbers of clerks and financial officers, all freedmen and slaves. The business dealt with must have been of vast range.... The Mint... the immediate head was a knight, in charge of the minting processes.... a freedman was placed under him, served freedmen and slaves.... From one branch of State service, at any rate, slaves were rigorously excluded, except on one or two occasions of exceptional stress. They were not allowed to fight in the Army because they were not thought worthy of honour. Doubtless other motives were present also; it would be dangerous experiment to train too many slaves systematically in the use of Arms. If, however, slaves served merely in the fighting line, they are regularly to be found in great numbers behind it employed as servants, and in the commissariat and transport. In the fleet slaves were common enough"

Such was the defacto position of the slave in Roman Society. Let us trun to the *defacto* position of the Negro in the United States during the period in which he was slave in the eye of the law. Here are some facts which shed a good deal of light on his position:

Lafayette himself had observed that white and black seamen and soldiers had fought and messed together in the Revolution without bitter difference. Down in Granville Country, North Carolina, a full blooded Negro, John Chavis, educated in Princeton University, was conducting a private school for white students and was a licentiate under the local Presbytary, preaching to white congregations in the State. One of his pupils became Governor of North Carolina, another the State's most prominent Whig senator. Two of his pupils were sons of the Chief Justice of North Carolina. The father of the founder of the greatest military academy of the State attended his school and boarded in his home....

Slave labour was used for all kinds of work and the more intelligent of the Negro slaves were trained as artisans to be used and leased. Slave artisans would bring twice as much as an ordinary field hand in the market. Master craftsmen owned their staff. Some masters, as the system became more involved, hired slaves to their slave artisans. Many slave artisans purchased their freedom by the savings allowed them above the normal labour expected."

The advertisements for runaways and sales are an index to this skill. They received the same or better wages than the poor white labourer and with the influence of the master got the best jobs. The Contractors for masons' and carpenters' work in Athens, Georgia in 1838 were petitioned to stop showing preference to Negro labourers. "The white man is the only real, legal, moral, and civil proprietor of this country and state. The right of his proprietorship reached from the date of the studies of those whitemen. Copernicus and Galileo, who indicated the sphericity of the earth; which sphericity hinted to another white man, Columbus, the possibility by a westerly course of sailing, of finding land.

Hence by whitemen alone was this continent discovered, the whitemen alone, aye, those to whom you decline to give money for bread or clothes for their famishing families, in the logical manner of withholding work from them defending Negroes too in the bargain." In Atlanta in 1858, a petition signed by 2 white mechanics and labourers sought protection against the black slave artisans of masters who resided in other sections. The very next year sundry white citizens were aggrieved that the City Council tolerated a Negro dentist to remain and operate in their midst. 'Injustice to ourselves and the community it ought to be abated. We, the residents of Atlanta, appeal to you for justice'. A Census of free Negroes in Richmond County, Georgia, in 1819 showed carpenters, barbers, boatcorkers, saddlers, spinners, millwrights, holsters, weavers, harness makers, sawmill attendants and steamboat pilots.

A Negro shoemaker made by hand the boots in which President Munrow was inaugurated. Harriet Martineau marvelled at the slave workmanship in the delicately tiled floors of Thomas Jefferson's home at Monticello. There still stands in the big house of the old plantation, heavy marks of the hands of these Negro craftsmen, strong mansions built of timber hewn from the original oak and pinned together by wooden pins. Negro women skilled in spinning and weaving worked in the mills. Buckingham in 1839 found them in Athens. Georgia, working alongside with white girls without apparent repugnance of objection.

Negro craftsmen in the South, slave and free fared better than their brothers in the North. In 1856 in Philadelphia, of 1637 Negro craftsmen recorded, less than two-thirds could use their trades; ' because of hostile prejudice '. The Irish who were pouring into America from the very beginning of the nineteenth century were being used in the North on approximately the same motives of preference which governed Negro slavery. 'An Irish Catholic', it was argued in their favour, ' seldom attempts to rise to a higher condition than that in which he is placed, while the Negro often makes the attempt with success.

Had not the old Puritan Oliver Cromwell, while the traffic in black slaves was on, sold all the Irish not killed in the Drogheda Massacre into Barbados? ' Free and fugitive Negroes in New York and Pennsylvania were in constant conflict with this group and the bitter hostility showed itself most violently in the draft riots of the New York. These Hibernians controlled the load carrying and the common labour jobs, opposing every approach of the Negro as a menace to their slight hold upon America and upon a means of livelihood."

Such was the *de facto* condition of the Roman slave and the American Negro slave. Is there anything in the condition of the Untouchables of India which is comparable with the condition of the Roman slave and the American Negro slave? It would not be unfair to take the same period of time for comparing the condition of the Untouchables with that of the slaves under the Roman Empire. But I am prepared to allow the comparison of the condition of the slaves in the Roman Empire to be made with the condition of the Untouchables of the present day.

It is a comparison between the worst of one side and the best of the other, for the present times are supposed to be the golden age for the Untouchables. How does the *defacto* condition of the Untouchables compare with the *defacto* condition of the slaves? How many Untouchables are engaged as the slaves in Rome were, in professions such as those of Librarians, Amanuenses, Shorthand writers? How many Untouchables are engaged, as the slaves in Rome were, in such intellectual occupations as those of rhetoricians, grammarians, philosophers, tutors, doctors and artists? How many untouchables are engaged in trade, commerce or industry as were the slaves in Rome? Even comparing his position with that of the Negro while he was a slave it cannot be said that the condition of the Untouchable has been better. Is their any instance of untouchables having been artisans?

Is there any instance of untouchable having maintained a school where Brahmin children have come to sit at his feet in search of learning? Why such a thing is unthinkable? But it has happened in the United States of America. In comparing the *defacto* condition of the Roman slave and the American Negro I have purposely taken the recent condition of the Untouchables as a basis of comparison for the simple reason that the present times are supposed to be the golden age for the untouchables. But comparing even the condition of the untouchables in modern times they are certainly a sunken community as compared with the condition of slaves in time which historians call barbarous.

There can therefore, be no doubt that untouchables have been worse off than slaves. This of course means that untouchability is more harmful to the growth of man than slavery ever was. On this there is a paradox. Slaves who were worse off in law than the untouchables were in fact better off than untouchables and untouchables who were better off in law than slaves were worse off in fact than slaves. What is the explanation of this paradox? The question of all questions is this; what is it which helped the slave to overcome the rigorous denial of freedom by law and enabled them to prosper and grow? What is it that destroyed the effect of the freedom which the law gave to the untouchables and sapped his life of all vitality and stunted his growth.

The explanation of this paradox is quite simple. It will be easily understood if one bears in mind the relation between law and public opinion. Law and public opinion are two forces which govern the conduct of men. They act and react upon each other. At times law goes ahead of public opinion and checks it and redirects in channels which it thinks proper. At times public opinion is ahead of the law. It rectifies the rigour of the law and moderates it. There are also cases where law and public opinion are opposed to each other and public opinion being the stronger of the two forces, disregards or sets at naught what the law-prescribes. Whether through compulsion arising out of convenience of commerce and industry or out of the selfish desire to make the best and the most profitable use of the slaves or out of considerations of humanity, public opinion and law were not in accord with regard to the position of the slave either in Rome or in the United States.

In both places the slave was not a legal person in the eye of the law. But in both places he remained a person in the sense of a human being in the eye of the society. To put it differently the personality which the law withheld from the slave was bestowed upon him by society. There lies a profound difference between slavery and untouchability. In the case of the untouchable just the opposite has happened. The personality which the law bestowed upon the untouchables is withheld by society.

In the case of the slave the law by refusing to recognise him as a person could do him no harm because society recognised him more amply than it was called upon to do. In the case of the untouchables the law by recognising him as a person failed to do him any good because Hindu society is determined to set that recognition at naught. A slave had a personality which counted notwithstanding the command of the law. An untouchable has no personality in spite of the command of the law. This distinction is fundamental. It alone can explain the paradox— the social elevation of the slave loaded though he was with the burden of legal bondage and the social degradation of the untouchable aided as he has been with the advantages of legal freedom.

Those who have condemned slavery have no doubt forgotten to take into consideration the fact that in a sense slavery was an apprenticeship in a business, craft or art, albeit compulsory. Unmitigated slavery with nothing to compensate the loss of freedom is of course to be condemned. But to enslave a person and to train him is certainly better than a state of barbarity accompanied by freedom. Slavery did mean an exchange of semi-barbarism for civilisation, a vague enough gift but none the less real. The full opportunities for civilised life could only be fully used in freedom, no doubt, but slavery was an apprenticeship, or in the words of Prof. Myres "an initiation into a higher culture".

This view of slavery is eminently a correct view. This training, this initiation of culture was undoubtedly a great benefit to the slave. Equally it involved considerable cost to the master to train his slave, to initiate him into culture. "There can have been little supply of slaves, educated or trained, before enslavement.

The alternative was to train them when young slaves in domestic work or in skilled craft, as was indeed done to some extent before the Empire, by Cato, the Elder, for example. The training was done by his owner and his existing staff indeed the household of the rich contained special pedagogy for this purpose. Such training took many forms: industry, trade, arts and letter".

The question is why was the slave initiated into the high culture and why did it not fall to the lot of the untouchable to be so initiated? The question is very pertinent and I have raised it because the answer to the question will further reinforce the conclusion that has been reached namely that untouchability is worse than slavery and that is because the slave had a personality and the untouchable has not.

The reason why the master took so much trouble to train the slave and to initiate him in the higher forms of labour and culture was undoubtedly the motive of gain. A skilled slave as an item was more valuable than an unskilled slave. If sold he would fetch better price, if hired out he would bring in more wages. It was therefore an Investment to the owner to train his slave. But this is not enough to account for the elevation of the slave and the degradation of the untouchable. Suppose Roman society had an objection to buy vegetables, milk, butter, water or wine from the hands of the slave?

Suppose Roman society had an objection to allow slaves to touch them, to enter their houses, travel with them in cars, etc. would it have been possible for the master to train his slave, to raise him from semi-barbarism to a cultured state? Obviously not. It is because the slave was not held to be an untouchable that the master could train him and raise him. We again come back therefore, to the same conclusion-namely, that what has saved the slave is that his personality was recognised by society and what has ruined the untouchable is that Hindu society did not recognise his personality, treated him as unfit for human association and common dealing.

That the slave in Rome was no less of a man because he was a slave, that he was fit for human intercourse although he was in bondage is proved by the attitude that the Roman Religion had towards the slave. As has been observed:

> *"Roman religion was never hostile to the slave. It did not close the temple doors against him; it did not banish*

*him from its festivals. If slaves were excluded from certain ceremonies, the same may be said of free men and women-being excluded from the rites of Bono Dea, Vesta and Ceres, women Jrom those of Hercules at the Ara Maxima. In the days when the old Roman divinities counted for something, the slave came to be informally included in the family, and could consider himself under the protection of the gods of the household.......Augustus ordered that freed women should be eligible as priestesses of Vesta. The law insisted that a slave's grave should be regarded as sacred and for his soul Roman mythology provided no special heaven and no particular hell. Even Juvenal agrees that the slave, soul and body is made of the same stuff as his master."*

## An Object Surrender

### *Congress Beats An Inglorious Retreat*

The Poona Paet was signed on the 24th September 1932. On 25th September 1932, a public meeting of the Hindus was held in Bombay to accord to it their support. At that meeting the following resolution was passed:

This Conference confirms the Poona agreement arrived at between the leaders of the Caste Hindus and Depressed Classes on September 24, 1932, and trusts that the British Government will withdraw its decision creating separate electorates within the Hindu community and accept the agreement in full.

The Conference urges that immediate action be taken by Government so as to enable Mahatma Gandhi to break his fast within the terms of his vow and before it is too late. The Conference appeals to the leaders of the communities concerned to realize the implications of the agreement and of this resolution and to make earnest endeavour to fulfil them.

This Conference resolves that henceforth, amongst Hindus, no one shall be regarded as an Untouchable by reason of his birth, and that those who have been so regarded hitherto will have the same right as other Hindus in regard to the use of public wells, public schools, public roads, and all other public institutions. This right shall have statutory recognition at the first opportunity and shall be one of the earliest Acts of the

Swaraj Parliament, if it shall not have received such recognition before that time.

It is further agreed that it shall be the duty of all Hindu leaders to secure, by every legitimate and peaceful means, an early removal of all social disabilities now imposed by custom upon the so-called Untouchable Classes, including the bar in respect of admission to temples.

This resolution was followed by a feverish activity on the part of the Hindus to throw open. Temples to the Untouchables. No week passed in which the Harijan a weekly paper started by Mr. Gandhi which did not publish a long list of temples thrown open, wells thrown open and schools thrown open to the Untouchables set out under special column headed "Week to Week" on the first page. As samples I produce below these "Week to Week" columns from two issues from the Harijan.

'Harijan' of 18th February 1933

Sri. V. R. Shinde, president, All – India Anti-Untouchability League and Founder – Trustee of the Depressed Mission Society of India, Poona, has addressed an open letter to the members of the Legislative Assembly on Sri. Ranga Iyer's Untouchability Bills, strongly urging them to support the two measures.

In Taikalwadi in 'G' Ward of Bombay, there was an outbreak of fire recently which caused very serious damage to the huts and belongings of 48 Mahar families, The President of the Bombay Provincial Board of the Servants of Untouchables Society sanctioned Rs.500/-for giving relief to these families, and the relief was organized by a sub committee of the 'G" Ward Committee of the Society. A sum of Rs. 402-8 was distributed as an urgent measure of help to the 48 families, containing in all 163 persons.

The Bombay Government has issued orders that requests from local bodies for assignment of Government lands for wells, tanks, Dharamshalas, etc., should not be granted except on condition that all castes alike will have equal use of such wells, tanks, etc.

"Harijan" of July 15, 1933

Week to Week

## Educational Facilities

Three reading rooms for Harijans have been opened in the North Arcot District by the S.U.S. In the Madura District S.U.S. workers got Harijan children admitted into the Viraganur taluq board school. Banians, towels, slates, etc. were distributed free to the children of the Melacheri school established by the Madura S.U.S Two Harijan, students of Ramjas College, Delhi, have been allowed free scholarship and free lodging and one a free scholarship by Principal Thadani of the College. One night school for adult Harijans was opened under the auspices of the Lahore Harijan Seva Sangh in the Harijan quarters outside. Mochi Gate. The opening ceremony was performed by Mrs. Brij Lal Nehru. It has been decided to start one more hostel for Harijan students in Brahmana Kodur (Guntur). The East Godavery District Harijan Seva Sangham has resolved to start a hostel for Harijan Girl Students studying in Coconada. A sum of Rs. 630/-20 bags of rice, fuel necessary for one year, have been already received as donations for the hostel, which will be started with 15 students. The Anantapur District Harijan Seva Sangam has decided to start a hostel for Harijan students in Uravakonda. Some provisions and money have already been collected and it is intended to start the hostel with 20 students. Owing to the unremitting efforts of the District Harijan Seva Sangham, Guntur, Harijan boys have been allowed into the savarna schools in a manner of villages and towns.

### *Wells*

Three wells in Coimbatore District which were in a bad condition, were cleaned and made available for use. The District Board President, South Arcot, has promised to dig four wells in cherries selected by the S.U.S During the fortnight ending 31-5-33, no less than 125 wells in all were opened to Harijans and 5 new ones constructed in Andhradesh.

### *General*

A shop has been opened in a bustee near Hogg Market (Calcutta) where Doms live, for supplying them with articles of food at cheap rates. Rs. 60 has been paid by the S.U.S. Bengal for paying up the debts of a Harijan family at Bibi

Bagan bustee (Calcutta). The Amrita Samaj (Calcutta) has given service to some Harijans. 450 Harijans of Bolpur (Birbhum) have given up drinking habits and 1,275 Muchis have taken a vow not to take beef. Three new district centres of S.U.S have been opened during the month in Bankura, Murshidabad, and 24 Parganas. Trichinopoly, Tanjore, Tinnevelley, Salem, Dindigal, North Arcot and Madura have all taken up the idea of a Gandhi Harijan Service corps for direct and personal service in the cheris.

Alandural, a Harijan village 12 miles from Coimbatore was given Rs. 25/-worth of grain, Rs. 100 worth of cloth and Rs. 5 worth of oil, as relief after a fire in the village. A Harijan Youth League has been formed in Chindambaram. A shop to supply provisions at cost price to the Harijans has been set up in Tenali and is being made use of by them. A sum of Rs.110/- was spent in giving help for rebuilding houses of Harijans in Valanna Palem (East Kistna) recently destroyed by fire. A sum of Rs.100/-was contributed by the Provincial Committee towards the relief of Harijans in Yellamanchili (Vizag) who lost their houses by a fire. The local Harijan Seva Sangham is endeavouring to erect new houses for the Harijans in a better locality and is collecting donations in cash and building materials. One Harijan has been employed as a servant by a Savarna Gentleman in Gollapalem.

When the owners or trustes of temples were not prepared to throw open their temples to the Untouchables, the Hindus actually started Satyagrah against them to compel them to fall in line. The Satyagrah by Mr. Kelappan for securing entry to the Untouchables in the temple at Guruvayur was a part of this agitation. To force the hands of the trustees of the temples who had the courage to stand against the current, many Hindu legislators came forward, tumbling over one another, with Bills requiring the trustees to throw open temples to the Untouchables if a referendum showed that the majority of the Hindu worshippers voted in favour.

There was a spate of such Bills and a race among legislators to take the first place. There was a Temple Entry Bill by Dr. Subbaroyan of the Madras Legislative Council. There were four Bills introduced in the Central Assembly. One was by Mr. C.S. Ranga Iyer, another by Mr. Harabilas Sarda, a third by Mr. Lalchand Navalrai, and a fourth one by Mr. M.R. Jayakar.

In this agitation Mr. Gandhi also joined. Before 1932, Mr. Gandhi was opposed to allow Untouchables to enter Hindu Temples. To quote his own words Mr. Gandhi said:

> *'How is it possible that the Antyajas (Untouchables) should have the right to enter all the existing temples? As long as the law of caste and Ashram has the chief place in Hindu Religion, to say that every Hindu can enter every temple is a thing that is not possible today."*

His joining the movement for Temple entry must therefore remain a matter of great surprise. Why Mr. Gandhi took this some sault it is difficult to imagine. Was it an honest act of change of heart, due to a conviction that he was in error in opposing the entry of the Untouchables in Hindu temples? Was it due to a realization that the political separation between the Hindus and the Untouchables brought about by the Poona Pact might lead to a complete severance of the cultural and religious ties and that it was necessary to counteract the tendency by some such measure as Temple Entry as will bind the two together? Or was his object in joining the Temple Entry movement to destroy the basis of the claim of the Untouchables for political rights by destroying the barrier between them and the Hindus which makes them separate from the Hindus? Or was it because Mr. Gandhi saw before him looming large a possibility of adding to his name and fame and rushed to make the most of it, as is his habit to do? The second or the third explanation may be nearer the truth.

What was the attitude of the Untouchables to this movement for Temple entry? I was asked by Mr. Gandhi to lend my support to the movement for Temple entry. I declined to do so and issued a statement on the subject to the Press. As it will help the reader to know the grounds for my attitude to this question I have thought it well to set it in full. Here it is!

Statement on Temple Entry Bill

14th February, 1933

Although the controversy regarding the question of Temple Entry is confined to the Sanatanists and Mahatma Gandhi, the Depressed Classes have undoubtedly a very important part to play in it, in so far as their position is bound to weigh the scales one way or the other when the issue comes up for a final settlement. It is, therefore, necessary that their view point should be defined and stated so as to leave no ambiguity about it, To the Temple-Entry of Mr. Ranga Iyer as now drafted, the Depressed Classes cannot possibly give their support. The principle of the Bill is that if a majority of Municipal and Local Board voters in the vicinity of any particular temple on a referendum decide by a majority that the Depressed Classes shall be allowed to enter the temple, the Trustees or the Manager of that temple shall give effect to that decision. The principle is an ordinary principle of Majority rule, and there is nothing radical or revolutionary about the Bill, and if the Sanatanists were a wise lot, they would accept it without demur.

The reasons why the Depressed Classes cannot support a Bill based upon this principle are two: One reason is that the Bill cannot hasten the day of temple-entry for the Depressed Classes any nearer than would otherwise be the case. It is true that under the Bill, the minority will not have the right to obtain an injunction against the Trustee, or the Manager who throws open the temple to the Depressed Classes in accordance with the decision of the majority. But before one can draw any satisfaction from this clause and congratulate the author of the Bill, one must first of all feel assured that when the question is put to the vote there will be a majority in favour the Temple Entry. If one is not suffering from illusions of any kind one must accept that the hope of a majority voting in favour of Temple-entry will be very rarely realized, if at all. Without doubt, the majority is definitely opposed today – a fact which is conceded by the author of the Bill himself in his correspondence with the Shankaracharya.

What is there in the situation as created after the passing of the Bill, which can lead one to hope that the majority will act differently? I find nothing. I shall, no doubt, be reminded of the results of the referendum with regard to the Guruvayur Temple. But I refuse to accept a referendum so over weighted as it was by the life of Mahatma Gandhi as the normal result. In any such calculations, the life of the Mahatma must necessarily be deducted.

Secondly, the Bill does not regard Untouchability in temples as a sinful custom. It regards Untouchability merely as a social evil not necessarily worse than social evils of other sorts. For, it does not declare Untouchability as such to be illegal. Its binding force is taken away, only, if a majority decides to do so. Sin and immorality cannot become tolerable because a majority is addicted to them or because the majority chooses to practise them. If Untouchability is a sinful and an immoral custom, then in the view of the Depressed Classes it must be destroyed without any hesitation even if it was acceptable to the majority. This is the way in which all customs are dealt with by Courts of Law, if they find them to be immoral and against public policy.

This is exactly what the Bill does not do. The author of the Bill takes no more serious view of the custom of Untouchability than does the temperance reformer of the habit of drinking. Indeed, so much is he impressed by the assumed similarity between the two that the method he has adopted is a method which is advocated by temperance reformers to eradicate the evil habit of drinking, namely, by local option. One cannot feel much grateful to a friend of the Depressed Classes, who holds Untouchability to be no worse than drinking. If Mr. Ranga Iyer had not forgotten that only a few months ago Mahatma Gandhi had prepared himself to fast unto death if Untouchability was not removed, he would have taken a more serious view of this curse and proposed a most thorough going reform to ensue its removal lock, stock and barrel. Whatever its shortcomings may be front the stand point of efficacy, the least that the Depressed classes could expect is for the Bill to recognize the principle that Untouchability is a sin.

I really cannot understand how the Bill satisfies Mahatma Gandhi who has been insisting that Untouchability is a sin. It certainly does not satisfy the Depressed Classes. The question whether this particular Bill is good or bad, sufficient or insufficient, is a subsidiary question.

The main question is; do the Depressed Classes desire Temple Entry or do they not? This main question is being viewed by the depressed Classes by two points of view. One is the materialistic point of view. Starting from it, the Depressed Classes think that the surest way for their elevation lies in higher education, higher employment and better ways of earning a living. Once they become well placed in the scale of social life, they would become respectable and once they become respectable the religious outlook of the orthodox towards them is sure to undergo change, and even if this did not happen, it can do no injury to their material interest. Proceeding on these lines the Depressed Classes say that they will not spend their resources on such an empty thing as Temple Entry.

There is also another reason why they do not care to fight for it. That argument is the argument of self-respect.

Not very long ago there used to be boards on club doors and other social resorts maintained by Europeans in Indian, which said "Dogs and Indians" not allowed. The temples of Hindus carry similar boards today, the only difference is that the boards on the Hindu temples practically say: "All Hindus and all animals including dogs are admitted, only Untouchables not admitted." The situation in both cases is on a parity. But Hindus never begged for admission in those places from which the Europeans in their arrogance had excluded them. Why should an Untouchable beg for admission in a place from which he has been excluded by the arrogance of the Hindus? This is the reason of the Depressed Class man who is interested in his material welfare. He is prepared to say to the Hindus, "to open or not to open your temples is a question for you to consider and not for me to agitate. If you think, it is bad manners not to respect the sacredness of human personality, open your temples and be a gentleman. If you rather be a Hindu than be gentleman, then shut the doors and damn yourself for I do not care to come."

I found it necessary to put the argument in this form, because I want to disabuse the minds of men like Pandit Madan Mohan Malaviya of their belief that the Depressed Classes are looking forward expectantly for their patronage.

The second point of view is the spiritual one. As religiously minded people, do the Depressed Classes desire temple entry or do they not? That is the question. From the spiritual point of view, they are not indifferent to temple entry as they would be, if the material point of view alone were to prevail. But their final answer must depend upon the reply which Mahatma Gandhi and the Hindus give to the question namely: What is the drive behind this offer of temple entry? Is temple entry to be the final goal of the advancement in the social status of the

Depressed Classes in the Hindu fold? Or is it only the first step and if it is the first step, what is the ultimate goal? Temple Entry as a final goal, the Depressed Classes can never support. Indeed they will not only reject it, but they would then regard themselves as rejected by Hindu society and free to find their own destiny elsewhere. On the other hand, if it is only to be a first step in the direction they be may be inclined to support it. The position would then be analogous to what is happening in the politics of India today. All Indians have claimed Dominion Status for India. The actual constitution will fall short of Dominion Status and many Indians will accept it. Why? The answer is that as the goal is defined, it does not matter much if it is to be reached by steps and not in one jump. But if the British had not accepted the goal of Monition Status, no one would have accepted the partial reforms which many are now prepared to accept.

In the same way, if Mahatma Gandhi and the reformers were to proclaim what the goal which they have set before themselves is for the advancement of the social Status of the Depressed Classes in the Hindu fold, it would be easier for the Depressed Classes to define their attitude towards Temple Entry. The goal of the depressed Classes might as well be stated here for the information and consideration of all concerned. What the Depressed Classes want is a religion, which will give them equality of social status.

To prevent any misunderstanding, I would like to elaborate the point by drawing a distinction between social evils which are the results of secular causes and social evils which are founded upon the doctrine of religion. Social evils can have no justification whatsoever in a civilized society. But nothing can be more odious and vile than that admitted social evils should be sought to be justified on the ground of religion. The Depressed Classes may not be able to overthrow inequities to which they are being subjected. But they have made up their mind not to tolerate a religion that will lend its support to the continuance of these inequities.

If the Hindu religion is to be their religion, then it must become a religion of Social Equality. The mere amendment of Hindu religious code by the mere inclusion in it of a provision to permit temple entry for all, cannot make it a religion of equality of social status. All that it can do is to recognize them as nationals and not aliens, if I may use in this connection terms which have become so familiar in politics. But that cannot mean that they would thereby reach a position where they would be free and equal, without being above or below any one else, for the simple reason that the Hindu religion does not recognize the principle of equality of social status; on the other hand it fosters inequality by insisting upon grading people as Brahmins, Kshatrias, Vaishyas and Sudras, which now stand towards one another in an ascending scale of hatred and descending scale of contempt.

If the Hindu religion is to be a religion of social equality then an amendment of its code to provide temple-entry is not enough. What is required is to purge it of the doctrine of Chaturvarna. That is the root cause of all in equality and also the parent of the caste system and Untouchability, which are merely forms of inequality. Unless it is done not only will the Depressed Classes reject Temple Entry, they will also reject the Hindu faith.

Chaturvarna and the Caste system are incompatible with the self-respect of the Depressed Classes. So long as they stand to be its cardinal doctrine the Depressed Classes must continue to be looked upon as low. The Depressed Classes can say that they are Hindus only when the theory of Chaturvarna and caste system is abandoned and expunged from the Hindu shastras.

Do the Mahatma and the Hindu reformers accept this as their goal and will they show the courage to work for it? I shall look forward to their pronouncements on this issue, before I decide upon my final attitude. But whether Mahatma Gandhi and the Hindus are prepared for this or not, let it be known once for all that nothing short of this will satisfy the Depressed Classes and make them accept Temple Entry. To accept temple entry and be content with it, is to temporize with evil and barter away the sacredness of human personality that dwells in them.

There is, however, one argument which Mahatma Gandhi and the reforming Hindus may advance against the position I have taken. They may say: acceptance by the Depressed Classes of Temple Entry now, will not prevent them from agitating hereafter for the abolition of Chaturvarna and Caste. If that is their view, I like to meet the argument right at this stage so as to clinch the issue and clear the road for future developments. My reply is that it is true that my right to agitate for the abolition of Chaturvarna and Caste System will not be lost, if I accept Temple Entry now. But the question is on what side will Mahatma Gandhi be at the time when the question is put. If he will be in the camp of my opponents, I must tell him that I cannot be in his camp now. If he will be in my camp he ought to be in it now.—B.R. Ambedkar.

Dewan Bahadur R. Srinivasan who along with me represented the untouchables at the Round Table Conference also did not support the movement for Temple entry. In a statement to the Press, he said:

> *"When a Depressed Classes member is permitted to enter into the caste Hindu temples he would not be taken into any one of the four castes, but treated as man of fifth or the last or the lower caste, a stigma worse than the one to be called an Untouchable. At the same time he would be subjected to so many caste restrictions and humiliations. The Depressed Classes shun the one who enters like that and exclude him as casteman. The crores of Depressed Classes would not submit to caste restrictions. They will be divided into sections if they do. 'Temple entry cannot be forced by law. The village castemen openly or indirectly defy the law. To the village Depressed Class man it would be like a scrap of paper on which the "Sugar" was written and placed in hands for him to taste. The above facts are placed before the public in time to save confusion and disturbance in the country."*

To the question I put to Mr. Gandhi in my statement he gave a straight reply. He said that though he was against untouchability he was not against caste. If at all, he was in favour of it and that he would not therefore carry his social reform beyond removing untouchability. This was enough for me to settle my attitude. I decided to take no further part in it.

The only leading member from the Untouchable community was the late Dewan Bahadur Rajah. One cannot help saying that he played a very regrettable part in this business. The Dewan Bahadur was a nominated member of the Central Assembly from 1927. He had nothing to do with the Congress either inside or outside the Assembly. Neither by accident nor by mistake did he appear on the same side of the Congress. Indeed, he was not merely a critic of the Congress but its adversary. He was the staunchest friend of the government and never hesitated to stand by the government. He stood for separate electorates for the Untouchables to which the Congress was bitterly opposed. In the crisis of 1932, the Dewan Bahadur suddenly decided to desert the Government and take sides with the Congress. He became the spearhead of the Congress movement for joint electorates and Temple entry.

It is impossible to discover a parallel in the conduct of any other public cause. The worst part of the business was that it had none but personal motive behind. The Dewan bahadur was deeply cut because the Government did not nominate his as a delegate to the Round Table Conference to represent the Untouchables and in his stead nominated Dewan Bahadur R. Srinivasan. The government of India had good ground for not nominating him. It was decided that neither the members of the Simon Commission not the members of the Central Legislative Committee should have a place in the Round Table Conference. The Dewan Bahadur was a member of the Central Legislative Committee and had therefore to be dropped.

This was quite a natural explanation. But the wounded pride of Dewan Bahadur Rajah could not let him see it. When the Congress Ministry took office in Madras, when he saw how the Poona Pact was being trampled upon, how his rival was made a Minister and how notwithstanding his services to the Congress he was left out, he bitterly regretted what he did. The fact, however, remains that in the critical year of 1932, Dewan Bahadur Rajah lent his full support to the Congress. He was not only running with the Congress crowd but he took care not to fall out in the race for legislation against untouchability. He too had sponsored two Bills. One of them was called the Removal of Untouchability Bill and the other was called the Criminal Procedure Amendment Bill.

Mr. Gandhi did not mind any opposition and was indifferent as to whether it came from the orthodox Hindus or from the

Untouchables. He went on in mad pursuit of his object. It is interesting to ask, what happened to this movement? Within the short compass of this book it is not possible to spread out this inquiry and cover everything that was done and claimed as evidence of the success of the movement.

To put it briefly, after a short spurt of activity in the direction of removing untouchability by throwing open temples and wells the Hindu mind returned to its original state. The reports appearing in the "Week to Week" columns of the Harijan subsided, became few and far between and ultimately vanished. For myself I was not surprised to find that the Hindu heart was so soon stricken with palsy. For I never believed that there was so much milk of human kindness locked up in the Hindu breast as the "Week to Week" column in the Harijan would have the world believe. As a matter of fact a large part of the news that appeared in the "Week to Week" was faked and was nothing but a lying propaganda engineered by Congressmen to deceive the world that the Hindus were determined to fight untouchability.

Few temples if any were really opened and those that were reported to have been opened most of them were dilapidated and deserted temples which were used by none but dogs and donkeys. One of the evil effects of the Congress agitation is that it has made the political minded Hindus a lying squad which will not hesitate to tell any lie if it can help the Congress. Thus ended the part which the Hindu public played or was made to appear to play in this Temple-Entry movement. The same fate overtook the Guruvayur Temple Satyagrah and the legislation for securing Temple-Entry for the Untouchables. As these are matters which were pursued by Mr. Gandhi and congressmen their history might be told in some detail inasmuch as it reveals the true mentality of Mr. Gandhi and the Congress towards the Untouchables.

To begin with the Guruvayur Temple Satyagrah. A temple of Krishan is situated at Guruvayur in the Ponnani taluk in Malabar. The Zamorin of Calicut is the trustee of the temple. One Mr. Kelappan, a Hindu who was working for the cause of the Untouchables of Malabar, began an agitation for securing the Untouchables entry into the temple. The Zamorin of Calicut as the trustee of the temple refused to throw open temple to the Untouchables and in support of his action cited Section 40 of the Hindu Religious Endowments Act which said that no trustee could do anything against the custom and usage of the temples entrusted to him.

On the 20th September 1932, Mr. Kelappan commenced a fast in protest lying in front of the temple in the sun till the Zamorin revised his views in favour of the Untouchables. To get rid of this annoyance and embarrassment the Zamorin appealed to Mr. Gandhi to request Mr. Kelappan to suspend his fast for a time. After a fast for ten days Mr. Kelappan at the request of Mr. Gandhi suspended the fast on 1st October 1932 for three months. The Zamorin did nothing. Mr. Gandhi sent him a wire telling him that he must move in the matter and get over all difficulties legal or otherwise. Mr. Gandhi also told the Zamorin that as Mr. Kelappan had suspended his fast on his advice he had become responsible for securing to the Untouchable entry into the temple to the extent of sharing the fast with Mr. Kelappan. On 5th November 1932, Mr. Gandhi issued the following statement to the press:

> *"There is another fast which is a near possibility and that in connection with the opening of the Guruvayur temple in Kerala. It was at my urgent request that Mr..Kelappan suspended his fast for three months, a fast that had well nigh brought him to death's door. I would be in honour bound to fast with him if on or before 1st January 1933 that temple is not opened to the Untouchables precisely on the same terms as to the Touchables, and if it becomes necessary for Mr. Kelappan to resume his fast."*

The Zamorin refused to yield and issue a counter-statement to the press in which he said:

> *"The various appeals that are being made for throwing open the temples to Avarnas proceed upon an inadequate appreciation of such difficulties. In these circumstances, there is hardly any justification for thinking that it is in my power to throw open the Guruvayur temple to the Avarnas as desired by the supporters of the temple-entry campaign"*

In these circumstances a fast by Mr. Gandhi became in evitable, and obligatory. But Mr. Gandhi did not go on fast. He modified his position and said that he would, refrain from fasting if a referendum was taken in Ponnani taluka in which the temple was situated and if the referendum showed that the majority was against the throwing open of the temple to the Untouchables. Accordingly, a referendum was taken. Voting was confined to those who were actual temple goers Those who were not entitled to enter the temple and those who would not enter it were excluded from the voters' list. It was reported that 73 per cent of eligible voters voted. The result of the poll was 56 per cent, were in favour of temple entry, 9 per cent, against, 8 percent were neutral and 27 percent abstained from recording their votes.

On this result of the referendum, Mr. Gandhi was bound to start the fast. But he did not. Instead, on the 29th of December 1932 Mr. Gandhi issued a statement to the press which he concluded by saying:

> *"In view of the official announcement that the Vice regal decision as to sanction for the introduction, in the Madras Legislative Council, of Dr. subbaroyan's permissive Bill with reference to the temple-entry could not possibly be announced before the 15th January, the fast contemplated to take place on the second day of the New Year will be indefinitely postponed and in any case up to the date of the announcement of the Viceregal decision. Mr. Kelappan concurs in this postponement."*

The Viceregal pronouncement mentioned by Mr. Gandhi had reference to the Viceroy's granting permission or refusing permission to the moving of the Temple Entry Bills in the Legislature. That permission was given by the viceroy. Yet Mr. Gandhi did not fast. Not only did he not fast, he completely forgot the matter as though it was of no moment. Since then nothing has been heard about Guruvayur Temple Satyagrah though the Temple remains closed to the Untouchables even today.

Thus ended Guruvayur. Let me now turn to the other project namely legislation for temple-Entry. Of the many bills the one in the name of Mr. Ranga Iyer in the Central Legislature was pursued. The rest were dropped. There was a storm at the very birth of the Bill. Under the Government of India Act as it then stood no legislative measure which affected religion and customs and usages based on religion could be introduced in the Assembly unless it had the previous sanction of the Governor-General. When the Bill was sent for such sanction another commotion was created by the reports that were circulated that the governor-General was going to refuse his sanction. Mr. Gandhi was considerably excited over these reports. In a statement to the press issued on the 21st January 1933, Mr. Gandhi said:

> *"If the report is an intelligent anticipation of the forth coming viceregal decision, I can only say that it will be a tragedy.... I emphatically repudiate the suggestion that there is any political objective behind these measures. If court decisions had not hardened a doubtful custom into law, no legislation would be required. I would myself regard State interference in religious matters as an intolerable nuisance. But here legislation becomes an imperative necessity in order to remove the legal obstruction and based as it will be on popular will, as far as I can see, there can be no question of clash between parties representing rival opinions."*

The decision of the Government was announced on the 23rd of January 1933. Lord Willingdon refused sanction to Dr. Subbaroyan's Temple-Entry Bill in the Madras Council, but His Excellency permitted the introduction, in the Legislative Assembly, of Mr. Ranga Iyer's Untouchability abolition Bill. The Government emphasized the need of ascertainment of Hindu opinion before they (Government) could decide what attitude to adopt. The announcement further stated that the Governor-General and the Government of India desired to make it plain that it was essential that consideration of any such measure should not proceed unless the proposals were subjected to the fullest examination in all their aspects, not merely in the Legislature but also outside it, by all who would be affected by them. This condition can only be satisfied if the Bill is circulated in the widest manner for the purpose of eliciting public opinion. It must also be understood that the grant of sanction to the introduction in the Central Legislature, Bills relating to temple entry do not commit the Government in any way to the acceptance or support of the principles contained therein. On the next day, Mr. Gandhi issued a statement in which he said:

*"I must try to trace the hand of god init. He wants to try me through and through. The sanction given to the all India Bill was an unintentional challenge to Hinduism and the reformer. Hinduism will take care of itself if the reformer will be true to himself. Thus considered the government of India's decision must be regarded as Godsend. It clears the issue. It makes it for India and the world to understand the tremendous importance of the moral struggle now going on in India. But whatever the Sanatanists may decide the movement for Temple-Entry now broadens from Guruvayur in the extreme south to Hardwar in the north and my fast, though it remains further postponed, depends not now upon ' Guruvayur only but extends automatically to temples in general."*

One can well realize under what fanfare the Bill began its legislative career. On the 24th of March 1933, Mr. Ranga Iyer formally introduced the Bill in the assembly. As it was a Bill for Mr. Gandhi the Congress members of the Assembly were of course ready to give it their support. Mr. Gandhi had appointed Mr. Rajagopalachari and Mr. G.D. Birla to canvass support for the Bill among the Non-congress members with a view to ensure safe passage for the Bill. He said they were better lobbyists than he was. The motion for introduction was opposed by the Rajah of Kollengode and Mr. Thampan raised a preliminary objection that the Bill was ultra vires of the legislature.

The latter objection was overruled by the President and the House allowed the Bill to be introduced. Mr. Ranga Iyer next moved that the Temple-Entry Bill be circulated to calicut public opinion by the 30th July. Raja Bahadur Krishnamachari opposed the circulation motion and condemned the proposed legislation in strong terms. At last he urged that the date for circulation should be 31st December instead of 31st July. Mr. Gunjal opposed the circulation motion and asked the House not to support the Bill. As it was already 5 p.m. and as that was the last day of the session for non-official business, the President wanted to take the sense of the House for a late sitting. As there was no over whelming majority for it, the President adjourned the House. So the Bill stood postponed to the autumn session of the Assembly.

The discussion of the Bill was resumed on 24th August 1933 during the Autumn session of the Central Legislature. Sir Harry Haig on behalf of the Government explained that their support to the motion for circulation of the Bill should in no way be construed as implying support to its provisions. It was true that the Government sympathized for the Depressed Classes and were anxious to do what they could for their social and economic improvement. He quoted from the communique issued in January last, wherein the government's view was fully explained. In his opinion circulation by the end of June was a fair and reasonable time to secure the widest possible circulation.

As regards the limit of circulation to temple going Hindus, Sir Harry Haig said from the practical viewpoint that it would really hardly be possible to impose the restriction as proposed. The government wanted the matter to be fully discussed by all classes of Hindus and were therefore prepared to give their support to the amendment of Mr. Sharma. Closure was moved and the House accepted Mr. Sharma's motion for circulation of the Bill by the end of June 1934. Opinions were duly received. They fill a whole volume of over a thousand fullscape pages. The Bill was ready for the next stage namely to move for the appointment of a Select Committee. Mr. Ranga Iyer had even given notice for such a motion. A strange thing happened. The government of India decided to dissolve the Assembly and order new election. The result of this announcement was a sudden change in the attitude of the Congress members in the Central Legislature towards Mr. Ranga's Bill. One and all stood out against it and refused to give any further support to the Bill. They were terrified of the electorates. Mr. Ranga Iyer's position was very pitiable. He described it in very biting language, the venom of which could hardly be improved upon. So well did he describe the situation that I make no apology for reproducing the following extract from his speech. Rising to move his motion Mr. Ranga Iyer said: Sir, I rise to move what is known as the Temple-Entry Bill, to remove the disabilities of the so-called Depressed Classes. Sir, I move:

> *"That the Bill to remove the disabilities of the so-called Depressed Classes in regard to entry into Hindu temples be referred to a Select Committee consisting of the*

*Honourable sir Nripendra Sircar, the Honourable Sir Henry Craik, Bhai Parma Naud, Rao Bahadur M.C. Rajah, Mr. T.N. Ramakrshna Reddi, Rao Bahadur B.L. Patil and the Mover,"*

I will delete with your permission, the words 'with instructions to report within a fortnight' and then I will continue the remaining portion of the motion: 'and that the number of members whose presence shall be necessary to constitute a meeting of the Committee shall be five' "Sir, at the time I gave notice of this motion, I did not think that before a fortnight we would be going into the wilderness. Therefore, I recognize the limitations of this motion, for there will be no time even to go to a Select Committee. I recognize that it gives us an opportunity to express our opinion on the subject.

"I have already stated that I owed an apology to Mr. Satyamurthi for while interrupting Mr. Mudaliar, I was not in a position naturally as he was rushing along with his speech to explain myself fully and he would have been at a disadvantage if I had done so. I recognize that Mr. Satyamurthi, who was at no time in favour of the Temple-entry Bill, has succeeded in making the Congress drop it. I read the following written statement of Mr. C. Rajagopalachari in the Hindu of Madras, dated the 16th august.

The Hindu is a very responsible newspaper, and as it is not a mere telegraphic interview but a written statement, I believe Mr. Rajagopalachari's statement can be taken as accurate. Mr. Rajagopalachari is apologizing to the public for his betrayal of the cause of the Untouchables, As the principal lieutenant of Mahatma Gandhi, his betrayal must be placed on record. He says:

*'The question has been asked by some Sanatanists whether Congress candidates will give an undertaking that Congress will not support any legislative interference with religious observances. Similar questions may be asked on a variety of topics by persons and groups interested in each one of them. That such questions are asked only of the Congress candidates and similar elucidation is not attempted in respect of other parties and independent candidates is a very great compliment paid to the Congress."*

"So, says, Sriman Rajagopalachari, And, instead of following up the compliment and arousing public opinion on an unpopular measure, here is a great Congress leader who sat dharna at our house with his son-in-law, Devidas Gandhi,, who repeatedly called on me at Delhi and said 'We seek joint support for this legislative measure,' here is a man who goes back 'like a crab' tomorrow the language of Shakespeare. Political parties, explains this subtle brain from the south, have distinctive policies on various questions covering a wide field:

"Not all of them, however, are made into election issues at any one time'

' Sir, this Congress leader is afraid of facing the public opinion which he has roused.

"Sir, are the congress people slaves?

"They are slaves who fear to speak,
For the fallen and the weak.'

"According to Milton, To say and straight unsay argues no liar but a coward traced,' Mr. Rajagopalachari unsays now what he had been saying long before the General Election from every platform in the following words:

*"the congress candidates go to the electorate in this election on well-defined political issues."*

"That is to say, they go to the electorate with a view to pandering to the prejudice of the masses whom they have misled, so much so, that they have got themselves into a bog. Lord Willingdon came to their rescue, to take them out of the bog by announcing the dissolution of this assembly and giving them an opportunity, as a Constitutional Viceroy, to return to the sheltered paths of constitutionalism. Therefore, they have run away from their own convictions and are playing every trick to come back to the Legislature with as large a number as possible. Had they gone on with the Temple entry Bill or the Untouchability question, they would have lost many votes, for it is not a popular issue. I said so, though Mahatma Gandhi contradicted me publicly at the time, I said so when Shankaracharya was staying in Malabar in my brother's house at Palghat. My brother came on a deputation to the Viceroy to oppose the Bill. I said: ' I know, the reformer is not in a majority in Malabar' Nowhere else are the reformers in a majority but the reformers believe, in persuading the majority to their way of thinking.

Then, I said-whatever the result of a referendum, the Congress people might have taken in guruvayur in Malabar, might be, I could not for a moment believe that the majority of the temple-going people in Malabar were in favour of admitting the Untouchables into the temples: but I was prepared to fight them, also to argue with them and to persuade them and to make them take an interest in the cause and the case of the Untouchables, for, I feel, the Untouchables are a part of my community. Sir, if one third of my community is to remain submerged in exclusion in the name of religion, I feel, as I have always felt and said, that community has no right to existence. It is with a view to the unification of the Hindu community, it is with a view to building up the greatness of the future of that community on the past of that community, when Untouchability was quite unknown as in the Vedic ages, that I have taken up their cause. And now, I find Congressmen, so keen about Untouchability yesterday, explaining why they are not taking it up today. Mr. Rajagopalachari has driven the last nail into the coffin of the Temple Entry Bill as Raja Bahadur Krishnamachari, the Raja Saheb of Kollengode or Sir Satya Charan Mukherji would perhaps like to say, representing as they do the various Sanatanist groups of the country.

"Sir. Mr. Rajagopalachari goes on to say that they asked to be returned' on no other issue,' that is to say, not on Temple Entry issue, but merely on a political Anglo-phobia issue, an anti-British issue, because, having traded on public feeling, having tried to give it as much racial antipathy as possible in the name of non-violence, in the name of religion itself, because non-violence was sometimes given a religious bias, having created that atmosphere might not help them in the election if they fought it on a bigger, a cleaner and higher issue, namely, the removal of Untouchability itself, they sidetrack the issue, they run away from their conviction:

'They are slaves who dare not be

In the right with two or three.'

"Then he, a principal lieutenant of Gandhiji goes on to say;

'If successful at the polls, they cannot believe they will receive the mandate of the electorate on any other questions.'

"That is to say, they are not receiving the mandate of the electorate on the Temple Entry Bill. This man, who came screaming at our doors, begging us for support-these beggars in the cause of the Congress—who just begged of us to proceed with this Temple Entry Bill, are not only betraying the cause of the Untouchables, but they are betraying the principles of the Mahatma himself, for, we know, that Mahatma's fast was directed toward the uplift of the Untouchables by giving them concession in regard to the Communal Award, which the Congress naturally has hesitated to repudiate, and we, therefore, know that has a direct bearing on the Untouchability question to approach which, to solve which, the Mahatma, the great Mahatma, wanted to tour the country, but today the Congress, who betrayed him first in the betrayal of the Congress boycott of the Councils, have, by seeking to come to the Councils, further betrayed him with the assistance of his own Samandhi, Rajagopalachari, and they say that they are not going to proceed with the Untouchability question and the Temple Entry Bill without a mandate from the people.

"Sir, where is the difference, I ask, between Raja Bahadur Krishnamachariar and Sriman Rajagopalachari? Raja Bahadur Krishnamachariar has always conceded – 'take a mandate from the people and then come and legislate,' Sir, he is not a coward; a great Sanatanist himself, he is willing to face the music. On the contrary, these people who pillory the Sanatanists up and down the country, forgetting that Sanatan Dharma is eternal truth itself, are behaving in a manner which even the Sanatanists will not appreciate, for Sanatan Dharma is eternal truth and the betrayal of truth is worthy only of untruthful people. Having betrayed many a principle which would lead us to our national goal, having taken up the case of the Untouchables only to save their faces, with no conviction behind them, as we now see, the great Congress leaders with the exception of Mahatma Gandhi, have said through Rajagopalachari, the Organizer-in-chief of the coming elections on behalf of the Congress;

'It will be open to all Congress men to have the matter duly considered before it is ever made into an official Congress Bill.'

"For this betrayal of the cause of the Untouchables, I hope constitutionalists will organize themselves, whether Hindus or

Musalmans. They can agree to differ later on communal issues, but they will unite and offer a great battle to the Congress and bring that organ of masqueraders down on its knees, Sir, I think here is a betrayal of the cause of the Untouchables and the Depressed Classes; and, if I did not believe in this movement before mahatma Gandhi could take it up or Mr. Rajagopalachari went from door to door in Delhi, I should not have been here to move this Bill." Here was a case of retreat from glory. And what an inglorious retreat? How did Mr. Gandhi react to it? In a statement issued on 4th November 1932, Mr. Gandhi said:

"Untouchables in the villages should be made to feel that their shackles have been broken, that they are in no way inferior to their fellow villagers, that they are worshippers of the same God as the other villagers and entitled to the same rights and privileges that the latter enjoy."

"But if these vital conditions of the Pact are not carried out by caste-Hindus, could I possibly live to face God and man? I ventured even to tell Dr. Ambedkar, Rao Bahadur M.C. Raja and other friends belonging to the suppressed group that they should regard me as a hostage for the due fulfilment by caste – Hindus of the conditions of the Pact.

The fast, if it is to come, will not be for coercion of those who are opponents of reform, but it will be intended to sting into action those who have been my comrades or who have taken pledges for the removal of Untouchability. If they believe their pledges or if they never meant to abide by them and their Hinduism was a mere camouflage, I should have no interest left in life."

He was never tired of repeating this. Exclusion of the Untouchables from the Hindu Temples, he described, as the agony of his soul. What did Mr. Gandhi do in this connection? Did he resent this betrayal by Mr. Rajagopalachari of this project without which he said he had no interest left in life? One would naturally expect. Mr. Gandhi to denounce this betrayal by the Congress Party to achieve success at the polls? Quite the contrary. Instead of blaming Mr. Rajagopalachari, he blamed Mr. Ranga Iyer for his violent denunciation of the Congress Party for withdrawing its support to the Bill. This is what Mr. Gandhi said in the issue of the Harijan dated August 31, 1934:

"The ill-fated Temple Entry Bill deserved a more decent burial, if it deserved it at all, than it received at the hands of the mover of the Bill. It was not a bill promoted by, and on behalf of, the reformers. The mover should, therefore, have consulted reformers and acted under instructions from them. So far as I am aware, there was hardly any occasion for the anger into which he allowed himself to be betrayed or the displeasure which he expressed towards Congressmen.

On the face of it, it was, and was designed to be, a measure pertaining to religion, framed in pursuance of the solemn declaration publicly made in Bombay at a meeting of representative Hindus, who met under the chairmanship of Pandit Malaviyaji on 25th September, 1932. The curious may read the declaration printed almost every week on the front page of Harijan. Therefore, every Hindu, caste or Harijan, was interested in the measure. It was not a measure in which Congress Hindus were more interested than the other Hindus. To have, therefore, dragged the Congress name into the discussion was unfortunate. The Bill deserved a gentler handling." The Temple Entry, what one is to say of, except to describe it a strange game of political acrobatics Mr. Gandhi begins as an opponent of Temple Entry. When the Untouchables put forth a demand for political rights, he changes his position and becomes a supporter of Temple Entry. When the Hindus threaten to defeat the Congress in the election, if it pursues the matter to a conclusion, Mr. Gandhi, in order to preserve political power in the hands of the Congress, gives up Temple Entry. Is this sincerity? Does this show conviction? Was the "agony of soul" which Mr. Gandhi spoke of more than a phrase?

## Political Demands of Scheduled Castes

Resolutions passed by the Working Committee of the All-India Scheduled Castes Federation held in Madras on the 23rd September 1944 under the Presidentship of Rao Bahadur N. Shiva Raj, B.A.B.L.M.L.A outlining the safeguards for the Untouchables in new constitution.

### Resolution No.1

***Subject:*** *Recognition of the Schedule Castes as a separate element.*

The Working Committee of the All India Scheduled Castes Federation has found a section of the Press in India making the allegation, that the statement made by H.E. the Viceroy in his letter to Mr. Gandhi dated the 15th August 1944 to the effect that the Scheduled Castes are one of the important and separate elements in the national life of India and requiring that the consent of the Scheduled Castes to the Constitution of India was a necessary condition precedent for transfer of power to Indians, is a departure from the position of His Majesty's Government as defined in the Cripps Proposals. The committee cannot help expressing its indignation at this propaganda and takes this occasion to state in most emphatic and categorical terms that the Scheduled Castes are a distinct and separate element in the national life of Indian and that they are a religious minority in a sense far more real than the Sikhs and Muslims can be and within the meaning of the Cripps Proposals. The Working Committee desires to point out that what has been stated by Lord Wavell in his letter to Mr. Gandhi has been the position of His Majesty's Government from the very beginning and was enunciated in clear terms as early as 1917 by the authors of the Montagu-Chelmsford Report simultaneously with the enunciation by them of Responsible Government as the goal of India's political evolution and has been confirmed by subsequent action of His Majesty's government such as the grant of separate representation to the Scheduled Castes at the Round Table Conference, Joint Parliamentary Committee and in the Government of India Act, 1935, as a recognized minority, separate from the Hindus.

The Working Committee has, therefore, no hesitation in saying that it is a false and malicious propaganda to allege that this is a departure from the policy of His Majesty's government and regards it as a manoeuvre on the part of the enemies of the Scheduled Castes to defeat their just claims for constitutional safeguards and calls upon Indian political leaders and particularly the Hindu leaders to accept this fact, in the interests of peace and goodwill between the Hindus and the Scheduled Castes, and for the speedy realization of India's political goal.

## Resolution No.2

Subject: Declaration by His Majesty's Government relating to the Scheduled Castes and the Constitution

The Working Committee of the All India Scheduled Castes Federation welcomes the declaration made by His Majesty's Government and recently reiterated by His Excellency the Viceroy that His Majesty's Government regards the consent of the Scheduled Castes, among others, to the Constitution of a free India, as a matter of vital importance and as a necessary condition precedent to the transfer of power to Indian hands. At the same time, the Working Committee wishes to draw the attention of His Majesty's Government to the attitude of the Congress and other political organizations in the country which treats this declaration of His Majesty's government as not being a bona fide declaration and made without any intention to honour it and as a mere matter of tactics adopted to postpone transfer of power, and which is in all probability responsible for the unwillingness of the Majority Community to seek for a settlement with the Scheduled Castes.

The Working Committee regards this allegation as baseless and calls upon His Majesty's Government not to give any ground for such suspicion and make it clear that they will stand by the declaration at all times and under all circumstances.

## Resolution No.3

***Subject:*** Nature of Constitutional Safeguards.

The working Committee declares that no constitution shall be acceptable to the Scheduled Castes unless:

(a) It has the consent of the Scheduled Castes;

(b) It recognizes the Scheduled Castes as distinct and separate element;

(c) It contains within itself provisions for securing the following purposes:

(1) For earmarking a definite sum in the Budgets of the Provincial and Central Governments for the Secondary. University and Advanced Education of the Scheduled Castes.

(2) For reservation of Government lands for separate settlements of the Scheduled Castes through a Settlement Commission.

(3) For Representation of the Scheduled Castes according to their needs, numbers and importance:

(i) in the Legislatures,
(ii) in the Executive,
(iii) in Municipalities and Local Boards,
(iv) in the Public Services,
(v) On the Public Service Commissions.

(4) For the recognition of the above provisions as fundamental rights beyond the powers of the Legislature or the Executive to amend or alter or abrogate.

(5) For the appointment of an Officer similar in status to that of the auditor-General appointed under Section 166 of the government of India Act of 1935 and removable from office in like manner and on the like grounds as a judge of the Federal Court to report on the working of the provisions relating to Fundamental Rights.

## Resolution No. 4

***Subject:*** Communal Settlement.

The Working Committee of the All –India Scheduled Caste Federation, while it is most eager for a settlement of the Communal problem, wholly disapproves of the secret negotiations which are being carried on by Mr. Gandhi and Mr. Jinnah for a settlement between the Hindus and the Muslims. The working Committee is of opinion that Communal Settlement of a sectional character is harmful in every way. It is harmful because it ignores the vital interest of other communities. It is harmful because it creates a feeling of suspicion in other communities that dishonest deal is being made between two communities to defeat their interests.

It is also harmful to the general interests of the country, inasmuch as the singling out of one special community from others for conferring special privileges, not necessary for its protection but demanded on the basis of prestige, creates differences in status which from the point of view of maintaining equal citizenship for all, are unjustifiable and must be deplored. The working Committee is surprised that Mr. Gandhi who has time and again proclaimed himself as an opponent of secrecy in public life should have entered into secret diplomacy to bring about Hindu-Muslim settlement. The Committee the communal question, which would give a sense of security and ensure fair and equal treatment to all is to discuss the demands put forth by each interest in public and in the presence of and with the representatives of other interests.

## Resolution No. 5

***Subject:*** Revision of the Constitution.

The Working Committee of the All-India Scheduled Castes Federation is of opinion that the provisions in the existing Constitution relating to minority representation are not based on any intelligible principle. The Committee finds that as the system now stands, some minorities have not received even their population ratio of representation, while other minorities have been given weightage over and above their population ratio as a concession to their claims based on historical and military importance. The Working Committee regards the recognition of such claims to be harmful to the interests of other minorities and inconsistent with the ideal of social and political democracy, which is the goal of all Indians and that they should never be tolerated. In this connection, the committee wishes to draw attention to the fact that the principle of giving weightage to specially selected minorities has been condemned by the authors of the Montagu-Chelmsford Report and also by the Simon Commission. The Committee demands that in view of the fact that the next Constitution of India will be for India as a Dominion, the provisions of the Constitution relating to minorities should be revised and should be brought in accord with the principle of equal treatment of all minorities.

## Resolution No. 6

***Subject:*** Representation in the Legislatures and in the Executive.

The Working Committee of the all-India Scheduled Castes Federation desires to state in categorical and emphatic terms that the Schedule Castes will not tolerate any discrimination between one community and another in the matter of representation and will insist upon their claim for seats in the Provincial and Central legislatures and in the Provincial and Central Executive being adjudged in the same manner and by the same principles that may be made applicable to the claims of the Muslim community.

## Resolution No.7

***Subject:*** Electorates.

The Working Committee of the all-India Scheduled Castes Federation is of opinion that the experience of the last elections held under the government of India Act has proved that the system of joint electorates has deprived the Scheduled Castes of the right to send true and effective representatives to the Legislatures and has given the Hindu Majority the virtual right to nominate members of the Scheduled Castes who are prepared to be the tools of the Hindu Majority. The working Committee of the federation therefore demands that the system of joint electorates and reserved seats should be abolished and the system of separate electorates be introduced in place thereof.

## Resolution No.8

***Subject:*** Framework of Executive Government.

The working Committee of the All-India Scheduled Castes Federation takes note of the fact that not only all wealth, property, trade and industry are in the hands of the Majority community, but even the whole administration of the State is controlled by the Majority Community whose members have monopolized all posts in the State Services both superior and inferior. The working committee of the All-India Scheduled Castes Federation regards this as the most dangerous situation which cannot but cause great apprehension to the minority communities since the combination of these circumstances gives the majority the fullest power to establish its strangle hold upon the minorities. The fear of a stranglehold is greatly augmented by the Constitutional provisions relating to the Executive contained, in the government of India Act of 1935 which permits the majority in the Legislature to form a Government without reference to the wishes of the minorities.

The Working Committee of the All –India Scheduled Castes Federation feels that while, in the absence of an alternative system, the Parliamentary system of Government may have to be accepted, the Committee is definitely opposed to the system of Parliamentary cabinet inasmuch as it automatically vests the Executive authority in the Majority Community and thereby strengthens the hold of the Majority Community which has entered into the steel frame of the administration and thus has become a source of great danger to the Minorities. The Working Committee has, therefore, come to the conclusion that the system of Parliamentary Cabinet is not suited to Indian conditions and that a different system under which Executive Government would be formed in consultation with the wishes of the Minorities must be designed to give them a better sense of security.

The working Committee insists that the Executive in the Provinces well as in the Centre should be constituted in the following manner:

(1) The Executive should consist of a Prime Minister and other ministers drawn from general community and from minority communities in a proportion to be specified in the constitution.

(2) The Prime Minister and Ministers drawn from the general community shall be elected to the Executive by the whole house by single transferable vote.

(3) The Ministers representing the minority communities shall be chosen by the members representing the different communities by single transferable vote.

(4) The Members of the Executive shall be members of the Legislature, shall answer questions, vote and take part in debates.

(5) Any vacancy in the Executive shall be filled in accordance with rules governing the original appointments.

(6) The period for which the Executive shall hold office shall be co-terminus with the life of the Legislature.

## Resolution No.9

***Subject:*** Public Services.

While it is desirable to plan for a Government which will be a government of Laws and not of men, it cannot be forgotten that no matter how government is organized, it must remain a Government of men. That being so, whether government is good or bad as distinguished from a merely efficient Government

(a) that so long as the Scheduled Castes continue to live on the outskirts of the Hindu village, as an alien people, with no source of livelihood and in small numbers as compared to Hindus, they will continue to remain Untouchables and subject to the tyranny and oppression of the Hindus and will not be able to enjoy free and full life, and

(b) that for the better protection of the Scheduled Castes from the tyranny and oppression of the Caste Hindus, which may take a worse form under Swaraj, and to enable the Scheduled Castes to develop to their fullest manhood, to give them economic and social security as also to pave the way for the removal of untouchability, the Working Committee demands that the Constitution should provide—

(1) For the transplantation of the Scheduled Castes from their present habitations and form separate Scheduled Caste villages away from and independent of Hindu villages;

(2) For the settlement of the Scheduled Castes in new villages a provision shall be made by the Constitution for the establishment of a Settlement Commission;

(3) All Government land which is cultivable and which is not occupied and land which may be reclaimed shall be handed over to the Commission to be held in trust for the purpose of making new settlements of the Scheduled Castes.

(4) The Commission shall be empowered to purchase new land under the Land Acquisition Act from private owners to complete the scheme of settlements of the Scheduled Castes.

(5) The constitution shall provide that the Central government shall grant to the Settlement Commission a minimum sum of rupees five crores per annum to enable it to carry out their duty in this behalf.

Mallik, Suneila: *Social Integration of the Scheduled Castes.* Abhinav, New Delhi, 1979.

Marriott, Mckim: *Village India: Studies in the Little Community*, The University of Chicago Press, Chicago, 1955.

Michael J.: *The Untouchables in Contemporary India*, University of Arizona Press, Arizona, 1972.

Mohan, P.E.: *Scheduled Castes: History of Elevation, Tamil Nadu, 1900-1955.* New Era Pub., Madras, 1993.

Nagaraj, D. R.: *The Flaming Feet: A Study of the Dalit Movement*, South Forum Press, Bangalore, 1993.

Nath, Trilok: *Politics of the Depressed Classes*, Deputy Publications, Delhi, 1987.

Neelam, G.: *Social Development and Dalit Women*, Gyan Pub. House, New Delhi, 1995.

Nim, H.L.: *Thoughts on Dr. Ambedkar*, Siddhartha Educational and Cultural Society, Agra, 1969.

Omprakash, S.: *Development of the Weaker Section: Problems, Policies and Issues*, Uppal Publishing House, New Delhi, 1989.

Omvedt, G.: *Dalits and the Democratic Revolution: Dr Ambedkar and the Dalit Movement in Colonial India*, Sage, New Delhi, 1994.

Owen M.: *The Politics of Untouchability: Social Mobility and Social Change in a City of India*, Columbia University Press, New York, 1969.

Pantavane, G.: *Patrikar Dr. Babasaheb Ambedkar*, Abhijit, Nagpur, 1987.

Paranjpe, A. C.: *Caste, Prejudice and the Individual*, Lalvani Publishing House, New Delhi, 1970.

Parmaji, S.: *Caste Reservations and Performance*, Mamata Publications, Warangal, 1985.

Partha, C.: *Caste and Subaltern Consciousness*, Oxford University Press, Delhi, 1994.

Pradhan, A. C.: *The Emergence of the Depressed Classes*, Bookland International, Bhubaneshwar, 1986.

Prahlad G.: *Dalit Movement in Maharashtra*, Kanak Publications, New Delhi, 1991.

Punalekar, S. P.: *Dalit Women in India: Issues and Perspectives*, Gyan Publishing House, New Delhi, 1995.

Rajasekharaiah, A.M.: *B.R. Ambedkar: the Politics of Emancipation*, Sindhu Publications, Bombay, 1971.

Ram, Jagivan: *Caste Challenge in India*, Vision Books, New Delhi, 1980.

Rege, Sharmila: *Sati: A Critical Analysis*, University of Poona, Poona, 1989.

Robb, Peter: *Dalit Movements and the Meanings of Labour in India*, Oxford University Press, New Delhi, 1993.

Sarkar, J.: *Caste, Occupation and Change*, B. R. Publishing Co., Delhi, 1984.

Sekhar, B: *Caste, Class and Politics in Colonial Bengal: A Case Study of the Namasudra Movement of 1872-1937*, Rawat Publications, New Delhi, 1994.

Shabbir, M.: *B.R. Ambedkar. Study in Law & Society*, Rawat, Jaipur, 1997.

Shah, Ghanshyam: *Caste Association and Political Processes in Gujarat*, Popular Prakashan, Bombay, 1975.

Shashi B.R.: *Ambedkar and Human Rights*, KK Publishers, New Delhi, 1981.

Shyam, L.: *Caste and Political Mobilisation: The Bhangis*, Panchsheel Prakashan, Jaipur, 1981.

Silverberg, James: *Social Mobility in the Caste System in India*, Mouton Publishers, The Hague, 1968.

Singh, K. K.: *Patterns of Caste Tensions*, Asia Publishing House, Bombay, 1967.

Singh, S. N.: *Reservation: Problems and Prospects*, Uppal Publishing House, New Delhi, 1987.

Tope, T.K.: *Dr. B.R. Ambedkar, A Symbol of Social Revolt*, Maharashtra Information Centre, New Delhi, 1964.

Varale, B.H.: *Dr. Babasaheb Ambedkarrancha Sangaki*, Shrividya Prakashan, Pune, 1988.

Venkateshwarlu, D.: *Harijan-Upper Class Conflicts*, Discovery, New Delhi, 1990.

## T



## U



## V



## W